INFLUENC B1

D0482693

A12431621001

DATE DUE

The Influence of the Enlightenment on the French Revolution

PROBLEMS IN EUROPEAN CIVILIZATION

Under the editorial direction of
John Ratté
Amherst College

The Influence of the Enlightenment on the French Revolution

Second Edition

Edited and with an introduction by

William F. Church
Brown University

D. C. HEATH AND COMPANY
Lexington, Massachusetts Toronto London

CONTENTS

I THE MOST FAMOUS DEBATE ON THE INFLUENCE OF THE ENLIGHTENMENT

II THE FUNDAMENTAL CRITICISMS OF THE ENLIGHTENMENT AND ITS INFLUENCE

III THE ENLIGHTENMENT AS THE SOURCE OF LIBERALISM AND PROGRESS

IV A SPECIAL STRAIN: ROUSSEAU'S INFLUENCE ON THE FRENCH REVOLUTION

V RECENT COMPREHENSIVE TREATMENTS OF THE PROBLEM

INTRODUCTION

Although the intellectual movement that is known as the Enlightenment occupies an important position in the growth of Western civilization, its total effect has been the subject of debate from its own time to the present. During the course of the eighteenth century, Voltaire, Montesquieu, Rousseau, Diderot and a host of lesser writers brought about a revolution in ways of thought and increasingly questioned the traditional legal, moral, and religious foundations of French society and government. The immediate import of the *philosophes'* ideas was therefore destructive, but it should be remembered that their ultimate objective was extensive reconstruction of French society and institutions along improved lines. This they believed to be feasible because they had great confidence in man's ability to change and control the world in which he lives. Especially during the last generation before the French Revolution, criticism of the established order became more and more virulent and utilitarian in nature, indicating widespread desire for practical, extensive, and thorough-going reforms. These ideas and attitudes were adopted by large sections of the French middle classes who were therefore thoroughly conversant with a genuine revolutionary ideology.

With the outbreak of the French Revolution in 1789, Europe witnessed the spectacle of the normally responsible elements of French society, the middle and professional classes, resorting to force in order to achieve the changes that they sought in French society and institutions. The first years of the Revolution are usually called the constructive years, since it was then that the revolutionaries did, in fact, accomplish many of their objectives. The French governmental system was radically altered on the national and local levels by the establishment of constitutional monarchy and decentralization of authority. The traditional position of the Roman Catholic church was destroyed by making the clergy state-supported and establishing religious toleration. The French social structure was drastically reorganized by the institution of equality before the law, extensive changes in land ownership, the abolition of the guilds and other corporations, and reforms in the administration of justice. Such matters as education, weights and measures, and the calendar also came under the scrutiny of the revolutionaries. Later, during the Terror and the Napoleonic dictatorship, there occurred a seeming perversion of the original ideals of the Revolution, yet many of its earlier accomplishments were in fact consolidated and made permanent elements of French life.

It is relatively simple to describe the essential features of the Enlightenment and the French Revolution respectively, but it is much more difficult to determine the exact causal relations between the two. Exactly what was the influence of the Enlightenment, a vast and exceedingly complex intellectual movement, upon the events, accomplishments, and general nature of the French Revolution? The argument *post hoc propter hoc* is clearly inadequate. The cry that was heard in certain quarters, "It's Voltaire's fault; it's Rousseau's fault," may express a point of view but proves nothing. Furthermore, the nature of intellectual forces in 1789 is one matter, whereas their continuing impact upon the course of the Revolution is quite another. The influence of the Enlightenment on the French Revolution is therefore a complex problem of historical interpretation which may not be solved without first giving tentative answers to a number of interrelated questions. What were the exact social and political objectives of the reformers before 1789? Did they merely seek specific though extensive reforms, or did they envisage a massive, fundamental reordering of French life? Should the various strands of thought in the Enlightenment be examined separately, or should they be lumped together and viewed as a single movement building a revolutionary ideology? Did the reformers think in terms of peaceful change, or were they prepared to resort to force if necessary to achieve their objectives? Does the fact that many of the accomplishments of the Revolution had been discussed for years before 1789 prove that ideas directed events, or is additional evidence necessary? Are such well known documents as the *philosophes'* treatises and pamphlets and the *cahiers* of the Estates General sufficient evidence of prevailing opinion in 1789? Do

FIGURE 1. Condorcet exemplifies the ties between the Enlightenment and the French Revolution. A leading *philosophe* and friend of the most learned men of his time, Condorcet was an outstanding leader in the Legislative Assembly (1791–1792) where he worked extensively for reforms, notably in education.

such factors as the presence of important thinkers (e.g. Condorcet) among the revolutionaries and their praise of earlier writers (e.g. Rousseau) indicate continuing intellectual influences upon the course of the Revolution? Also, what was the fundamental nature of the revolutionary ideology? Was it overly rationalized, naively optimistic, immoral, irresponsible, and destructive of governmental authority, or was it constructive, pragmatic, matured by generations of debate, based upon fundamental concepts of right and justice in human affairs, and "the wave of the future"? What was the relative importance of this ideology in the matrix of factors that led to the Revolution? Were ideas as influential as French participation in the American Revolution, the crisis in French finances, and the continued mistakes and ineptitudes of Louis XVI? Is it possible to weigh the various "causes" of the French Revolution one against another? These and many other interrelated question will be analyzed in the selections in this volume.

In spite of the evident complexities of our problem, its overriding elements may be reduced to two. First, was there in fact any positive influence of the Enlightenment on the French Revolution? And second, if this influence is admitted, was it for good or for bad? These issues are interrelated and yet distinct. The first is essentially a problem of investigating the evidence and arriving at a reasonable conclusion. The differences of opinion in this area are extensive, but they merely reflect honest disagreement among experts and give little cause for aroused feelings. The second, however, is more fundamental and goes to the heart of the frictions between schools of interpretation, since it is not a matter of objective historical analysis but of personal convictions and belief.

The entry of the moral issue at once changes the nature of the debate and goes far to explain the intransigence that has been exhibited by both sides. There is a fundamental difference between the traditionalist mentality, so well represented by Burke, and the empirical, libertarian cast of mind of Paine; and the strong feelings of both can be explained only by recalling that both believed their positions to be morally superior. Even more important is the role that religion has played in the controversy. The *philosophes* were as much concerned with religious problems as with social and political, and the Revolution quickly exhibited a strong antireligious (i.e. anti-Catholic) character, inflicting upon the Roman church one blow after another and permanently ending its favored position in French society. The result was that the Revolution split French opinion along political *and* religious lines, and the division has survived to this day.

For this reason it has been extremely difficult for French scholars to view the Enlightenment and the Revolution objectively. The strict and more conservative Catholic scholars usually reject the principles of the Enlightenment and view its influence as detrimental, if not disastrous. On the other hand, the liberal-minded historians generally accept the principles of the Enlightenment and regard its influence during the Revolution and later as beneficial. A few scholars, such as Mornet, seem to have succeeded in maintaining their objectivity, but the large majority view the problem from the liberal or conservative standpoint in both religion and politics.

The existence of schools of thought concerning the influence of the Enlightenment on the French Revolution is at once apparent from a glance at our series of selections. Interestingly enough, the two most powerful writers who are represented in this book, Burke and Taine, are those who best articulated the conservative, anti-Enlightenment position. Their works contain massive criticisms of the movement which both regarded as extremely influential and decidedly calamitous. Representative of the opposing, liberal school are such men as Michelet, Aulard and Lefebvre who accepted the contributions of the Enlightenment to French life as good. There is, moreover, a further distinction between these schools in the degree of influence that they ascribe to the Enlightenment. The conservative writers generally view the *philosophes'* ideas as the primary cause of the Revolution and the explanation of its excesses, whereas the liberal scholars, while recognizing the importance of ideas, tend to view them merely as one element among many, with relatively less influence than the conservative writers would assign them. This may be surprising in view of the fact that the Enlightenment is the fountainhead of the liberal scholars' political heritage. It may also indicate that the conservative writers tend to argue more exclusively from principle.

Although there are certain clear patterns in the debate on our problem, every author who is excerpted in this book presented his own personal interpretation. Remarkably early in the course of the Revolution, Edmund Burke and Thomas Paine engaged in their famous literary debate concerning the merits and defects of the movement. Burke, whose attack on the Revolution was one of the most famous and influential ever penned, strongly presented the view that society grows and evolves only through accumulated experience and the working of time-tested tradition. Using the unwritten British constitution as his model, he argued that the present generation should revere the established order, alter it only with great caution, and recognize that true liberty consists of enjoying one's rights within the framework of traditional law and institutions. Burke had earlier championed the cause of the American colonists precisely because he felt their claims to be justified by British tradition. Now, however, he condemned the Enlightenment as antitraditional, doctrinaire speculation and denounced the French revolutionaries as self-interested fanatics who were recklessly destroying living institutions and whose new, written, rationally conceived constitution for France would never survive. He even predicted accurately the rise of a single tyrant in France.

For Burke, therefore, the basic flaw of the Revolution stemmed from faulty ideology which provided its fundamental motivation and would surely bring France to ruin. In answer, Paine argued that the interests of the present generation should take precedence over any traditions that might be inherited from the past. The living are perpetually sovereign and may not be bound by a generation that is dead and gone. Any true constitution, he said, should be built upon and protect man's natural rights as well as his civil rights that spring from living in organized society. These rights had been increasingly lost in England whose constitution was based on conquest. In contrast, the American and French constitutions represented recovery of those rights through justified rebellion. Paine believed the ideas of the *philosophes* to be the great source of these concepts in recent times, and he hailed the era of revolution that was just beginning as the fulfillment of their precepts.

Four critics of the Enlightenment and its influence—de Maistre, de Tocqueville, Taine, and Gaxotte—may be grouped together under this heading, although their fundamental positions were very different. De Maistre was certainly the most uncompromising critic of the Enlightenment to be represented in this book. Adopting a strictly theocratic position, he insisted that all human works are vain unless God-centered. The Enlightenment and the Revolution were doubly disastrous in that they not only destroyed tradition, including religion, but represented supreme confidence in man's autonomous reason to build without divine aid. The impact of these pernicious ideas had been extremely extensive, but their fruits would come to naught, and he predicted the collapse of man-centered, rationally conceived institutions not only in France but also in the new United

States of America. He also went so far as to assert that the violence of the Revolution was directly and personally inspired by the *philosophes.*

For de Maistre, the matter was simple. The influence of the Enlightenment on the Revolution was extremely powerful and entirely bad. De Tocqueville, on the other hand, has rightly been classified as a proponent of nineteenth-century liberalism. His attitude toward the Enlightenment and its influence, however, was mixed, in certain ways very critical. In our selection, he repeats the charge that the *philosophes'* ideas were rootless and doctrinaire, and that the men who held them lacked experience and the responsibilities of office, with disastrous consequences for the Revolution. His statements show that acceptance of liberalism did not necessarily preclude an awareness of serious flaws in the Enlightenment.

In several ways, de Tocqueville echoed Burke, yet the two men held to fundamentally different positions. Burke totally rejected the Enlightenment and the Revolution as destructive, whereas de Tocqueville criticized only certain elements in both movements. Burke found the chief cause of the Revolution in the powerful influence of the Enlightenment, while de Tocqueville distinctly subordinated ideas to social and political factors when explaining the upheaval. In commenting on Burke's views, de Tocqueville said that Burke was an excellent judge of specific developments during the Revolution and the philosophical weaknesses that had produced them, but he entirely missed the Revolution's general character, its universal significance, and its meaning for all mankind.[1] In sum, de Tocqueville was critical of the intellectual origins of the Revolution but regarded it as ultimately beneficial.

Our third critic of the Enlightenment, Hippolyte Taine, was one of the most influential anti-republican historians of the nineteenth century. Writing after the French debacle in the Franco-Prussian War, Taine sought to discover where France had gone wrong in her historical development. He concluded that she had done so during the eighteenth century largely because of the evil nature of the Enlightenment. His resulting work is the classic statement of the weaknesses of the movement. Using a metaphor that was to become famous, he wrote that the philosophy of the Enlightenment contained

[1] De Tocqueville, *Œuvres complètes,* edited by J. P. Mayer, Vol. 2.2 (Paris, 1953), pp. 340–341.

a poison which was a compound of scientific rationalism and the classic spirit. These combined to discredit traditions, laws, institutions, morality, and religion, and to promote a shallow view of human nature and a false confidence in reason. The result was an unleashing of brutal and dangerous forces that led inevitably to destruction and to a despotism which was much more tyrannical than that of any monarch.

Taine's views, which attributed great weight to the force of ideas, were repeated by many later critics of the Enlightenment. Pierre Gaxotte, a prolific twentieth-century conservative historian, has summarized the major criticisms that have been leveled at the Enlightenment since the time of Burke. Gaxotte even reinforced his position by introducing such questionable elements as the role of the Freemasons and the idea that the Enlightenment stemmed from foreign sources and was not truly French. His summary of the argument from the conservative standpoint is a fitting conclusion of this section of the readings.

During the period between 1815 and 1914, the liberal historians in France expressed their approval of the Enlightenment and its influence in many diversified writings, only two of which are excerpted here. One of their favorite themes was expressed by Michelet in his colorful treatment of the background of the Revolution. Michelet was the ablest representative of the liberal, romantic school of French historians. He loved the French people, had a strong sense of justice and equity in human affairs, and was capable of recapturing the emotional qualities of the movements that he described. The old regime he regarded as a period when everything was rotten and justice was the only remaining hope. The *philosophes* were among the first to reassert fundamental concepts of justice, and they became the leaders of a great crusade for its reestablishment in French society. Thus the Enlightenment was the true inspiration of the Revolution, and one of its most important accomplishments was to put the *philosophes'* ideas into effect.

Considerably later in the century, Alphonse Aulard began his very extensive reexamination of the Revolution and became the first French historian to apply modern methods of analysis to its documentary sources. When examining the background of the Revolution, Aulard addressed himself to one of the thorniest problems relative to the role of ideas. What was the source of the political radicalism that was so apparent in the initial phases of the Revolution, and why did the Revolution rapidly assume an even more radical character? Republican and democratic ideas were almost totally lacking in the writings of the *philosophes* before 1789, Aulard found, but he insisted that the total impact of the Enlightenment had the effect of developing a republican state of mind. This "republican spirit" was widely accepted when the Revolution began and accounts for its rapid evolution toward democracy. Thus Aulard attempted to go beyond the specific evidences of intellectual history and to assess the impact of the Enlightenment as a whole. Its influence he found to be crucial in guiding the course of the Revolution.

The fact that historical scholarship has attained new heights of perfection in the twentieth century is well illustrated by the work of Daniel Mornet. Although he was primarily a student of literary history, Mornet set himself the task of determining the exact role of ideas leading to the Revolution. His research was unbelievably extensive and covered not only the usual evidences of opinion but also such lesser sources as the records of provincial academies and discussion groups, periodical literature, newspapers, pamphlets, the contents of libraries, editions of key works, educational reforms, etc. So thorough was his research that it remains fundamental in spite of the appearance of many later statistical studies.

In weighing the influence of ideas against other causes of the Revolution, Mornet concluded that while such practical matters as endemic famine were of greater moment, ideas played a very important role which he delineated in carefully chosen terms. The constant and growing criticism of French society and institutions led men increasingly to associate thought with the cause of reform. The widespread diffusion of these ideas accounts for their strength and caused France to be more inclined toward drastic upheaval than any other European state. The broad currents of opinion were more concerned with practical reforms than philosophical speculation, yet the greatest thinkers dominated the intellectual life of the century and channeled its currents, thereby crystallizing opinion. Intelligence led the movement of reform and was therefore the key element that was needed to spark a revolution.

Considerably broader were the research interests of Georges Lefebvre, the ablest historian of the French Revolution in this century. Lefebvre's writings touched upon almost every phase of eighteenth-century historical experience, and he was a leading expert in many. His approach to the Revolution stressed the multiplicity of factors that went into its making, and of these, ideas were not the most important. Certain statements in Lefebvre's writings, however, indicate that he went far toward recognizing the importance of ideas in shaping events. The *Encyclopédie,* he said, not only sharpened contemporaries' views and broadened their insights into current problems; it also set forth many of the later revolutionaries' principles such as man's ability to control nature and society, and it even foreshadowed many actual achievements of the Revolution in such areas as freedom of thought and the press and religious toleration.[2] Lefebvre's fundamental position seems to be that while a great many different factors went into the making of the Revolution, its guiding principles were provided by the Enlightenment. The *Declaration of the Rights of Man and the Citizen* he viewed as both the essence of the *philosophes'* thought and the "incarnation" of the Revolution. The document demonstrated the continuity between the Enlightenment and the Revolution, and epitomized much of the latter's work by marking the end of the old regime. To this extent Lefebvre recognized the influence of the Enlightenment during the Revolution and regarded the ideological factor as a significant element in the pattern of causation.

The problem of Jean-Jacques Rousseau's influence during the French Revolution presents special difficulties both because he stood apart from the main stream of the Enlightenment and because of the very unusual nature of his appeal to the eighteenth-century mentality. Analysis of his place in pre-revolutionary thought has demonstrated that his political ideas found only limited response before 1789. At that time his wide popularity stemmed not from his *Contrat social* but from such works as his *Emile* and *La Nouvelle Héloise,* that is, his back-to-nature romanticism. This he effectively combined with idealization of the common man and insistence upon human perfectability. With the Revolution his political writings and ideals were rediscovered, as much evidence proves, but his influence upon the course of events has been variously interpreted as both libertarian and authoritarian. Our two selections present these viewpoints. After examining the evidence that Rousseau was

[2] G. Lefebvre, "L'Encyclopédie et la Révolution française," *Annales de l'Université de Paris,* XXII[2] (1952), pp. 81–90.

widely known and idealized during the Revolution, Joan McDonald concludes that the cult of Rousseau—something more than the mere sum of his political ideas—was influential in a libertarian way. Lester Crocker, on the other hand, argues that Rousseau's concepts of the general will and forcing a man to be free had totalitarian implications that could be realized only in despotism. Tentative solutions to this problem of interpretation may be reached only by careful examination of the evidence.

The fact that the relationships between the Enlightenment and the French Revolution remain unresolved and a lively subject of debate is illustrated by our last group of selections, in which three outstanding authorities present comprehensive treatments of the problem. Henri Peyre, whose eminence in literary studies is well known, gives an excellent survey of the controversy together with his own views of the matter. Interestingly, he finds reasons for ascribing greater influence to ideas during the Revolution than many historians are willing to admit. Professor Peyre's preoccupation with intellectual matters may explain his viewpoint, but his statements carry the weight of very considerable authority. The late Alfred Cobban, on the other hand, examines the problem more from the standpoint of political ideology in relation to the several phases of the Revolution. He concludes that the patent divergence of the course of events from the values and objectives of the *philosophes* indicates that currents of thought were of minor practical import in determining both the nature of the upheaval and the characteristics and policies of the various French regimes. Finally, Norman Hampson returns to the broader role of ideas in the revolutionaries' motivation. By recalling that the leaders of the Revolution during its early years were thoroughly imbued with the *philosophes'* precepts, he finds significant ideological influences in shaping events. These initial ideals, however, were increasingly abandoned as France embarked upon war and imperial ventures.

The controversy concerning the influence of the Enlightenment on the French Revolution is ultimately insoluble in absolute terms because it is a problem of historical interpretation. As such it will always be treated differently by individual investigators. One's answer will depend on one's examination of the evidence, personal viewpoint and values, and above all the significance that one ascribes to ideas as an element of human experience. The only certainty in the picture is that knowledge of the issues has increased and they are now more thoroughly understood. Beyond this, the debate remains very much alive. As a subject for investigation, the influence of the Enlightenment on the French Revolution retains considerable value because of its extensive ramifications in eighteenth-century history and its importance for understanding the development of modern civilization. It is one of the best test cases to examine when grappling with the question: Do ideas have consequences?

Conflict of Opinion

Compute your gains; see what is got by those extravagant and presumptuous speculations which have taught your leaders to despise all their predecessors, and all their contemporaries, and even to despise themselves, until the moment in which they became truly despicable. By following those false lights, France has bought undisguised calamities at a higher price than any nation has purchased the most unequivocal blessings! . . . The fresh ruins of France, which shock our feelings wherever we can turn our eyes, are not the devastation of civil war; they are the sad but instructive monuments of rash and ignorant counsel in time of profound peace.

EDMUND BURKE

The only signs which appeared of the spirit of liberty during those periods are to be found in the writings of the French philosophers. . . . All those writings and many others had their weight; and by the different manner in which they treated the subject of government, Montesquieu by his judgment and knowledge of laws, Voltaire by his wit, Rousseau and Raynal by their animation, and Quesnay and Turgot by their moral maxims and systems of economy, readers of every class met with something to their taste, and a spirit of political inquiry began to diffuse itself through the nation at the time the dispute between England and the then colonies of America broke out.

THOMAS PAINE

At bottom, the glory of having caused the Revolution belongs exclusively to neither Voltaire nor Rousseau. The entire philosophical sect claims its part, but these two men should be regarded as its leaders. While one undermined politics by corrupting morals, the other corrupted morals by undermining politics. . . . After this, let no one go into raptures over the influence of Voltaire and his ilk; let no one speak of the power which they wielded over their century. Yes, they were powerful, like poison and fire.

JOSEPH DE MAISTRE

Montesquieu is the writer, the interpreter of Right; Voltaire weeps and clamors for it; and Rousseau found it. . . . Rousseau spoke by the mouth of another, by Mirabeau, yet it is no less the soul of Rousseau's genius. When once he severed himself from the false science of the time, and from a no less false society, you behold in his writings the dawn of a celestial effulgence—Duty, Right! . . . Is it the power of an idea, of a new inspiration, of a revelation from above? Yes, there has been a revelation. . . . Nobody knows why, but since that glowing language impregnated the air, the temperature has changed; it seems as though a breath of life had been wafted over the world; the earth begins to bear fruits that she would never else have borne.

JULES MICHELET

The philosophy of the eighteenth century contained a poison, and of a kind as potent as it was peculiar, for, not only is it a long historic elaboration, the final and condensed essence of the tendency of the thought of the century, but again, its two principal ingredients have this peculiarity that, separate, they are salutary and in combination they form a venomous compound.

                                                                    HIPPOLYTE A. TAINE

No one on the eve of the Revolution had ever dreamed of the establishment of a republic in France; it was a form of government that seemed impossible in a great state in course of unification. . . . Men wished to organize the monarchy, not to destroy it. . . . However, the future date of democracy was announced in the proclamation of the principle of the sovereignty of the people; and the republic, the logical form of democracy, was prepared by the diffusion of republican ideas. . . . The ruling classes of society were steeped in republicanism.

                                                                    ALPHONSE AULARD

Surely if the old regime had been threatened only by ideas, it would have run no risk. Ideas needed a fulcrum, the people's misery and political unrest, in order to be effective. But these political causes would not have sufficed to bring about the Revolution as rapidly as it came. It was ideas that demonstrated and systematized the consequences of political unrest and gradually initiated the movement for the Estates General. And it was from the Estates General, without, however, denying the role of ideas, that the Revolution came.

                                                                    DANIEL MORNET

The *Declaration of the Rights of Man and the Citizen* stands as the incarnation of the Revolution as a whole. . . . The whole philosophic movement in France in the eighteenth century pointed to such an act; Montesquieu, Voltaire and Rousseau had collaborated in its making. . . . It is a direction of intention; it therefore requires of the citizens an integrity of purpose, which is to say a critical spirit, patriotism in the proper sense of the word, respect for the rights of others, reasoned devotion to the national community, 'virtue' in the language of Montesquieu, Rousseau and Robespierre.

                                                                    GEORGES LEFEBVRE

The Revolution strayed from the primrose path of enlightened happiness to the strait and narrow road of Jacobin virtue, from the principle of representative and constitutional government to the rule of an authoritarian elite, from the *philosophes'* ideal of peace to the revolutionaries' crusading war and the Napoleonic dream of conquest. Nothing could have been more alien to the Enlightenment than this transition from the ideals of democracy and peace to a policy of dictatorship and war. . . . The influence of the Enlightenment cannot be disregarded in any history of the French Revolution; but the revolutionaries did not set their course by its light in the beginning, nor did they steer the ship of state into the haven of the Enlightenment in the end.

ALFRED COBBAN

If the first phase of the Revolution, from 1789 to 1791, was not directly caused by the Enlightenment, it nevertheless transferred political power in France to the men who had been most influenced by the Enlightenment. . . . The real rulers of France at the time of the Constituent Assembly came from those sections of society most influenced by the writing of the *philosophes:* members of the court nobility such as Lafayette, Noailles and La Rochefoucauld, intellectuals like the astronomer, Bailly, now mayor of Paris, Duport from the Paris *parlement,* Barnave, a lawyer from Grenoble. The Assembly reorganized the entire political shape of the country on principles of secularism, rationality, uniformity and election to office.

NORMAN HAMPSON

Eighteenth Century French Names

Mentioned in the Selections*

D'ALEMBERT, 1717–1783. A preeminent mathematician, *philosophe*. Member of the French Academy. Early editor of the *Encyclopédie*.

D'ANTRAIGUES, COUNT, 1755–1812. Enlightened nobleman. Supported the Revolution in its early phases, but soon went into exile.

D'ARGENSON, MARQUIS, 1694–1757. Minister of Foreign Affairs, 1744–1747. Writings expressed very advanced political ideas.

D'ARGENTAL, 1700–1788. Counsellor in Parlement of Paris. Close friend of Voltaire.

AUBERT DE VITRY, FRANÇOIS, 1765–1849. Economist. Supported the Revolution, including the Girondins, until his flight during the Terror.

BABEUF, 1760–1797. Publicist. Noted for his strongly communist ideas and program for putting them into practice.

BAILLY, JEAN-SYLVAIN, 1736–1793. Astronomer and politician. Friend of Lafayette. Elected to Estates General. Chosen first Mayor of Paris, summer of 1789. Resigned, 1791. Executed, 1793.

BARBIER, 1689–1771. His *Journal* on the period 1718–1763 illustrates the advanced ideas and critical spirit of the time.

BARNAVE, 1761–1793. Active revolutionary. Strongly democratic ideas. Executed, 1793.

BARÈRE or BARRÈRE, 1755–1841. Jurist, politician. Active in Constituent Assembly, Convention; member of Committee of Public Safety. Supported Robespierre at first; later turned against him.

BARRY, MME DU, 1743–1793. Official mistress of Louis XV beginning in 1769. Executed in 1793 for alleged royalist sympathies.

BARTHÉLEMY, ABBÉ, 1716–1795. Scholar, antiquarian. Member of French Academy. Enemy of the Revolution, but was not persecuted.

BEAUMARCHAIS, 1732–1799. Dramatist, promoter. Purchased noble status. His *Barber of Seville* and *Marriage of Figaro* are noted for the audacity and success of their social criticism.

BILLAUD-VARENNE, JACQUES, 1756–1819. Radical political leader. President of the Convention and member of the Committee of Public Safety.

BODEAU or BAUDEAU, ABBÉ, 1730–1792. Economist, author. Supported ideas of the Physiocrats.

BOULAINVILLERS, COUNT, 1658–1722. Historian, political analyst. Known for study of the French nobility and insistence on its existence as a distinct class since the fifth century.

BRISSOT, 1754–1793. Politician, humanitarian. Founded Société des amis des noirs, 1788. In Legislative Assembly. Directed foreign affairs, 1791–1793. Leader of the Girondist Party. Executed, 1793.

BUFFON, COUNT, 1707–1788. Most famous naturalist of the century. His *Histoire Naturelle* was a landmark in its field.

BUZOT, FRANÇOIS, 1760–1793. Lawyer and revolutionary. Member of the

* A few of the most obscure names have been omitted from this list.

Constituent Assembly and the Convention. Died under mysterious circumstances.

CABANIS, 1757–1808. Empiricist *philosophe.* Held to atheism and materialism. Supported much of the Revolution.

CALAS, 1698–1762. Calvinist merchant of Toulouse. Falsely accused of murdering his son because he wished to turn Catholic. Executed after a trial enflamed by religious passions. Voltaire secured reversal of the decree and protected widow and two children.

CALONNE, 1734–1802. Controller General of Finance, 1783–1787.

CÉRUTTI, 1738–1792. Jesuit, author, successful teacher. Supporter of Mirabeau.

CHABANON, 1730–1792. Author, musician. Member of French Academy. Works were mediocre.

CHAMFORT, 1741–1794. Author, literary critic. Member of French Academy. Hailed the Revolution. Supported Mirabeau but not Robespierre. Suicide, 1794.

CHÂTELET, MME DU, 1706–1749. One of most learned ladies of the age. Friend of Voltaire. Wrote on religious, scientific subjects.

CHASTELLEUX, FRANÇOIS-JEAN, MARQUIS DE, 1734–1788. Military man; fought with Rochambeau in America. Also important man of letters. Wrote with great success in support of the ideology of the late Enlightenment, stressing reason, progress, humanity.

CHÉNIER, 1762–1794. Ablest poet during the Revolution. Materialist, atheist. Supported the Revolution but was executed for Girondist associations, 1794.

COLLOT D'HERBOIS, 1750–1796. Actor, ardent revolutionary. Member of Convention, Committee of Public Safety. Supported all violent measures. Arrested during reaction after fall of Robespierre; died in prison in French Guiana.

CONDILLAC, ABBÉ, 1715–1780. Empiricist *philosophe.* Member of French Academy. Believed that sensations are the source of all human knowledge, ideals, character. Enjoyed wide following.

CONDORCET, MARQUIS, 1743–1794. Advanced *philosophe,* mathematician. Member of French Academy. Active in Legislative Assembly. Girondist. Died in prison during the Terror. Famous for his idea of progress.

DANTON, 1759–1794. One of the most important and effective leaders of the Revolution, 1791–1793. Executed because of Girondist connections, 1794.

DE BROSSES or DES BROSSES, 1709–1777. Jurist, historian, man of letters. First President of Parlement of Dijon. Wrote many types of works. Noted for intellectual independence.

DELILLE, 1738–1813. Poet. Member of French Academy. Disliked the Revolution but was not persecuted.

DELISLE DE SALES, 1741–1816. Writer. Member of Academy of Inscriptions. Many semi-popular works on history, philosophy, politics.

DESMOULINS, 1760–1794. Active revolutionary through writing and agitation from 1789 to his execution for Girondist sympathies, 1794.

DESTUTT DE TRACY, 1754–1836. Active *philosophe.* Member of the Constituent Assembly, then withdrew to private life. Many works on philosophy, chiefly post-revolutionary.

DIDEROT, 1713–1784. One of the most learned *philosophes*. Absorbed most of the knowledge of his age. Leader of the Encyclopedists. Wrote many scattered, often experimental works.

DORAT, 1743–1780. Poet. Friend of Voltaire. Wrote many able but facile dramatic and poetic works.

DUCLOS, 1704–1772. Writer, moralist. Member of French Academy. Works on history, philosophy; noted for intellectual independence.

DUMONT, ETIENNE, 1759–1829. Swiss publicist. In France during the first years of the Revolution. Partisan of democratic ideas. Friend of Mirabeau.

DUPORT-DUTERTRE, 1754–1793. Lawyer. Minister of Justice, 1790–1792. Executed, 1793.

D'ESCHERNY, FRANÇOIS-LOUIS, 1733–1815. Swiss writer. Friend of many French authors, especially Rousseau. Supported the Revolution.

D'EYMAR, COUNT, c. 1750–1803. Administrator and writer. Friend of Rousseau. Deputy to Estates General where he was one of the first nobles to join the Third Estate.

FAVART, 1710–1792. Dramatist. His works were much in vogue.

FONTANES, MARQUIS, 1757–1821. Statesman, man of letters. Works were mediocre but widely read. Hailed the Revolution, but soon went into exile.

FONTENELLE, 1657–1757. Able *philosophe*. Perpetual Secretary of the Academy of Sciences. Known for his Cartesian views.

FRÉRON, 1754–1802. Journalist, politician. Combatted the Encyclopedists. Hailed the Revolution; served most of its regimes.

FRONSAC, DUKE, 1736–1791. Son of a Marshal of France. In high favor at court. Known for his lawless way of life.

GILBERT, 1751–1780. Poet. Actively combatted the Encyclopedists.

GINGUENÉ, PIERRE-LOUIS, 1748–1816. Celebrated essayist and literary critic. Supported Rousseau's ideas and the Revolution. Imprisoned during the Terror.

GIRARDIN, MARQUIS DE, 1735–1808. Successful military man. Close friend of Rousseau who was buried on his estate at Ermenonville.

GOEFFRIN, MME, 1699–1777. Patroness of letters. Presided over the most fashionable salon in Paris.

GOSSEC, 1733–1829. Composer. Wrote many patriotic hymns praising the Revolution.

GOSSIN, 1744–1794. Member of Constituent Assembly. Executed, 1794.

GOUY D'ARSY, 1753–1794. General, politician. Member of National Assembly. Active in colonial affairs. Executed for counterrevolutionary activity, 1794.

GRÉGOIRE, BISHOP, 1750–1831. Active in National Assembly, Convention. Supported Civil Constitution of the Clergy.

GUILLOTIN, JOSEPH, 1738–1814. Doctor. Elected to the Estates General.

Active in reforming criminal law. Favored execution by the guillotine, but was not its inventor.

HARDY, 1756–1823. Political leader. Member of the Convention. Opposed the Terror.

HELVÉTIUS, 1715–1771. Empiricist *philosophe*. Stressed importance of the sensations. Strongly utilitarian. For a universal religion.

HÉRAULT DE SÉCHELLES, 1759–1794. Writer, politician. Member of Legislative Assembly, Convention, Committee of Public Safety. Executed for Girondist leanings, 1794.

HOLBACH, 1723–1789. A leading, late *philosophe*. His many powerful writings supported materialism, atheism, individual liberty.

ISNARD, MAXIMIN, 1751–1830. Member of the Legislative Assembly and Convention, where he supported the Girondins. Went into hiding during the Terror.

JAUCOURT, LOUIS, CHEVALIER DE, 1704–1779. Highly educated nobleman; learned in many fields. Contributed extensively to the *Encyclopédie*.

KERSAINT, 1742–1793. Naval officer. Member of Legislative Assembly. Disapproved of execution of Louis XVI. Executed for royalist sympathies, 1793.

LA BARRE, 1747–1766. Youthful prank caused him to be accused of sacrilege. Victim of miscarriage of justice due to religious intolerance.

LACLOS, 1741–1803. General, writer. Supported the Revolution. Most famous work: *Les Liaisons Dangereuses,* a licentious commentary on the age.

LAFAYETTE, MARQUIS, 1757–1834. General, political leader. Participated in American Revolution. A moderating influence in early phases of French Revolution. Later turned against it.

LALANDE, 1732–1807. Astronomer, mathematician. One of ablest in his time.

LAMARCK, 1744–1829. Naturalist. Especially famous for work in zoology.

LANJUINAIS, 1753–1827. Jurist. Member of National Assembly, Convention.

LA REVELLIÈRE-LÉPEAUX, LOUIS, 1753–1824. Active politician. Admirer of Rousseau. Deputy to Estates General; took part in various phases of the Revolution.

LA ROCHEFOUCAULD-LIANCOURT, DUC DE, 1747–1827. Noble courtier; intimate of Louis XVI. Elected to the Estates General; President of the National Assembly.

LETRONNE or LETROSNE, 1728–1780. Jurist, economist. Followed the Physiocrats' ideas.

LIGNE, PRINCE DE, 1735–1814. Austrian military man; wrote extensively in French. Friend of many outstanding persons in government and literary circles.

LINGUET, 1736–1794. Lawyer, publicist. Wrote extensively against d'Alembert and his followers. Also wrote against Mirabeau; defended Louis XVI. Executed in 1794.

LOUVET, JEAN-BAPTISTE, 1760–1797. Writer and political leader. Supported the Girondins against the radicals in the Convention.

MABLY, ABBÉ, 1709–1785. *Philosophe,* historian. Many successful works, noted for their materialism, communism, internationalism.

MALLET DU PAN, JACQUES, 1749–1800. Swiss publicist. Wrote extensively on current affairs.

MARAT, 1743–1793. Journalist, politician. Noted for humanitarian views, violence of attacks on all enemies of the Revolution. Assassinated by a Girondist sympathizer, 1793.

MARÉCHAL, 1750–1803. Mediocre writer. Noted for socialist views. Supported the Revolution throughout.

MARMONTEL, 1723–1799. Man of letters. His *Memoirs* give intimate details of the social life of the period.

MAUPEOU, 1714–1792. Chancellor late under Louis XV. Famous for exiling the Parlement of Paris to the provinces, 1771–1774.

MAURY, JEAN-SIFFREIN, 1746–1817. Ecclesiastic. Court preacher under Louis XVI. Elected to Estates General. Opposed many acts of the Constituent Assembly, especially the Civil Constitution of the Clergy. Soon went into exile.

MERCIER, 1740–1814. Man of letters. Member of the Convention. Opposed Robespierre. Imprisoned, but survived.

MERCIER DE LA RIVIÈRE, 1720–1793. Economist, publicist. Supported ideas of the Physiocrats.

MIRABEAU (ELDER), MARQUIS, 1715–1789. Economist. Followed ideas of the Physiocrats.

MIRABEAU, COUNT, 1749–1791. Leader of the Revolution, 1789–1791. Its greatest orator. Favored constitutional monarchy.

MONTESQUIEU, BARON, 1689–1755. One of the greatest *philosophes.* Known for his social criticism, ideas on law, constitutions, separation of powers, theory of climate.

MORELLET, 1727–1819. *Philosophe,* economist. Followed ideas of the Physiocrats. Collaborated in the *Encyclopédie.* Member of French Academy.

MORELLY (dates unknown). Several works, strongly communistic.

MOUNIER, 1758–1806. Jurist, politician. Active in initial phase of the Revolution. Elected President of Constituent Assembly but went into exile, 1790. Known for judicious political opinions.

NECKER, 1732–1804. Swiss Protestant. Financier, author, statesman. Finance Minister of France, 1777–1781, 1788–1790. Favored a conservative revolution.

NOAILLES, LOUIS-MARIE, VICOMTE DE, 1756–1804. French general and political leader. Elected to Estates General as deputy for the nobility. Vigorously supported reforms by the Constituent Assembly.

PALISSOT, 1730–1814. Man of letters. Critic of Encyclopedists. Satirized them in several works, but respected Voltaire.

POMPADOUR, MME DE, 1721–1764. Official mistress of Louis XV after 1745. Influential in governmental affairs. Patron of artists, writers. Supported Encyclopedists.

POMPIGNAN, 1709–1784. Poet. Member of French Academy. Sharp critic of the new ideas.

PREVOST, ABBÉ, 1697–1763. Successful novelist. Masterpiece: *Manon Lescaut.*

QUESNAY, 1694–1774. Physician, economist. Leader of the Physiocrats. Proponent of natural economic law. Collaborated in the *Encyclopédie.*

RABAUT DE SAINT-ETIENNE, 1743–1793. Protestant. Proponent of religious toleration. President of Constituent Assembly; member of Convention. Executed for Girondist affiliations, 1793.

RACINE, LOUIS, 1692–1763. Lawyer, poet. Poetic works were elegant but uninspired.

RAYNAL, ABBÉ, 1713–1796. *Philosophe,* historian. Wrote many successful, popular works. Most famous: *History of the Indies.*

REGNAUD, 1762–1819. Ardent revolutionary. Imprisoned during the Terror.

RESTIF, 1734–1806. Man of letters, novelist. Disciple of Rousseau. Wrote many mediocre novels.

RIVAROL, ANTOINE, 1756–1804. Writer and publicist. Wrote in defense of the monarohy during the first years of the Revolution.

ROBESPIERRE, 1758–1794. Major political leader. Took radical position throughout early Revolution; all-powerful during the Terror. His execution in 1794 ended the Terror.

ROLAND, MME, 1754–1793. Cultured, learned lady. Leaders of the Revolution frequented her salon. Executed, 1793.

ROUSSEAU, 1712–1778. One of the greatest *philosophes.* Enjoyed enormous following. Influential in romantic movement, religious revival, education, ideas of democracy.

SADE, MARQUIS, 1740–1814. Writer. Known for his licentious novels.

SAINT-JUST, 1764–1794. Ardent revolutionary. Supported Robespierre. Member of the Committee of Public Safety and a major influence during the Terror. Executed, 1794.

SAINT-SIMON, DUKE, 1675–1755. Courtier, historian. Known for his famous *Memoirs,* ideas on rightful place of nobility in government.

SERVAN, 1737–1807. Jurist. Sacrificed his career by defending religiously unpopular causes.

SIEYÈS, ABBÉ, 1748–1836. Publicist, politician. Served many regimes during the Revolution and Napoleonic era. Known for efforts to write and reform constitutions.

TOUSSAINT, 1715–1772. Jurist, author. Proponent of natural morality and religion. Contributed to the *Encyclopédie.*

TURGOT, BARON, 1727–1781. *Philosophe,* economist. One of the ablest Physiocrats. Controller General of Finance, 1774–1776. Attempted many useful but unsuccessful reforms.

VERGENNES, COUNT, 1717–1787. Statesman. Foreign Minister, 1774–1787. Last great foreign minister of the monarchy.

VERGNIAUD, 1753–1793. Active revolutionary. In Legislative Assembly, Convention. Leader of the Girondists; opposed the Terror. Executed, 1793.

VOISENON, ABBÉ, 1708–1755. Man of letters. Member of French Academy. Wrote many licentious works of fiction.

VOLLAND, SOPHIE. Lady friend and inspiration of Diderot.

VOLNEY, 1757–1820. Learned *philosophe*. Great knowledge of languages, history, geography. In National Assembly; later withdrew his support from the Revolution.

VOLTAIRE, 1694–1778. Greatest and most widely read *philosophe*. Proponent of civil liberties, natural rights, enlightened despotism. Enemy of religious fanaticism; held to deism, natural religion. Sought judicial reforms. Able historian.

I THE MOST FAMOUS DEBATE ON THE INFLUENCE OF THE ENLIGHTENMENT

Edmund Burke

REFLECTIONS ON THE REVOLUTION IN FRANCE

It was Edmund Burke (1729–1797) who first extensively articulated certain basic criticisms of the Enlightenment and its influence during the French Revolution. Burke's arguments were so fundamental and so convincing that they were repeated by many generations of like-minded writers. Distrusting pure reason and abstract ideas as keys to human affairs, Burke insisted that the constitution of every state was a natural, organic growth and that individual rights were meaningful only if they rested upon legal and traditional foundations. Thus he supported the cause of the colonists during the American Revolution, but denounced the leaders of the French Revolution as presumptuous doctrinaires who misunderstood the true nature of political institutions and were sowing the seeds of anarchy and destruction. It was from this point of view that he criticized the Enlightenment and its influence in his widely read Reflections on the Revolution in France.

You are pleased to call again, and with some earnestness, for my thoughts on the late proceedings in France. I will not give you reason to imagine that I think my sentiments of such value as to wish myself to be solicited about them. They are of too little consequence to be very anxiously either communicated or withheld. It was from attention to you, and to you only, that I hesitated at the time when you first desired to receive them. . . .

You imagined, when you wrote last, that I might possibly be reckoned among the approvers of certain proceedings in France, from the solemn public seal of sanction they have received from two clubs of gentlemen in London, called the Constitutional Society, and the Revolution Society.[1] . . .

I flatter myself that I love a manly, moral, regulated liberty as

From *Reflections on the Revolution in France, and on the Proceedings in Certain Societies in London, Relative to that Event. In a Letter Intended to Have Been Sent to a Gentleman in Paris (1790).* In *The Works of Edmund Burke,* Vol. 3 (Boston, 1839).

[1] The Revolution Society to which Burke refers was founded to honor the Glorious Revolution of 1688. However, it was composed chiefly of religious dissenters who resented their political disabilities and supported the cause of reform. Dr. Richard Price, who gave his famous address before this group in November, 1789, praised the French Revolution as the successor to the Glorious Revolution and advocated open resistance to oppression.—Ed.

well as any gentleman of that society, be he who he will; and perhaps I have given as good proofs of my attachment to that cause,
in the whole course of my public conduct. I think I envy liberty as
little as they do, to any other nation. But I cannot stand forward,
and give praise or blame to anything which relates to human actions, and human concerns, on a simple view of the object, as it
stands stripped of every relation, in all the nakedness and solitude
of metaphysical abstraction. Circumstances (which with some gentlemen pass for nothing) give in reality to every political principle its
distinguishing color, and discriminating effect. The circumstances are
what render every civil and political scheme beneficial or noxious to
mankind. Abstractedly speaking, government, as well as liberty, is
good; yet could I, in common sense, ten years ago, have felicitated
France on her enjoyment of a government (for she then had a government) without inquiry what the nature of that government was,
or how it was administered? Can I now congratulate the same nation
upon its freedom? Is it because liberty in the abstract may be
classed among the blessings of mankind, that I am seriously to
felicitate a madman, who has escaped from the protecting restraint
and wholesome darkness of his cell, on his restoration to the enjoyment of light and liberty? Am I to congratulate a highwayman and
murderer, who has broke prison, upon the recovery of his natural
rights? . . . I must be tolerably sure, before I venture publicly to
congratulate men upon a blessing, that they have really received one.
Flattery corrupts both the receiver and the giver; and adulation is
not of more service to the people than to kings. I should therefore
suspend my congratulations on the new liberty of France, until I
was informed how it had been combined with government; with
public force; with the discipline and obedience of armies; with the
collection of an effective and well-distributed revenue; with morality
and religion; with solidity and property; with peace and order; with
civil and social manners. All these (in their way) are good things too;
and, without them, liberty is not a benefit whilst it lasts, and it is
not likely to continue long. The effect of liberty to individuals is,
that they may do what they please: we ought to see what it will
please them to do, before we risk congratulations, which may be
soon turned into complaints. Prudence would dictate this in the case
of separate insulated private men; but liberty, when men act in
bodies, is *power*. Considerate people, before they declare them-

selves, will observe the use which is made of *power;* and particularly of so trying a thing as *new* power in *new* persons, of whose principles, tempers, and dispositions they have little or no experience, and in situations, where those who appear the most stirring in the scene may possibly not be the real movers. . . .

Kings, in one sense, are undoubtedly the servants of the people, because their power has no other rational end than that of the general advantage; but it is not true that they are, in the ordinary sense, (by our constitution, at least) anything like servants; the essence of whose situation is to obey the commands of some other, and to be removable at pleasure. But the king of Great Britain obeys no other person; all other persons are individually, and collectively too, under him, and owe to him a legal obedience. The law, which knows neither to flatter nor to insult, calls this high magistrate, not our servant, as this humble divine calls him, but *"our sovereign lord the king;"* and we, on our parts, have learned to speak only the primitive language of the law, and not the confused jargon of their Babylonian pulpits.

As he is not to obey us, but as we are to obey the law in him, our constitution has made no sort of provision towards rendering him as a servant in any degree responsible. . . . In this he is not distinguished from the commons and the lords; who, in their several public capacities, can never be called to an account for their conduct; although the Revolution Society chooses to assert, in direct opposition to one of the wisest and most beautiful parts of our constitution, that "a king is no more than the first servant of the public, created by it, *and responsible to it."*

III would our ancestors at the Revolution [of 1688] have deserved their fame for wisdom, if they had found no security for their freedom, but in rendering their government feeble in its operations, and precarious in its tenure; if they had been able to contrive no better remedy against arbitrary power than civil confusion. Let these gentlemen state who that *representative* public is to whom they will affirm the king, as a servant, to be responsible. It will be then time enough for me to produce to them the positive statute law which affirms that he is not. . . . The Revolution was made to preserve our *ancient* indisputable laws and liberties, and that *ancient* constitution of government which is our only security for law and liberty. If you are desirous of knowing the spirit of our constitution, and the policy which predominated in that great period which has secured it to this hour, pray look for both in our histories, in our records, in our acts of Parliament, and journals of Parliament, and not in the sermons of the Old Jewry, and the after-dinner toasts of the Revolution Society. In the former you will find other ideas and another language. Such a claim is as ill-suited to our temper and wishes as it is unsupported by any appearance of authority. The very idea of the fabrication of a new government, is enough to fill us with disgust and horror. We wished at the period of the Revolution, and do now wish, to derive all we possess as *an inheritance from our forefathers.* Upon that body and stock of inheritance we have taken care not to inoculate any scion alien to the nature of the original plant. All the reformations we have hitherto made, have proceeded upon the principle of reference to antiquity; and I hope, nay I am persuaded, that all those which possibly may be made hereafter, will be carefully formed upon analogical precedent, authority, and example. . . .

This policy appears to me to be the result of profound reflection; or rather the happy effect of following nature, which is wisdom without reflection, and above it. A spirit of innovation is generally the result of a selfish temper and confined views. People will not look forward to posterity, who never look backward to their ancestors. Besides, the people of England well know, that the idea of inheritance furnishes a sure principle of conservation, and a sure principle of transmission; without at all excluding a principle of improvement. It leaves acquisition free; but it secures what it acquires. Whatever advantages are obtained by a state proceeding on these maxims, are locked fast as in a sort of family settlement; grasped as in a kind of mortmain forever. By a constitutional policy, working after the pattern of nature, we receive, we hold, we transmit our government and our privileges, in the same manner in which we enjoy and transmit our property and our lives. The institutions of policy, the goods of fortune, the gifts of Providence, are handed down, to us and from us, in the same course and order. Our political system is placed in a just correspondence and symmetry with the order of the world, and with the mode of existence decreed to a permanent body composed of transitory parts; wherein, by the disposition of a stupendous wisdom, molding together the great mysterious incorporation of the human race, the whole, at one time, is never old, or middle-aged, or young, but in a condition of unchangeable constancy, moves on through the varied tenor of perpetual decay, fall, renovation, and progression. Thus, by preserving the method of nature in the conduct of the state, in what we improve we are never wholly new; in what we retain, we are never wholly obsolete. By adhering in this manner and on those principles to our forefathers, we are guided not by the superstition of antiquarians, but by the spirit of philosophic analogy. In this choice of inheritance we have given to our frame of polity the image of a relation in blood; binding up the constitution of our country with our dearest domestic ties; adopting our fundamental laws into the bosom of our family affections; keeping inseparable, and cherishing with the warmth of all their combined and mutually reflected charities, our state, our hearths, our sepulchres, and our altars.

Through the same plan of a conformity to nature in our artificial institutions, and by calling in the aid of her unerring and powerful instincts, to fortify the fallible and feeble contrivances of our reason, we have derived several other, and those no small benefits, from considering our liberties in the light of an inheritance. Always acting as if in the presence of canonized forefathers, the spirit of freedom, leading in itself to misrule and excess, is tempered with an awful gravity. This idea of a liberal descent inspires us with a sense of habitual native dignity, which prevents that upstart insolence almost inevitably adhering to and disgracing those who are the first acquirers of any distinction. By this means our liberty becomes a noble freedom. It carries an imposing and majestic aspect. It has a pedigree and illustrating ancestors. It has its bearings and its ensigns armorial. It has its gallery of portraits; its monumental inscriptions; its records, evidences, and titles. We procure reverence to our civil institutions on the principle upon which nature teaches us to revere individual men; on account of their age; and on account of those from whom they are descended. All your sophisters cannot produce anything better adapted to preserve a rational and manly freedom than the course that we have pursued, who have chosen our nature rather than our speculations, our breasts rather than our inventions, for the great conservatories and magazines of our rights and privileges.

You might, if you pleased, have profited of our example, and have given to your recovered freedom a correspondent dignity. Your privileges, though discontinued, were not lost to memory. Your con-

stitution, it is true, whilst you were out of possession, suffered waste
and dilapidation; but you possessed in some parts the walls, and in
all the foundations of a noble and venerable castle. You might have
repaired those walls; you might have built on those old foundations.
Your constitution was suspended before it was perfected; but you
had the elements of a constitution very nearly as good as could be
wished. In your old states [Estates General] you possessed that
variety of parts corresponding with the various descriptions of which
your community was happily composed; you had all that combination, and all that opposition of interests, you had that action and
counteraction which, in the natural and in the political world, from
the reciprocal struggle of discordant powers, draws out the harmony
of the universe. These opposed and conflicting interests, which you
considered as so great a blemish in your old and in our present
constitution, interpose a salutary check to all precipitate resolutions. . . .

You had all these advantages in your ancient states; but you
chose to act as if you had never been molded into civil society,
and had everything to begin anew. You began ill, because you began
by despising everything that belonged to you. You set up your trade
without a capital. If the last generations of your country appeared
without much lustre in your eyes, you might have passed them by,
and derived your claims from a more early race of ancestors. Under
a pious predilection for those ancestors, your imaginations would
have realized in them a standard of virtue and wisdom, beyond the
vulgar practice of the hour: and you would have risen with the example to whose imitation you aspired. . . . You would have rendered
the cause of liberty venerable in the eyes of every worthy mind in
every nation. You would have shamed despotism from the earth, by
showing that freedom was not only reconcilable, but as, when well
disciplined, it is, auxiliary to law. You would have had an unoppres-
sive but a productive revenue. You would have had a flourishing
commerce to feed it. You would have had a free constitution; a
potent monarchy; a disciplined army; a reformed and venerated
clergy; a mitigated but spirited nobility, to lead your virtue, not to
overlay it; you would have had a liberal order of commons, to
emulate and to recruit that nobility; you would have had a protected,
satisfied, laborious, and obedient people, taught to seek and to recognize the happiness that is to be found by virtue in all conditions;

in which consists the true moral equality of mankind, and not in that monstrous fiction, which, by inspiring false ideas and vain expectations into men destined to travel in the obscure walk of laborious life, serves only to aggravate and embitter that real inequality, which it never can remove; and which the order of civil life establishes as much for the benefit of those whom it must leave in an humble state, as those whom it is able to exalt to a condition more splendid, but not more happy. You had a smooth and easy career of felicity and glory laid open to you, beyond anything recorded in the history of the world; but you have shown that difficulty is good for man.

Compute your gains; see what is got by those extravagant and presumptuous speculations which have taught your leaders to despise all their predecessors, and all their contemporaries, and even to despise themselves, until the moment in which they became truly despicable. By following those false lights, France has bought undisguised calamities at a higher price than any nation has purchased the most unequivocal blessings! France has bought poverty by crime! France has not sacrificed her virtue to her interest; but she has abandoned her interest, that she might prostitute her virtue. . . . France, when she let loose the reins of regal authority, doubled the license of a ferocious dissoluteness in manners, and of an insolent irreligion in opinions and practices; and has extended through all ranks of life, as if she were communicating some privilege, or laying open some secluded benefit, all the unhappy corruptions that usually were the disease of wealth and power. This is one of the new principles of equality in France. . . .

[All men] have seen the French rebel against a mild and lawful monarch, with more fury, outrage, and insult, than ever any people has been known to rise against the most illegal usurper, or the most sanguinary tyrant. Their resistance was made to concession; their revolt was from protection; their blow was aimed at a hand holding out graces, favors, and immunities.

This was unnatural. The rest is in order. They have found their punishment in their success. Laws overturned; tribunals subverted; industry without vigor; commerce expiring; the revenue unpaid, yet the people impoverished; a church pillaged, and a state not relieved; civil and military anarchy made the constitution of the kingdom; everything human and divine sacrificed to the idol of public credit, and national bankruptcy the consequence; and to crown all, the paper securities of new, precarious, tottering power, the discredited paper securities of impoverished fraud, and beggared rapine, held out as a currency for the support of an empire. . . .

Were all these dreadful things necessary? Were they the inevitable results of the desperate struggle of determined patriots, compelled to wade through blood and tumult, to the quiet shore of a tranquil and prosperous liberty? No! nothing like it. The fresh ruins of France, which shock our feelings wherever we can turn our eyes, are not the devastation of civil war; they are the sad but instructive monuments of rash and ignorant counsel in time of profound peace. They are the display of inconsiderate and presumptuous, because unresisted and irresistible authority. The persons who have thus squandered away the precious treasure of their crimes, the persons who have made this prodigal and wild waste of public evils (the last stake reserved for the ultimate ransom of the state) have met in their progress with little, or rather with no opposition at all. Their whole march was more like a triumphal procession than the progress of a war. Their pioneers have gone before them, and demolished and laid everything level at their feet. Not one drop of *their* blood have they shed in the cause of the country they have ruined. They have made no sacrifice to their projects of greater consequence than their shoe buckles, whilst they were imprisoning their king, murdering their fellow citizens, and bathing in tears, and plunging in poverty and distress, thousands of worthy men and worthy families. Their cruelty has not even been the base result of fear. It has been the effect of their sense of perfect safety, in authorizing treasons, robberies, rapes, assassinations, slaughters, and burnings, throughout their harassed land. But the cause of all was plain from the beginning. . . .

Whilst they are possessed by these notions, it is vain to talk to them of the practice of their ancestors, the fundamental laws of their country, the fixed form of a constitution, whose merits are confirmed by the solid test of long experience, and an increasing public strength and national prosperity. They despise experience as the wisdom of unlettered men; and as for the rest, they have wrought underground a mine that will blow up at one grand explosion all examples of antiquity, all precedents, charters, and acts of Parliament. They have "the rights of men." Against these there can be no prescription; against these no argument is binding: these admit no temperament, and no compromise: anything withheld from their full demand is so much of fraud and injustice. Against these their rights of men let no government look for security in the length of its continuance, or in the justice and lenity of its administration. The objections of these speculatists, if its forms do not quadrate with their theories, are as valid against such an old and beneficent government as against the most violent tyranny, or the greenest usurpation. . . .

Far am I from denying in theory; full as far is my heart from withholding in practice (if I were of power to give or to withhold) the *real* rights of men. In denying their false claims of right, I do not mean to injure those which are real, and are such as their pretended rights would totally destroy. If civil society be made for the advantage of man, all the advantages for which it is made become his right. It is an institution of beneficence; and law itself is only beneficence acting by a rule. Men have a right to live by that rule; they have a right to justice; as between their fellows, whether their fellows are in politic function or in ordinary occupation. They have a right to the fruits of their industry; and to the means of making their industry fruitful. They have a right to the acquisitions of their parents; to the nourishment and improvement of their offspring; to instruction in life, and to consolation in death. Whatever each man can separately do, without trespassing upon others, he has a right to do for himself; and he has a right to a fair portion of all which society, with all its combinations of skill and force, can do in his favor. In this partnership all men have equal rights; but not to equal things. He that has but five shillings in the partnership, has as good a right to it, as he that has five hundred pounds has to his larger proportion. But he has not a right to an equal dividend in the product of the joint stock; and as to the share of power, authority, and direction which each individual ought to have in the management of the state, that I must deny to be amongst the direct original rights of man in civil society; for I have in my contemplation the civil social man, and no other. It is a thing to be settled by convention. . . .

Government is not made in virtue of natural rights, which may and do exist in total independence of it; and exist in much greater clearness, and in a much greater degree of abstract perfection: but their abstract perfection is their practical defeat. By having a right to everything, they want everything. Government is a contrivance of human wisdom to provide for human *wants*. Men have a right that these wants should be provided for by this wisdom. Among these wants is to be reckoned the want, out of civil society, of a sufficient restraint upon their passions. Society requires not only that the passions of individuals should be subjected, but that even in the mass and body as well as in the individuals, the inclinations of men should frequently be thwarted, their will controlled, and their passions brought into subjection. This can only be done *by a power out of themselves;* and not, in the exercise of its function, subject to that will and to those passions which it is its office to bridle and subdue. In this sense the restraints on men, as well as their liberties, are to be reckoned among their rights. But as the liberties and the restrictions vary with times and circumstances, and admit of infinite modifications, they cannot be settled upon any abstract rule; and nothing is so foolish as to discuss them upon that principle. . . .

The pretended rights of these theorists are all extremes; and in proportion as they are metaphysically true, they are morally and politically false. The rights of men are in a sort of *middle,* incapable of definition, but not impossible to be discerned. The rights of men in governments are their advantages; and these are often in balances between differences of good; in compromises sometimes between good and evil, and sometimes, between evil and evil. Political reason is a computing principle; adding, subtracting, multiplying, and dividing, morally and not metaphysically or mathematically, true moral denominations. . . .

I almost venture to affirm, that not one in a hundred amongst us participates in the "triumph" of the Revolution Society. . . . We are not the converts of Rousseau; we are not the disciples of Voltaire; Helvetius has made no progress amongst us. Atheists are not our preachers; madmen are not our lawgivers. We know that *we* have made no discoveries; and we think that no discoveries are to be made, in morality; nor many in the great principles of government, nor in the ideas of liberty, which were understood long before we were born, altogether as well as they will be after the grave has heaped its mold upon our presumption, and the silent tomb shall have imposed its law on our pert loquacity. . . .

Your literary men, and your politicians, and so do the whole clan of the enlightened among us, essentially differ in these points. They have no respect for the wisdom of others; but they pay it off by a very full measure of confidence in their own. With them it is a sufficient motive to destroy an old scheme of things, because it is an old one. As to the new, they are in no sort of fear with regard to the duration of a building run up in haste; because duration is no object to those who think little or nothing has been done before their time, and who place all their hopes in discovery. They conceive, very systematically, that all things which give perpetuity are mischievous, and therefore they are at inexpiable war with all establishments. They think that government may vary like modes of dress, and with as little ill effect: that there needs no principle of attachment, except a sense of present convenience, to any constitution of the state. They always speak as if they were of opinion that there is a singular species of compact between them and their magistrates, which binds the magistrate, but which has nothing reciprocal in it, but that the majesty of the people has a right to dissolve it without any reason, but its will. Their attachment to their country itself is only so far as it agrees with some of their fleeting projects; it begins and ends with that scheme of polity which falls in with their momentary opinion.

These doctrines, or rather sentiments, seem prevalent with your new statesmen. But they are wholly different from those on which we have always acted in this country. . . .

The effects of the incapacity shown by the popular leaders in all the great members of the commonwealth are to be covered with the "all-atoning name" of liberty. In some people I see great liberty indeed; in many, if not in the most, an oppressive degrading servitude. But what is liberty without wisdom, and without virtue? It is the greatest of all possible evils; for it is folly, vice, and madness, without tuition or restraint. Those who know what virtuous liberty is, cannot bear to see it disgraced by incapable heads, on account of their having high-sounding words in their mouths. Grand, swelling sentiments of liberty, I am sure I do not despise. . . . But in such an undertaking as that in France, all these subsidiary sentiments and artifices are of little avail. To make a government requires no great prudence. Settle the seat of power; teach obedience: and the work is done. To give freedom is still more easy. It is not necessary to guide; it only requires to let go the rein. But to form a *free government;* that is, to temper together these opposite elements of liberty and restraint in one consistent work, requires much thought, deep reflection, a sagacious, powerful, and combining mind. This I do not find in those who take the lead in the National Assembly. . . .

But am I so unreasonable as to see nothing at all that deserves commendation in the indefatigable labors of this assembly? I do not deny that among an infinite number of acts of violence and folly, some good may have been done. They who destroy everything certainly will remove some grievance. They who make everything new, have a chance that they may establish something beneficial. . . . Some usages have been abolished on just grounds; but they were such, that if they had stood as they were to all eternity, they would little detract from the happiness and prosperity of any state. The improvements of the National Assembly are superficial, their errors fundamental.

Whatever they are, I wish my countrymen rather to recommend to our neighbors the example of the British constitution, than to take models from them for the improvement of our own. . . .

I would not exclude alteration either; but even when I changed, it should be to preserve. I should be led to my remedy by a great grievance. In what I did, I should follow the example of our ancestors. I would make the reparation as nearly as possible in the style of the building. A politic caution, a guarded circumspection, a moral rather than a complexional timidity, were among the ruling principles of our forefathers in their most decided conduct. Not being illuminated with the light of which the gentlemen of France tell us they have got so abundant a share, they acted under a strong impression of the ignorance and fallibility of mankind. He that had made them thus fallible, rewarded them for having in their conduct attended to their nature. Let us imitate their caution, if we wish to deserve their fortune or to retain their bequests. Let us add, if we please, but let us preserve what they have left; and, standing on the firm ground of the British constitution, let us be satisfied to admire, rather than attempt to follow in their desperate flights the aëronauts of France. . . .

Thomas Paine
THE RIGHTS OF MAN

Among the writers who answered Burke's criticisms of the Enlightenment, Thomas Paine (1737–1809) was by far the most important. A minor partici- pant in both the American and French Revolutions, he was chiefly known as a skillful and very influential controversialist. Paine was fired with the crusad- ing zeal of a reformer who believed in man's natural rights and in revolution as a means of achieving social and political betterment. Contrary to Burke, he argued that the needs and desires of the living should prevail regardless of tradition, that the people were perpetually sovereign, and that government was for the purpose of implementing man's inalienable rights. Thus Paine thoroughly accepted the philosophy of the Enlightenment and applauded its influence during the French Revolution.

Among the incivilities by which nations or individuals provoke and irritate each other, Mr. Burke's pamphlet on the French Revolution is an extraordinary instance. Neither the people of France, nor the National Assembly, were troubling themselves about the affairs of England, or the English Parliament; and that Mr. Burke should commence an unprovoked attack upon them, both in Parliament and in public, is a conduct that cannot be pardoned on the score of man- ners, nor justified on that of policy.

There is scarcely an epithet of abuse to be found in the English language, with which Mr. Burke has not loaded the French nation and the National Assembly. Everything which rancor, prejudice, ignorance or knowledge could suggest, is poured forth in the copious fury of nearly four hundred pages. In the strain and on the plan Mr. Burke was writing, he might have written on to as many thousands. When the tongue or the pen is let loose in a frenzy of passion, it is the man, and not the subject, that becomes exhausted. . . .

As Mr. Burke occasionally applies the poison drawn from his horrid principles, not only to the English nation, but to the French Revolution and the National Assembly, and charges that august, il- luminated and illuminating body of men with the epithet of *usurpers,* I shall, *sans cérémonie,* place another system of principles in opposi- tion to his.

From Thomas Paine, *Rights of Man*, in *The Writings of Thomas Paine*, edited by M. D. Conway, Vol. 2 (New York, 1895).

The English Parliament of 1688 did a certain thing, which, for themselves and their constituents, they had a right to do, and which it appeared right should be done. But, in addition to this right, which they possessed by delegation, *they set up another right by assumption,* that of binding and controlling posterity to the end of time. The case, therefore, divides itself into two parts; the right which they possessed by delegation, and the right which they set up by assumption. The first is admitted; but with respect to the second, I reply—

There never did, there never will, and there never can, exist a Parliament, or any description of men, or any generation of men, in any country, possessed of the right or the power of binding and controlling posterity to the *"end of time,"* or of commanding forever how the world shall be governed, or who shall govern it; and therefore all such clauses, acts or declarations by which the makers of them attempt to do what they have neither the right nor the power to do, nor the power to execute, are in themselves null and void. Every age and generation must be as free to act for itself *in all cases* as the age and generations which preceded it. The vanity and presumption of governing beyond the grave is the most ridiculous and insolent of all tyrannies. Man has no property in man; neither has any generation a property in the generations which are to follow. The Parliament or the people of 1688, or of any other period, had no more right to dispose of the people of the present day, or to bind or to control them *in any shape whatever*, than the parliament or the people of the present day have to dispose of, bind or control those who are to live a hundred or a thousand years hence. Every generation is, and must be, competent to all the purposes which its occasions require. It is the living, and not the dead, that are to be accommodated. When man ceases to be, his power and his wants cease with him; and having no longer any participation in the concerns of this world, he has no longer any authority in directing who shall be its governors, or how its government shall be organized, or how administered.

I am not contending for nor against any form of government, nor for nor against any party, here or elsewhere. That which a whole nation chooses to do it has a right to do. Mr. Burke says, No. Where, then, does the right exist? I am contending for the rights of the *living*, and against their being willed away and controlled and contracted for by the manuscript assumed authority of the dead, and Mr. Burke is contending for the authority of the dead over the rights and freedom of the living. There was a time when kings disposed of their crowns by will upon their death beds, and consigned the people, like beasts of the field, to whatever successor they appointed. This is now so exploded as scarcely to be remembered, and so monstrous as hardly to be believed. But the Parliamentary clauses upon which Mr. Burke builds his political church are of the same nature. . . .

It requires but a very small glance of thought to perceive that although laws made in one generation often continue in force through succeeding generations, yet they continue to derive their force from the consent of the living. A law not repealed continues in force, not because it *cannot* be repealed, but because it is *not* repealed; and the non-repealing passes for consent. . . .

The circumstances of the world are continually changing, and the opinions of men change also; and as government is for the living, and not for the dead, it is the living only that has any right in it. That which may be thought right and found convenient in one age may be thought wrong and found inconvenient in another. In such cases, who is to decide, the living or the dead?

As almost one hundred pages of Mr. Burke's book are employed upon these clauses, it will consequently follow that if the clauses themselves, so far as they set up an *assumed usurped* dominion over posterity forever, are unauthoritative, and in their nature null and void; that all his voluminous inferences, and declamation drawn therefrom, or founded thereon, are null and void also; and on this ground I rest the matter. . . .

Before anything can be reasoned upon to a conclusion, certain facts, principles, or data, to reason from, must be established, admitted, or denied. Mr. Burke with his usual outrage, abused the *Declaration of the Rights of Man,* published by the National Assembly of France, as the basis on which the constitution of France is built. This he calls "paltry and blurred sheets of paper about the rights of man." Does Mr. Burke mean to deny that *man* has any rights? If he does, then he must mean that there are no such things as rights anywhere, and that he has none himself; for who is there in the world but man? But if Mr. Burke means to admit that man has rights, the question then will be: What are those rights, and how man came by them originally?

The error of those who reason by precedents drawn from antiquity, respecting the rights of man, is that they do not go far enough into antiquity. They do not go the whole way. They stop in some of the intermediate stages of an hundred or a thousand years, and produce what was then done, as a rule for the present day. This is no authority at all. If we travel still farther into antiquity, we shall find a direct contrary opinion and practice prevailing; and if antiquity is to be authority, a thousand such authorities may be produced, successively contradicting each other; but if we proceed on, we shall at last come out right; we shall come to the time when man came from the hand of his Maker. What was he then? Man. Man was his high and only title, and a higher cannot be given him. . . .

If any generation of men ever possessed the right of dictating the mode by which the world should be governed forever, it was the first generation that existed; and if that generation did it not, no succeeding generation can show any authority for doing it, nor can set any up. The illuminating and divine principle of the equal rights of man (for it has its origin from the Maker of man) relates, not only to the living individuals, but to generations of men succeeding each other. Every generation is equal in rights to generations which preceded it, by the same rule that every individual is born equal in rights with his contemporary.

Every history of the creation, and every traditionary account, whether from the lettered or unlettered world, however they may vary in their opinion or belief of certain particulars, all agree in establishing one point, *the unity of man;* by which I mean that men are all of *one degree,* and consequently that all men are born equal, and with equal natural right, in the same manner as if posterity had been continued by *creation* instead of *generation,* the latter being the only mode by which the former is carried forward; and consequently every child born into the world must be considered as deriving its existence from God. The world is as new to him as it was to the first man that existed, and his natural right in it is of the same kind. . . .

Hitherto we have spoken only (and that but in part) of the natural rights of man. We have now to consider the civil rights of man, and to show how the one originates from the other. Man did not enter into society to become *worse* than he was before, nor to have fewer rights than he had before, but to have those rights better secured. His natural rights are the foundation of all his civil rights. But in order to pursue this distinction with more precision, it will be necessary to mark the different qualities of natural and civil rights.

A few words will explain this. Natural rights are those which appertain to man in right of his existence. Of this kind are all the intellectual rights, or rights of the mind, and also all those rights of acting as an individual for his own comfort and happiness, which are not injurious to the natural rights of others. Civil rights are those which appertain to man in right of his being a member of society. Every civil right has for its foundation some natural right pre-existing in the individual, but to the enjoyment of which his individual power is not, in all cases, sufficiently competent. Of this kind are all those which relate to security and protection.

From this short review it will be easy to distinguish between that class of natural rights which man retains after entering into society and those which he throws into the common stock as a member of society. . . .

To possess ourselves of a clear idea of what government is, or ought to be, we must trace it to its origin. In doing this we shall easily discover that governments must have arisen either *out* of the people or *over* the people. Mr. Burke has made no distinction. He investigates nothing to its source, and therefore he confounds everything; but he has signified his intention of undertaking, at some future opportunity, a comparison between the constitutions of England and France. . . . The English government is one of those which arose out of a conquest, and not out of society, and consequently it arose over the people; and though it has been much modified from the opportunity of circumstances since the time of William the Conqueror, the country has never yet regenerated itself, and is therefore without a constitution. . . .

The present National Assembly of France is, strictly speaking, the personal social compact. The members of it are the delegates of the nation in its *original* character; future assemblies will be the delegates of the nation in its *organized* character. The authority of the present Assembly is different from what the authority of future Assemblies will be. The authority of the present one is to form a constitution; the authority of future assemblies will be to legislate according to the principles and forms prescribed in that constitution; and if experience should hereafter show that alterations, amendments, or additions are necessary, the constitution will point out the mode by which such things shall be done, and not leave it to the discretionary power of the future government. . . .

In contemplating the French Constitution, we see in it a rational order of things. The principles harmonize with the forms, and both with their origin. It may perhaps be said as an excuse for bad forms, that they are nothing more than forms; but this is a mistake. Forms grow out of principles, and operate to continue the principles they grow from. It is impossible to practice a bad form on anything but a bad principle. It cannot be ingrafted on a good one; and wherever the forms in any government are bad, it is a certain indication that the principles are bad also. . . .

As Mr. Burke has not written on constitutions so neither has he written on the French Revolution. He gives no account of its commencement or its progress. He only expresses his wonder. "It looks," says he, "to me, as if I were in a great crisis, not of the affairs of France alone, but of all Europe, perhaps of more than Europe. All circumstances taken together, the French Revolution is the most astonishing that has hitherto happened in the world."

As wise men are astonished at foolish things, and other people at wise ones, I know not on which ground to account for Mr. Burke's astonishment; but certain it is, that he does not understand the French Revolution. It has apparently burst forth like a creation from a chaos, but it is no more than the consequence of a mental revolution priorily existing in France. The mind of the nation had changed beforehand, and the new order of things has naturally followed the new order of thoughts. I will here, as concisely as I can, trace out the growth of the French Revolution, and mark the circumstances that have contributed to produce it.

The despotism of Louis XIV, united with the gaiety of his court, and the gaudy ostentation of his character, had so humbled, and at the same time so fascinated the mind of France, that the people appeared to have lost all sense of their own dignity, in contemplating that of their grand monarch; and the whole reign of Louis XV, remarkable only for weakness and effeminacy, made no other alteration than that of spreading a sort of lethargy over the nation, from which it showed no disposition to rise.

The only signs which appeared of the spirit of liberty during those periods, are to be found in the writings of the French philosophers. Montesquieu, president of the Parliament of Bordeaux, went as far as a writer under a despotic government could well proceed; and being obliged to divide himself between principle and prudence, his mind often appears under a veil, and we ought to give him credit for more than he has expressed.

Voltaire, who was both the flatterer and the satirist of despotism, took another line. His forte lay in exposing and ridiculing the superstitions which priest-craft, united with statecraft, had interwoven with governments. It was not from the purity of his principles, or his love of mankind (for satire and philanthropy are not naturally concordant), but from his strong capacity of seeing folly in its true shape, and his irresistible propensity to expose it, that he made those attacks. They were, however, as formidable as if the motive had been virtuous; and he merits the thanks rather than the esteem of mankind.

On the contrary, we find in the writings of Rousseau, and the Abbé Raynal, a loveliness of sentiment in favor of liberty, that excites respect, and elevates the human faculties; but having raised this animation, they do not direct its operation, and leave the mind in love with an object, without describing the means of possessing it.

The writings of Quesnay, Turgot, and the friends of those authors, are of the serious kind; but they labored under the same disadvantage with Montesquieu; their writings abound with moral maxims of government, but are rather directed to economize and reform the administration of the government, than the government itself.

But all those writings and many others had their weight; and by the different manner in which they treated the subject of government, Montesquieu by his judgment and knowledge of laws, Voltaire by his wit, Rousseau and Raynal by their animation, and Quesnay and Turgot by their moral maxims and systems of economy, readers of every class met with something to their taste, and a spirit of political inquiry began to diffuse itself through the nation at the time the dispute between England and the then colonies of America broke out.

In the war which France afterwards engaged in, it is very well known that the nation appeared to be beforehand with the French ministry. Each of them had its view; but those views were directed to different objects; the one sought liberty, and the other retaliation on England. The French officers and soldiers who after this went to America, were eventually placed in the school of freedom, and learned the practice as well as the principles of it by heart.

As it was impossible to separate the military events which took place in America from the principles of the American Revolution, the publication of those events in France necessarily connected themselves with the principles which produced them. Many of the facts were in themselves principles; such as the Declaration of American Independence, and the treaty of alliance between France and America, which recognized the natural rights of man, and justified resistance to oppression.

The then Minister of France, Count Vergennes, was not the friend of America; and it is both justice and gratitude to say, that it was the Queen of France who gave the cause of America a fashion at the French court. Count Vergennes was the personal and social friend of Dr. Franklin; and the Doctor had obtained, by his sensible gracefulness, a sort of influence over him; but with respect to principles Count Vergennes was a despot.

The situation of Dr. Franklin, as Minister from America to France, should be taken into the chain of circumstances. The diplomatic character is of itself the narrowest sphere of society that man can act in. It forbids intercourse by the reciprocity of suspicion; and a diplomatic is a sort of unconnected atom, continually repelling and repelled. But this was not the case with Dr. Franklin. He was not the diplomatic of a Court, but of MAN. His character as a philosopher had been long established, and his circle of society in France was universal.

Count Vergennes resisted for a considerable time the publication in France of American constitutions, translated into the French language: but even in this he was obliged to give way to public opinion, and a sort of propriety in admitting to appear what he had undertaken to defend. The American constitutions were to liberty what a grammar is to language: they define its parts of speech, and practically construct them into syntax.

The peculiar situation of the then Marquis de Lafayette is another link in the great chain. He served in America as an American officer under a commission of Congress, and by the universality of his acquaintance was in close friendship with the civil government of America, as well as with the military line. He spoke the language of the country, entered into the discussions on the principles of government, and was always a welcome friend at any election.

When the war closed, a vast reinforcement to the cause of liberty spread itself over France, by the return of the French officers and soldiers. A knowledge of the practice was then joined to the theory; and all that was wanting to give it real existence was opportunity.

Man cannot, properly speaking, make circumstances for his purpose, but he always has it in his power to improve them when they occur, and this was the case in France. . . .

The opinions of men with respect to government are changing fast in all countries. The Revolutions of America and France have thrown a beam of light over the world, which reaches into man. The enormous expense of governments has provoked people to think, by making them feel; and when once the veil begins to rend, it admits not of repair. Ignorance is of a peculiar nature: once dispelled, it is impossible to reestablish it. It is not originally a thing of itself, but is only the absence of knowledge; and though man may be *kept* ignorant, he cannot be *made* ignorant. The mind, in discovering truth, acts in the same manner as it acts through the eye in discovering objects; when once any object has been seen, it is impossible to put the mind back to the same condition it was in before it saw it. Those who talk of a counterrevolution in France, show how little they understand of man. There does not exist in the compass of language an arrangement of words to express so much as the means of effecting a counterrevolution. The means must be an obliteration of knowledge; and it has never yet been discovered how to make man *unknow* his knowledge, or *unthink* his thoughts.

Mr. Burke is laboring in vain to stop the progress of knowledge; and it comes with the worse grace from him, as there is a certain transaction known in the city which renders him suspected of being a pensioner in a fictitious name. This may account for some strange doctrine he has advanced in his book, which though he points it at the Revolution Society, is effectually directed against the whole nation. . . .

From the Revolutions of America and France, and the symptoms that have appeared in other countries, it is evident that the opinion of the world is changing with respect to systems of government, and that revolutions are not within the compass of political calculations. The progress of time and circumstances, which men assign to the accomplishment of great changes, is too mechanical to measure the force of the mind, and the rapidity of reflection, by which revolutions are generated: All the old governments have received a shock from those that already appear, and which were once more improbable, and are a greater subject of wonder, than a general revolution in Europe would be now.

When we survey the wretched condition of man, under the monarchical and hereditary systems of government, dragged from his home by one power, or driven by another, and impoverished by taxes more than by enemies, it becomes evident that those systems are bad, and that a general revolution in the principle and construction of governments is necessary.

What is government more than the management of the affairs of a nation? It is not, and from its nature cannot be, the property of any particular man or family, but of the whole community, at whose expense it is supported; and though by force and contrivance it has been usurped into an inheritance, the usurpation cannot alter the right of things. Sovereignty, as a matter of right, appertains to the nation only, and not to any individual; and a nation has at all times an inherent indefeasible right to abolish any form of government it finds inconvenient, and to establish such as accords with its interest, disposition and happiness. The romantic and barbarous distinction of men into kings and subjects, though it may suit the condition of courtiers, cannot that of citizens; and is exploded by the principle upon which governments are now founded. Every citizen is a member of the sovereignty, and, as such, can acknowledge no personal subjection; and his obedience can be only to the laws. . . .

What were formerly called revolutions, were little more than a change of persons, or an alteration of local circumstances. They rose and fell like things of course, and had nothing in their existence or their fate that could influence beyond the spot that produced them. But what we now see in the world, from the revolutions of America and France, are a renovation of the natural order of things, a system of principles as universal as truth and the existence of man, and combining moral with political happiness and national prosperity.

    I. *Men are born, and always continue, free and equal in respect of their rights. Civil distinctions, therefore, can be founded only on public utility.*

    II. *The end of all political associations is the preservation of the natural and imprescriptible rights of man; and these rights are liberty, property, security, and resistance of oppression.*

    III. *The nation is essentially the source of all sovereignty; nor can any INDIVIDUAL, or ANY BODY OF MEN, be entitled to any authority which is not expressly derived from it.*

In these principles, there is nothing to throw a nation into confusion by inflaming ambition. They are calculated to call forth wisdom and abilities, and to exercise them for the public good, and not for the emolument or aggrandizement of particular descriptions of men or families. Monarchical sovereignty, the enemy of mankind, and the source of misery, is abolished; and the sovereignty itself is restored to its natural and original place, the nation. . . .

II THE FUNDAMENTAL CRITICISMS OF THE ENLIGHTENMENT AND ITS INFLUENCE

Joseph de Maistre
THE NECESSITY OF THE THEOCRATIC STATE

Joseph de Maistre (1754–1821) was one of the most important spokesmen for the conservative and Catholic minded critics of the Enlightenment. Forced into exile from his native Savoy by the armies of the Revolution, he wrote most of his works abroad. De Maistre believed in the absolute necessity of order and authority in human society which should be hierarchical in structure and should permit a minimum of individualism. The supreme expression of organized society he found in the Roman Catholic church, and he insisted on unqualified papal absolutism. He further believed that all human activity should have a religious foundation and purpose, and that the absence of these would vitiate man's efforts. It is therefore not surprising that he was fundamentally opposed to the philosophy of the Enlightenment and regarded it as primarily responsible for the French Revolution and its excesses.

There is a *satanic* quality to the French Revolution that distinguishes it from all earlier events and perhaps from everything that will occur in the future.

Recall the great assemblies, the speeches of Robespierre against the priesthood, the solemn apostasy of the clergy, the profanation of objects of worship, the festivals to the goddess of reason, and the innumerable orgies when the provinces sought to outdo Paris. All this goes beyond ordinary crimes and seems to belong to another world.

Now that the Revolution has become less violent, the great excesses have disappeared but its principles remain. . . . Certain men of our age have occasionally seemed to succeed in hating the Divinity, but this horrible feat is not necessary to vitiate the greatest human efforts. Mere indifference to God is an irrevocable curse upon the works of men who are thus blighted. All conceivable institutions either represent a religious concept or merely wither away. They are strong and durable to the extent that they are *deified*, if I may use the term. Not only is human reason, which is ignorantly called philosophy, incapable of supplying these foundations which with

From Joseph de Maistre, *Considérations sur la France* and *Étude sur la souveraineté* in *Œuvres complètes,* Vol. 1 (Lyon, 1884). Italics in the original. [Editor's translation]

equal ignorance are called *superstitions;* philosophy is, on the contrary, an essentially disruptive influence.

In a word, man cannot resemble the Creator without placing himself in contact with Him. Mad as we are, if we wish a mirror to reflect the sun, would we turn it toward the earth?

These observations are addressed to all, to the believer as well as the skeptic. It is a fact that I am asserting, not a hypothesis. Whether one ridicules or venerates religious concepts makes no difference; they nonetheless form the unique basis of all durable institutions. . . .

When we reflect on the attested facts of all history and recall that in the chain of human establishments from the greatest institutions of entire epochs to the smallest social organization, from an empire to a brotherhood, all have a divine basis, and that isolated human power has succeeded in endowing its works with only a false and temporary existence, what shall we think of the new French government and the power that built it? As for myself, I shall never believe in the fertility of nothingness. . . .

Whenever man, according to his power, places himself in contact with the Creator and produces an institution in the name of God, no matter what may be his personal weaknesses, ignorance, poverty, obscurity of birth, in a word, his complete lack of human resources, he participates somehow in the supreme power whose instrument he has become. He produces works whose strength and duration defy reason. . . .

What more is needed to judge the French system? If its nullity is not clear, there is nothing certain in the universe. . . .

The Constitution of 1795, like all the earlier ones, is made for *man.* Now, there is no *man* in the world. In my life I have seen Frenchmen, Italians, Russians, etc. I am even aware, thanks to Montesquieu, that one may be a Persian. But as for *man,* I declare that I have never in my life met him. If he exists, I am unaware of it. . . .

Modern philosophy is at once too materialistic and too presumptuous to perceive the true limitations of politics. One of its follies is to maintain that an assembly of men may organize a nation and that a *constitution,* which is a body of fundamental laws that are proper to a nation and give it a certain form of government, may be created like anything else that requires understanding, knowledge, and application. It maintains that one may acquire the skills necessary for membership in the Constituent Assembly, and that a group of men, whenever they choose, may say to each other, "Let us make a government," as they say to a workman, "Make a steam pump or a stocking-frame."

However, it is as true in its way as a mathematical proposition that *no great institution results from deliberation,* and that human works are fragile in proportion to the number of men who take part in them and the extent to which they apply reason and science in *a priori* fashion. . . .

The inventor of a system of physics would doubtless be praised if he were supported by all the facts of nature, as I cite all the facts of history in support of my contentions. I have carefully examined all the evidence which history furnishes us, and have found nothing that justifies this visionary system of deliberation and political construction by abstract reasoning. At best, one might cite the example of the United States of America, but I have already said that I do not wish to discuss it here. However, I shall make a few observations.

1. British America had a king but never saw him. The splendor of monarchy was foreign to her, and her sovereign was like a supernatural power that is not experienced by the senses.

2. She possessed an element of democracy which existed in the constitution of the mother country.

3. She also possessed many people who came as colonists during the religious and political troubles, and almost all were republican minded.

4. The Americans built with these elements and according to the plan of the three powers which they received from their ancestors rather than reducing all to *tabula rasa* as did the French.

However, all that is genuinely new in the American constitution, all that stems from common deliberation is the most fragile thing in the world. It would be impossible to assemble more symptoms of weakness and decay.

Not only do I refuse to believe in the stability of the American government; the individual elements of the American system inspire me with no confidence. The cities, for example, are unreasonably jealous of each other and have been unable to agree on the location of Congress; none is willing to concede the honor to another. In consequence, it has been decided to build a new city which will be the seat of government. They have chosen the most advantageous location on the banks of a great river, and have decided to name the city *Washington.* The location of all public buildings has been indicated; construction has begun, and the plan of this queen city is already circulating throughout Europe. Essentially, there is nothing in this that surpasses human power; it is quite possible to build a city. However, there is too much deliberation, too much of the *human* in this affair, and one may wager a thousand to one that the city will not be built, that it will not be called *Washington,* and that the Congress will not meet there. . . .

*   *   *

Throughout the entire moral and political world, what do we know? What are we able to do? We *know* the morality which we have received from our forefathers as a body of dogmas and useful prejudices that have been accepted by the national mentality. But we owe nothing of this to the individual reason of any man. On the contrary, whenever this type of reason enters the picture, it perverts morality.

In politics, we *know* that we must respect the powers that have been established from time immemorial. When time brings abuses that may alter the principles of government, we *know* that these abuses must be eliminated without touching fundamental principles. This requires great dexterity. We *are capable* of bringing about salutary reforms without reaching the point where the principle of life is vitiated and the death of the body politic becomes inevitable. . . .

Let no one be mistaken. The successes of the *philosophes* may dazzle inattentive eyes, and must therefore be evaluated. If you ask these men what they have accomplished, they will tell you of their influence over opinions. They will say that they have destroyed *prejudice* and especially *fanaticism,* for that is their key word; they will extoll in glowing terms the type of leadership that Voltaire exercised over his century during his long career. But these words, *prejudice* and *fanaticism,* signify in the last analysis the beliefs of many nations. Voltaire eliminated these beliefs from many minds; that is, he destroyed, and this is precisely what I am saying. Philosophy functions in such a way that a man who follows his individual reason is dangerous in the moral and political order exactly in proportion to his ability. The more spirit, activity and perseverance he has, the more disastrous is his influence. He merely augments a destructive power and strives in nothingness.

Whenever a writer who befriends religion criticizes philosophy, he becomes suspect to a great many readers who obstinately find fanaticism wherever they do not find incredulity or *indifferentism.* It may therefore not be inappropriate to borrow the exact words with which the public prosecutor reproached the *philosophes:*

"And you, mad *philosophes* who in your presumptuous wisdom claim to guide the universe; apostles of tolerance and humanity; *you who prepared our* GLORIOUS *revolution* and extoll the progress of intelligence and reason:

"Leave your tombs. Walk among these many corpses and explain to us how, in this celebrated century, thirty tyrants who decreed murder could find three hundred thousand executioners to carry out their will. Your writings are in the pockets of the tyrants; your maxims are on their lips; your pages shine forth in their testimony in court. In the name of virtue the most horrible thievery is committed; in the name of humanity two million men perish; in the name of liberty a thousand bastilles are built. There is not one of your works that is not on the desks of our forty thousand revolutionary committees. They left you only a moment, Diderot, to sign the order for mass drownings! . . . The only fruit of your labors has been to gloss over crimes with fine language so as to permit more telling blows. Injustice and violence are called *strong measures;* floods of spilled blood are called *purging the body politic. . . .* Did you believe, O pretended sages, that the seed of philosophy might germinate in barren soil without cultivation? And in your wild paradoxes and metaphysical abstractions, did you count human passions as nothing? . . ."

There is a book entitled *De Jean-Jacques Rousseau considéré comme auteur de la Révolution.* This book and the bronze statue that the National Convention dedicated to Rousseau are perhaps the greatest shame ever to dishonor the memory of any writer.

However, Voltaire vies with Rousseau for the frightful honor of having caused the French Revolution and has weighty authorities on his side. To him Frederick the Great wrote, "The fabric of superstition is tottering on its foundations and is about to collapse. The nations will write in their histories that Voltaire was the promoter of the revolution that took place in men's minds during the eighteenth century. . . ."

At bottom, the glory of having caused the Revolution belongs ex-

FIGURE 2. Voltaire. The greatest of the *philosophes* and spokesman for advanced opinion in his time, Voltaire combined brilliant criticism of existing institutions and beliefs with unremitting efforts for human betterment in many spheres. *(Courtesy of the Fogg Art Museum, Harvard University)*

clusively to neither Voltaire nor Rousseau. The entire philosophical sect claims its part, but these two men should be regarded as its leaders. While one undermined politics by corrupting morals, the other corrupted morals by undermining politics. For sixty years, Voltaire's destructive works sapped the foundations of the superb edifice whose fall has caused Europe to tremble. Rousseau's seductive eloquence deluded the mob, which is controlled more by imagination than reason. Everywhere he disseminated distrust of authority and the spirit of revolt. It was he who systematized ideas of anarchy, and, while mouthing sterile and isolated truths that are known to all, proclaimed the disastrous principles which gave rise to the horrors that we have seen. The bodies of both men have been interred in the Pantheon according to a decree of the National Convention, thus condemning their memory to a final disgrace.

After this, let no one go into raptures over the influence of Voltaire and his ilk; let no one speak of the *power* which they wielded over their century. Yes, they were powerful, like poison and fire.

Wherever individual reason predominates, nothing great can exist; for everything that is great rests on belief, and the shock of irresponsible personal opinions merely produces a skepticism that destroys all. Of general and personal morality, religion, laws, respected customs and useful prejudices, nothing survives and all collapses before this skepticism. It is universal destruction.

Let us always return to first principles. Any *institution* whatsoever is merely a public structure. In physics and morality the laws are the same; you cannot build a great edifice on a weak foundation nor a permanent one on a moving and temporary base. In politics, if you wish to build in grand style and for the ages, you must build upon an opinion, a *great* and profound belief. If opinion is not accepted by the majority and is not deeply rooted, it will provide only a weak and temporary base.

When one looks for the great and permanent foundations of all institutions, large and small, one always finds religion and patriotism. And if one looks more closely, one will find that these are united, for there is no true patriotism without religion. Patriotism flourishes only in an age of belief and declines and dies with it. As soon as man divorces himself from God, he corrupts himself and all that he touches. His acts are false and he merely destroys. As this bond is weakened in a state, conservative virtues proportionally decline; all character is degraded and even good works are unavailing. Murderous egotism ceaselessly motivates the public spirit against all else, like an enormous Alpine glacier that imperceptibly covers fruitful areas of life and vegetation.

However, as soon as the concept of the Divinity is the principle of human action, such action becomes fertile, creative, invincible. An unknown power is felt everywhere; it animates, enflames and vivifies all. Regardless of the errors and crimes with which human ignorance and corruption may stain this august concept, it nonetheless preserves its inconceivable influence. In the midst of massacres, men multiply and nations display astounding vigor. "Greece," says Rousseau, "flourished in the midst of the cruelest wars; blood was shed in torrents and yet the whole land was filled with inhabitants." No doubt, but that was an age of prodigies and oracles, an age of *faith* after the manner of the time, that is, exalted patriotism. When one says of the Supreme Being that He exists, one says nothing; one must say that He is *Existence.* "It is a *living Being* which in a *single instant* fulfills *eternity.*" A drop of this immeasurable ocean of existence seems to fall on men who speak and act in the name of God; its effects astound and give an idea of creation. Centuries pass, but its work remains. Everything that is great, good, desirable, true and permanent among men stems from the *Existence that is the source of all existences;* outside there is naught but error, decay and nothingness.

I should forestall an objection. In criticizing human philosophy for all the ills that it has brought us, do we not risk being unfair and going too far toward the opposite extreme?

It is doubtless necessary to avoid excess, but in this regard there seems to be an infallible rule for judging philosophy. It is useful when it does not transcend its rightful sphere, the natural sciences. In this area, all efforts are useful and deserve our gratitude. But as soon as philosophy enters the world of morality, it is outside its domain. In morality, general reason holds sway, while philosophy or individual reason becomes destructive and therefore guilty if it dares to question or contradict sacred laws and national beliefs. Its duty in this sphere is to follow these beliefs.

This distinction suffices to judge our century and the preceding one. All the great men of the seventeenth century were characterized by their respect for, and submission to, the civil and religious laws of their country. In their writings you will find nothing reckless, paradoxical or contrary to the national dogmas which for them were definitive, sacred maxims that were not to be questioned.

They were distinguished by an excellent good sense whose great merit may be appreciated only by those who have been spared the influence of false modern taste. Since they always address themselves to the reader's conscience which is infallible, it seems as though they echo our thoughts. Sophistical men complain that they find nothing new in their works, whereas their special merit was to paint in brilliant colors the universal truths upon which the welfare of empires, families and individuals is founded.

That which is now called *new ideas, bold thought, great concepts* the writers of the past century would have called *criminal daring, frenzy* or *outrage.* The facts show on which side reason is found.

I know that philosophy, ashamed of its frightful success, has attempted to disown the violence that we have seen, but this is not the way to escape condemnation by the wise. Fortunately for humanity, destructive theories are rarely found among men who possess the power to put them into effect. But what does it matter that Spinoza lived peacefully in a Dutch village or that timid, feeble Rousseau had neither the will nor the power to excite sedition? What does it matter that Voltaire defended Calas in order to gain publicity? What does it matter that during the recent dreadful tyranny over France the *philosophes* feared for their heads and prudently hid themselves? From the moment they set forth maxims capable of producing crimes, these crimes became their work and the criminals their disciples. . . .

Philosophes! Never will you absolve yourselves of the cause by minimizing the effect. *You detest crimes,* you say. *You have never murdered.* Well! *You have never murdered;* such is the only praise that may be given you. But you have caused murders. It is you who said to the people, *"The people, as sole author of political government and distributor of power to bodies and magistrates, are forever within their rights in interpreting their contract, or rather their gifts, changing and abolishing clauses and establishing a new order of things."* [Mably] It is you who said to them, *"Laws are always useful to those who have and injurious to those who have not. Thus organized society is advantageous to men only when all have something and none has too much."* [Rousseau] It is you who said, *"You are sovereign. You may change laws at will, even your best fundamental laws and the social contract, for if you desire to harm yourself, who has the right to stop you?"* [Rousseau] All the rest follows. The detestable Lebon, the butcher of Arras, the monster *who checked the fall of the guillotine's blade on his outstretched victims in order to read them the latest news, and then executed them,* what did he answer when he was interrogated at the bar of the National Convention by the only men who could never rightfully condemn him? *"I enforced the laws,"* he said, *"laws which make one shudder. I was wrong. . . . I should be treated as I treated the others. When I met men of principle, I allowed myself to be guided by them.* IT IS ABOVE ALL THE PRINCIPLES OF ROUSSEAU THAT KILLED ME."

He was right. The tiger that destroys merely fulfills his role; the guilty one is he who unleashes the tiger and turns it on society. Do not think that you may absolve yourselves with your feigned lamentations over Marat and Robespierre. Hear the truth. Wherever you are and others have the misfortune to believe you, there will be similar monsters, for every society harbors scoundrels who merely await release from the force of law to destroy society. Without you, Marat and Robespierre would never have done evil because they would have been restrained by the bonds that you have broken.

Alexis de Tocqueville
THE LIMITATIONS OF THE ENLIGHTENMENT

Although Alexis de Tocqueville (1805–1859) was aristocratic by birth and instinct, he became famous as a proponent of liberty and, to a lesser extent, democracy. He was among the first to do extensive archival research on the background of the French Revolution, and developed a complex interpretation concerning its causes and significance. Although he concluded that violent change was both necessary and inevitable, he found fundamental continuities between the old regime and the Revolution in the growth of administrative centralization, the trend toward equality, and the influence of the Enlightenment. He also praised the universal significance of the Revolution for all peoples. These views, however, did not prevent his emphasizing certain fundamental weaknesses and limitations in the Enlightenment and their consequent ill effects during the course of the Revolution.

France had long been the most literary nation of Europe, but her men of letters had never exhibited the mental peculiarities, or occupied the rank which distinguished them in the eighteenth century. Nothing of the kind had ever been witnessed either here or abroad.

They took no part in public business, as English authors did; on the contrary, they had never lived so much out of the world. They held no public office, and, though society teemed with functionaries, they had no public functions to discharge.

But they were not strangers to politics, or wholly absorbed in abstract philosophy and belles-lettres, as most of the German literary men were. They paid sedulous, and, indeed, special attention to the subject of government. They were to be heard day after day discoursing of the origin and primitive form of society, of the primordial rights of the governed and governing power, of the natural and artificial relations of men one to the other, of the soundness or the errors of the prevailing customs, of the principles of the laws. They made thorough inquiries into the Constitution, and criticized its structure and general plan. They did not invariably devote particular or profound studies to these great problems. Many merely glanced at them in passing, often playfully, but none omitted them altogether. Abstract and literary

From Alexis de Tocqueville, *The Old Regime and the Revolution*, translated by John Bonner (New York, 1856).

views on political subjects are scattered throughout the works of that day; from the ponderous treatise to the popular song, none are wholly devoid of this feature.

The political systems of these writers were so varied that it would be wholly impossible to reconcile them together, and mold them all into a theory of government.

Still, setting details aside, and looking only to main principles, it is readily discerned that all these authors concurred in one central point, from whence their particular notions diverged. They all started with the principle that it was necessary to substitute simple and elementary rules, based on reason and natural law, for the complicated and traditional customs which regulated society in their time.

It will be ascertained, on close inquiry, that the whole of the political philosophy of the eighteenth century is really comprised in that single notion.

It was not new. For 3,000 years it had been floating backward and forward through the minds of men without finding a resting place. How was it that it contrived to engross the attention of all the authors of the day just at this time? How did it happen that, instead of lying buried in the brain of philosophers, as it had done so often, it became so absorbing a passion among the masses, that idlers were daily heard discussing abstract theories on the nature of human society, and the imaginations of women and peasants were fired by notions of new systems? How came it that literary men, without rank, or honors, or riches, or responsibility, or power, monopolized political authority, and found themselves, though strangers to the government, the only leading politicians of the day? I desire to answer these queries briefly, and to show how facts which seem to belong to the history of our literature alone exercised an influence over our revolution that was both extraordinary and terrible, and is still felt in our time.

It was not chance which led the philosophers of the eighteenth century to advocate principles so opposed to those on which society rested in their day. They were naturally suggested by the spectacle they had before them. They had constantly in view a host of absurd and ridiculous privileges, whose burden increased daily, while their origin was growing more and more indistinct; hence they were driven toward notions of natural equality. They beheld as many irregular and strange old institutions, all hopelessly jarring together and unsuited to the time, but clinging to life long after their virtue had departed;

and they naturally felt disgusted with all that was ancient and traditional, and—each taking his own reason for his guide—they sought to rebuild society on some wholly new plan.

These writers were naturally tempted to indulge unreservedly in abstract and general theories of government. They had no practical acquaintance with the subject; their ardors were undamped by actual experience; they knew of no existing facts which stood in the way of desirable reforms; they were ignorant of the dangers inseparable from the most necessary revolutions, and dreamed of none. There being no approach toward political liberty, the business of government was not only ill understood, it was not understood at all. Having no share in it themselves, and seeing nothing that was done by those who had, these writers lacked the superficial education which the habit of political freedom imparts even to those who take no part in politics. They were hence bolder in their projects of innovation, fonder of theory and system, more prone to despise the teaching of antiquity and to rely on individual reason than is usually the case with speculative writers on politics.

Ignorance of the same kind insured their success among the masses. If the French people had still participated in the government by means of the Estates General, if they had still taken part in the administration of the public business in provincial assemblies, it is certain that they would have received the lucubrations of these authors with more coolness; their business habits would have set them on their guard against pure theory.

Had they seen a possibility of changing the spirit without wholly destroying the form of their old institutions, as the English did, they might have been reluctant to adventure upon absolute novelties; but there was not a man whose fortune, or whose comfort, or whose person, or whose pride was not daily interfered with by some old law, or old institution, or old decayed authority, and each particular grievance seemed altogether incurable short of the total destruction of the constitution of the country.

We had, however, saved one right from the general wreck—that was the right of philosophizing freely on the origin of society, on the natural principles of government, and the primitive rights of man.

A rage for this political literature seized all who were inconvenienced by the legislation of the day, including many who were naturally but little prone to indulge in abstract speculations. Taxpayers, wronged by the unjust distribution of the taille, warmed over the principle of the natural equality of man. Farmers, whose harvests were spoiled by rabbits kept by their noble neighbors, rejoiced to hear that reason repudiated all privileges without exception. Popular passions thus disguised themselves in a philosophic garb; political aspirations were forcibly driven into a literary channel, and men of letters, taking the direction of public opinion, temporarily occupied the position which in free countries belongs to party leaders.

Nor could their claim to that place be disputed. A vigorous aristocracy will not only conduct public business, but will make public opinion, and give the keynote to authors, and authority to principles; but these prerogatives had passed away from the French nobility long before the eighteenth century; they had lost credit and power together. The place they had occupied in the public mind was vacant, and no one could gainsay the authors for seizing upon it.

The aristocracy rather favored than impeded their usurpation. Forgetting that established theories, sooner or later, inevitably become political passions, and find expression in acts, they made no objection to the discussion of doctrines that were wholly subversive of their private rights, and even of their existence. They considered them ingenious exercises for the mind, amused themselves by taking part in them, and peacefully enjoyed their immunities and privileges, while they serenely discoursed on the absurdity of all existing customs.

Astonishment is expressed at the blindness with which the upper classes of the old regime helped to ruin themselves; but where could they have learned better? Ruling classes can no more acquire a knowledge of the dangers they have to avoid without free institutions, than their inferiors can discern the rights they ought to preserve in the same circumstances. More than a century had elapsed since the last trace of public life had disappeared in France. During the interval, no noise or shock warned conservatives of the impending fall of the ancient edifice. Appearances remaining unchanged, they suspected no internal revolution. Their minds had stood still at the point where their ancestors had left off. The nobility were as jealous of the royal prerogative in 1789 as they had been in the fifteenth century, as the reports of the Estates General prove. On the other hand, on the very eve of his wreck in the democratic storm, the unhappy Louis XVI, as Burke very truly observes, could see no rival to the throne outside the ranks of the aristocracy; he was as suspicious of the nobles as if he had been living in the time of the Fronde. He felt as certain as any of his ancestors that the middle and lower classes were the surest supports of the throne.

But of all the strange phenomena of these times, the strangest to us, who have seen so many revolutions, is the absence of any thought of revolution from the mind of our ancestors. No such thing was discussed, because no such thing had been conceived. In free communities, constant vibrations keep men's minds alive to the possibility of a general earthquake, and hold governments in check; but in the old French society that was so soon to topple over, there was not the least symptom of unsteadiness.

I have read attentively the cahiers of the Three Estates presented to the Estates General in 1789; I say tho Three Estates—nobility and clergy as well as Third Estate. I observe that here a law and there a custom is sought to be changed, and I note it. Pursuing the immense task to the end, and adding together all the separate demands, I discover with terror that nothing less is demanded than the simultaneous and systematic repeal of all the laws, and abolition of all the customs prevailing in the country; and I perceive at once that one of the greatest revolutions the world ever saw is impending. Those who are to be its victims tomorrow suspect nothing; they delude themselves with the notion that this elaborate old society can be transformed without a shock, and with the help of reason alone. Unhappy creatures! how had they forgotten the quaint old maxim of their fathers four hundred years ago, "He that is too desiring of liberty and franchise must needs fall into serfage."

That the nobles and middle classes, shut out as they had been for so long from public life, should exhibit this singular inexperience, was not surprising; but it was singular that the members of the government, ministers, magistrates, and intendants, should be equally blind. Of these, many were able men at their trade; they were thoroughly versed in the administrative science of the period; but of the great science of government in the abstract, of the art of watching social movements and foreseeing their results, they were as ignorant as the people themselves; for this branch of the business of public men can only be taught by the practical working of free institutions. . . .

Now when it is borne in mind that this French nation, which had so little experience of business, and so little to do with its own government, was, at the same time, the most literary of all the nations of the world, it may be easily understood how writers became a power in the state, and ended by ruling it.

In England, political writers and political actors were mixed, one set working to adapt new ideas to practice, the other circumscribing theory by existing facts; whereas in France, the political world was divided into two separate provinces without intercourse with each other. One administered the government, the other enunciated the principles on which government ought to rest. The former adopted measures according to precedent and routine, the latter evolved general laws, without ever thinking how they could be applied. The one conducted business, the other directed minds.

There were thus two social bodies: society proper, resting on a framework of tradition, confused and irregular in its organization, with a host of contradictory laws, well-defined distinctions of rank and station, and unequal rights; and above this, an imaginary society, in which everything was simple, harmonious, equitable, uniform, and reasonable.

The minds of the people gradually withdrew from the former to take refuge in the latter. Men became indifferent to the real by dint of dwelling on the ideal, and established a mental domicile in the imaginary city which the authors had built.

Our revolution has often been traced to American example. The American Revolution, no doubt, exercised considerable influence over ours, but that influence was less a consequence of the deeds done in America than an inference from the prevailing ideas in France. In other European countries the American Revolution was nothing more than a strange and new fact; in France it seemed a striking confirmation of principles known before. It surprised them, it convinced us. The Americans seemed merely to have carried out what our writers had conceived; they had realized what we were musing. It was as if Fénelon had been suddenly transported into the midst of the Sallentines.

It was something entirely new for men of letters to direct the political education of a great nation: this, more perhaps than anything else, contributed to form the peculiar character and results of our revolution.

The people imbibed the temper and disposition of the authors with their principles. They were so long sole tutors of the nation, and their lessons were so wholly unchecked and untried by practical experience, that the whole nation acquired, by dint of reading them, their instincts, their mental complexion, their tastes, and even their natural defects. When the time for action came, men dealt with political questions on literary principles.

The student of our revolution soon discovers that it was led and managed by the same spirit which gave birth to so many abstract treatises on government. In both he finds the same love for general theories, sweeping legislative systems, and symmetrical laws; the same confidence in theory; the same desire for new and original institutions; the same wish to reconstruct the whole Constitution according to the rules of logic, and in conformity with a set plan, instead of attempting partial amendments. A terrible sight! For what is a merit in an author is often a defect in a statesman, and characteristics which improve a book may be fatal to a revolution.

The political style of the day was somewhat indebted to the prevailing literature; it bristled with vague expressions, abstract terms, ambitious words, and literary phrases. The political passions of the day gave it currency among all classes, even the lowest. Long before the Revolution, the edicts of Louis XVI often spoke of natural laws and the rights of man. Peasants, in petitions, styled their neighbors "fellow-citizens;" the intendant, "a respectable magistrate;" the parish curate, the "minister of the altar;" and God, the "Supreme Being." They might have become sorry authors had they but known orthography.

These peculiarities have taken such root in the French mind that they have been mistaken for its natural characteristics, whereas they are, in fact, only the result of a strange system of education. I have heard it stated that the taste, or, rather, the rage we have shown during the last sixty years for general principles, systems, and grand verbiage in political matters, proceeded from an idiosyncracy of our race—a peculiarity of the French mind; as though a feature of this kind would be likely to remain hidden for ages, and only to see the light at the close of last century.

It is singular that we should have retained the habits which literature created, though we have almost entirely lost our old love for letters. I was often surprised, during the course of my public life, to see men who hardly ever read the works of the eighteenth century, or, indeed, any others, and who despised literary men, exhibit a singular fidelity to leading defects to which the old literary spirit gave birth.

Hippolyte Adolphe Taine

THE SPIRIT AND DOCTRINE OF THE ENLIGHTENMENT

Among the many nineteenth-century writers who severely criticized the Enlightenment and its influence on the French Revolution, the name of Hippolyte Adolphe Taine (1828–1893) stands preeminent. Taine was endowed with great intellectual ability and wrote extensively in the fields of literary criticism, philosophy and history. Profoundly shocked by the defeat of France in 1871, he determined to discover the flaws in French national life which had caused her downfall. After extensive investigation of the record of the eighteenth century, he concluded that the philosophy of the Enlightenment contained fundamental, indeed fatal, defects which divorced thought from reality, gave rise to the violence and tyranny of the French Revolution, and underlay the weaknesses of all later French regimes. Taine's formulation of his criticisms of the Enlightenment was one of the most powerful and influential ever penned.

The Composition of the Revolutionary Spirit. Science, the First Element

On seeing a man with a somewhat feeble constitution, but healthy in appearance and of steady habits, greedily swallow some new kind of cordial and then suddenly fall to the ground, foam at the mouth, act deliriously and writhe in convulsions, we at once surmise that this agreeable beverage contained some dangerous substance; but a delicate analysis is necessary to detect and decompose the poison. The philosophy of the eighteenth century contained poison, and of a kind as potent as it was peculiar; for, not only is it a long historic elaboration, the final and condensed essence of the tendency of the thought of the century, but again, its two principal ingredients have this peculiarity that, separate, they are salutary and in combination they form a venomous compound.

The first is scientific discovery, admirable on all sides, and beneficent in its nature; it is made up of masses of facts slowly accumulated and then summarily presented or in rapid succession. For the first time in history the sciences expand and affirm each other to the

From Hippolyte Adolphe Taine, *The Ancient Regime*, translated by John Durand (New York, 1876).

extent of providing, not, as formerly, under Galileo and Descartes, constructive fragments, or a provisional scaffolding, but a definite and demonstrated system of the universe, that of Newton. Around this capital fact, almost all the discoveries of the century, either as complementary or as prolongations, range themselves. . . . In the picture of nature which the human mind portrays, the science of the eighteenth century has drawn the general outline, the perspective, and the principal masses so correctly, that, at the present day, all its grand lines remain intact. Except for a few partial changes we have nothing to efface.

This vast supply of positive or probable facts, either demonstrated or anticipated, furnishes food, substance and impulse to the intellect of the century. Consider the leaders of public opinion, the promoters of the new philosophy: they are all, in various degrees, versed in the physical and natural sciences. Not only are they familiar with theories and authorities but again they have personal knowledge of facts and objects. . . . Prophets of a superior or inferior kind, masters or pupils, specialists or simple amateurs, all draw directly or indirectly from the living source that has just burst forth. From this they all start to teach man what he is, from whence he came, where he is going, what he may become and what he should be. A new point of departure leads to new points of view, and hence the idea which was then entertained of man is to undergo a complete transformation. . . .

What is life, what is organic substance in this monstrous universe but an indifferent mass, a passing accident, the corruption of a few epidermic particles? And if this be life, what is that humanity which is so small a fragment of it? Such is man in nature, an atom, an ephemeral particle; let this not be lost sight of in our theories concerning his origin, his importance, and his destiny. . . . If he is unique he is not isolated, being an animal among other animals; in him and with them, substance, organization and birth, formation and renewal, functions, senses and appetites, are similar, while his superior intelligence, like their rudimentary intelligence, has for an indispensable organ a nervous matter whose structure is the same with him and with them. Thus surrounded, brought forth and borne along by nature, is it to be supposed that in nature he is an empire within an empire? He is there as the part of a whole, by virtue of being a physical body, a chemical composition, an animated organism, a sociable animal, among other bodies, other compositions, other social animals, all analogous to him; and, by virtue of these classifications, he is, like them, subject to laws. For, if the first cause is unknown to us, and we dispute among ourselves to know what it is, whether innate or external, we affirm with certainty the mode of its action, and that it operates only according to fixed and general laws. Every circumstance, whatever it may be, is conditioned, and, its conditions being given, it never fails to conform to them. Of two links forming a chain, the first always draws on the second. There are laws for numbers, forms, and motions, for the revolutions of the planets and the fall of bodies, for the diffusion of light and the radiance of heat, for the attractions and repulsions of electricity, for chemical combinations, and for the growth, equilibrium and dissolution of organized matter. They exist for the growth, support, and development of human societies, for the formation, conflict, and direction of the ideas, the passions and the wills of human individuals. In all this, man continues nature; from which it follows that, to know him, it is necessary to study him in her, after her, and like her, with the same independence, the same precautions, and in the same spirit. Through this remark alone the method of the moral sciences is fixed. In history, in psychology, in morals, in politics, the thinkers of the preceding century, Pascal, Bossuet, Descartes, Fénelon, Malebranche, and La Bruyère, still start from dogma; it is plain to everyone qualified to read them that their position is already determined. Religion provided them with a complete theory of the moral order of things; according to this theory, latent or exposed, they described man and accommodated their observations to the preconceived type. The writers of the eighteenth century reverse this method: they dwell on man, on the observable man, and on his surroundings; in their eyes, conclusions about the soul, its origin, and its destiny, must come afterwards and depend wholly, not on that which revelation, but on that which observation furnishes. The moral sciences are divorced from theology and attach themselves, as if a prolongation of them, to the physical sciences.

Through this substitution and this combination they become sciences. In history, every foundation is laid on which we of the present day build. Compare Bossuet's *Discours sur l'histoire universelle,* and Voltaire's *Essai sur les mœurs,* and we at once see how new and deep these foundations were. Criticism at once obtains its fundamental principle: considering that the laws of nature are universal and immutable it concludes from this that, in the moral world, as in the physical world, there can be no infringement of them and that no arbitrary or foreign force intervenes to disturb the regular course of things, which affords a sure means of discerning myth from truth. . . . Human history is a thing of natural growth like the rest; its direction is due to its own elements; no external force guides it, but the inward forces that create it: it is not tending to any prescribed end but developing a result. And the chief result is the progress of the human mind. . . . Man thus possesses "a principle of reason," namely, a "mechanical instinct" suggesting to him useful implements; also an instinct of right suggesting to him his moral conceptions. These two instincts form a part of his organization; he has them from his birth, "as the birds have their feathers, and bears their hair." Hence he is perfectible through nature and merely conforms to nature in improving his mind and in bettering his condition. . . . Extend the idea farther along with Turgot and Condorcet, and with all its exaggerations, we see arising, before the end of the century, our modern theory of progress, that which founds all our aspirations on the boundless advance of the sciences, on the increase of comforts which their applied discoveries constantly bring to the human condition, and on the increase of good sense which their discoveries, popularized, slowly deposit in the human brain.

A second principle has to be established to complete the foundations of history. Discovered by Montesquieu it still today serves as a constructive support, and, if we resume the work, as if on the substructure of the master's edifice, it is simply owing to accumulated erudition placing at our disposal more substantial and more abundant materials. In human society all parts are interdependent; no modification of one can take place without effecting proportionate changes in the others. Institutions, laws and customs are not mingled together, as in a heap, through chance or caprice, but connected one with the other through convenience or necessity as in a harmony. . . . A multitude of subordinate wheels depend on the great central wheel. For, if the clock goes, it is owing to the harmony of its various parts, from which it follows that, on this harmony ceasing, the clock gets out of order. But, besides the principal spring, there are others which, acting on or in combination with it, give to each clock a special character and a peculiar movement. Such, in the first place, is climate, that is to say, the degree of heat or cold, humidity or dryness, with its infinite effects on man's physical and moral attributes, followed by its influence on political, civil and domestic servitude or freedom. Likewise the soil, according to its fertility, its position and its extent. Likewise, the physical régime according as a people is composed of hunters, shepherds or agriculturists. Likewise the fecundity of the race, and the consequent slow or rapid increase of population, and also the excess in number, now of males and now of females. And finally, likewise, are national character and religion. All these causes, each added to the other, or each limited by the other, contribute together to form a total result, namely society. Simple or complex, stable or unstable, barbarous or civilized, this society contains within itself its explanations of its being. Strange as its structure may be, it can be explained, also its institutions however contradictory. Neither prosperity, nor decline, nor despotism, nor freedom, is a cast of the die brought on by the vicissitudes of chance, nor so many passages of theatrical display improvised by individual wills. They are conditions from which we cannot abstract ourselves. In any event it is serviceable to know these conditions, either to better ourselves or take all things patiently, now to carry out opportune reforms, now to renounce impracticable reforms, now to acquire the skill which enables us to succeed and now to acquire the prudence which leads us to abstain.

The center of the moral sciences is herein reached; the question now is concerning man in general. The natural history of the soul has to be set forth, and this must be done as we have done the others, by discarding all prejudice and adhering to facts, taking analogy for our guide, beginning with origins and following, step by step, the development by which the infant, the savage, the uncultivated primitive man, is converted into the rational and cultivated man. Let us consider life at the outset, the animal at the lowest degree on the scale, man as soon as he is born. The first thing we find is sensation, of this or that species, agreeable or painful, and next a want, tendency or desire, and next after these, through physiological mechanism, voluntary or involuntary movements, more or less exactly and more or less quickly appropriated and coordinated. And this elementary fact is not merely primitive; it is, again, constant and universal since we encounter it at each moment of each life, and in the most complicated as well as in the simplest. . . . Locke had already stated that our ideas all originate in outward or inward experience. Condillac shows additionally that the *actual elements* of perception, memory, idea, imagination, judgment, reasoning, knowledge are sensations, properly so called, or revived sensations; our loftiest ideas are derived from no other materials, for they can be reduced to signs which are themselves sensations of a certain kind. Sensations accordingly form the substance of human or of animal intelligence; but the former infinitely surpasses the latter in this, that, through the creation of signs, it succeeds in isolating, abstracting and noting fragments of sensations, that is to say, of forming, combining, and employing general conceptions. This being granted, we are able to verify all our ideas, for, through reflection, we can revive and reconstruct the ideas we had formed without any reflection. No abstract definitions exist at the outset; abstraction is ulterior and derivative; at the head of each science must be placed examples, experiences, concrete facts; from these we derive our general idea. In like manner we derive from several general ideas of the same degree a more general idea, and so on successively, step by step, always proceeding according to the natural order of things, by constant analysis, using expressive signs, as with mathematicians who pass from calculation by the fingers to calculation by numerals and from this to calculation by letters, and who, calling upon the eyes to aid reason, depict the inward analogy of quantities by the outward analogy of symbols. In this way science becomes complete by means of a properly organized language. Through this reversal of the usual method we summarily dispose of disputes about words, escaping the illusions of human speech, simplifying study, remodelling education, insuring discoveries, subjecting every assertion to control and bringing all truths within reach of all understandings.

Such is the course to be pursued with all the sciences and especially with the moral and political sciences. To consider in turn each distinct province of human activity, to decompose the leading notions out of which we form our conceptions, those of religion, society and government, those of utility, wealth and exchange, those of justice, right and duty; to revert to palpable facts, to first experiences, to the simple circumstances harboring the elements of our ideas; to derive from these the precious ore without loss or alloy; to recompose our ideas with this, to fix its meaning and determine its value; to substitute for the vague and vulgar notion with which we started, the precise scientific definition we arrive at, the base metal we receive for the refined metal we obtain, constituted the prevalent method taught by the philosophers under the name of analysis, and which sums up the whole progress of the century. Up to this point, and no farther, they are right: truth, every truth, is found in observable objects and only from thence can it be derived; there is no other pathway leading to discovery. The operation, undoubtedly, is productive only when the vein is rich and we possess the means of extracting the ore. To obtain a just notion of government, of religion, of right, of wealth, a man must be a historian beforehand, a jurisconsult and economist, and have gathered up myriads of facts; and, besides all this, he must possess a vast erudition and practiced and special acuteness. If these conditions are only partially complied with, the operation again doubtless affords but incomplete results or a dubious alloy, a few rough drafts of the sciences, the rudiments of pedagogy along with Rousseau, of political economy with Quesnay, Smith, and Turgot, of linguistics with Des Brosses, and of arithmetical morals and criminal legislation with Bentham. Finally, if none of these conditions are ·complied with, the same operation in the hands of closet speculators, drawing-room amateurs, and oratorical charlatans in public places, will undoubtedly end only in mischievous compounds and in destructive explosions. Nevertheless a good law remains good even when the ignorant and the impetuous make a bad use of it, and if we of today resume the abortive effort of the eighteenth century it is within the lines it transmitted to us.

The Classic Spirit, the Second Element

This grand and magnificent edifice of new truths resembles a tower of which the first story, quickly finished, at once becomes accessible to the public. The public ascends the structure and is requested by its constructors to look about, not at the sky and at surrounding space, but right before it and on the ground, so as to know the country on which it dwells. The point of view is certainly favorable and the recommendation is judicious. To conclude, however, that the public will see accurately would not be warranted, for the state of its eyes must be examined, to ascertain whether it is near- or far-sighted, or if the retina naturally, or through habit, is sensitive to certain colors. In like manner the French of the eighteenth century must be considered, the structure of their inward vision, that is to say, the fixed form of understanding they bear with them, unconsciously and undesignedly into the tower.

This fixed form consists of the classic spirit and this, applied to the scientific acquisitions of the period, produces the philosophy of the century and the doctrines of the Revolution. . . . Fully to comprehend it let us study its formation.

Its establishment is coeval with that of the regular monarchy and polished intercourse, and it accompanies these, not accidentally but in the natural order of things. For it is the work of the new public which the new régime and new habits then formed, consisting of an aristocracy rendered listless by the encroaching monarchy, of people well born and well educated who, withdrawn from activity, fall back on conversation and devote their leisure to enjoying the calm or refined pleasures of the intellect. At last they find no other occupation or interest: to talk, to listen, to entertain themselves agreeably and with ease, on all subjects, grave or gay, of any interest to the men, and especially to the women, of society is their great affair. In the seventeenth century they are styled "honest folks" and thenceforth a writer, even the most abstract, addresses himself to them. "The honest man," says Descartes, "need not have read all books nor have studiously acquired all that is taught in the schools"; and he entitles his last treatise, "A search for Truth according to natural light which alone, without the aid of Religion or Philosophy, determines the truths an *honest man* should possess on all matters forming the subjects of his thoughts." In short, from one end of his philosophy to the other, the only qualification he demands of his readers is "natural good sense" added to the common stock of experience acquired by contact with the world. As these form the auditory they are likewise the judges. "One must study the taste of the court," says Molière, "for in no place are verdicts more just. . . ." In the eighteenth century they constitute the sovereign authority. In the great crowd of "imbeciles," sprinkled with vulgar pedants, there is, says Voltaire, "a small group apart called *good society,* which group, rich, well brought up, well informed and polished, forms, so to say, the flower of humanity; for it the greatest men have labored; it is that which creates fame." Admiration, favor, importance, belong not to those who are worthy of it but to those who address themselves to this group. . . . Under a strong pressure of this kind the mind necessarily accommodates itself to the exigencies, the proprieties, the tastes, and the degree of attention and of instruction of its public. Hence the classic mold—formed out of the habit of speaking, writing and thinking for a drawing-room audience. . . .

There is, accordingly, a radical defect in the classic spirit, the defect of its qualities, and which, at first kept within proper bounds, contributes towards the production of its purest masterpieces, but which, in accordance with the universal law, goes on increasing and turns into a vice through the natural effect of age, use, and success. Contracted at the start, it is to become yet more so. In the eighteenth century the portrayal of living realities, an actual individual, just as he is in nature and in history, that is to say, an undefined unit, a rich plexus, a complete organism of peculiarities and traits, superimposed, commingled and coordinated, is improper. The capacity to receive and contain all these is wanting. Whatever can be discarded is cast aside, and to such an extent that nothing is left at last but a condensed extract, an evaporated residuum, an almost empty name, in short, what is called a hollow abstraction. . . .

To pursue in every research, with the utmost confidence, without either reserve or precaution, the mathematical method; to derive, limit and isolate a few of the simplest generalized notions; and then, setting experience aside, comparing them, combining them, and, from the artificial compound thus obtained, deducing all the consequences they involve by pure reasoning, is the natural process of the classic spirit. It is so deeply implanted as to be equally encountered in both centuries, as well with Descartes, Malebranche and the partisans of innate ideas as with the partisans of sensation, of physical needs and of primary instinct, Condillac, Rousseau, Helvétius, and, later, Condorcet, Volney, Sieyès, Cabanis and Destutt de Tracy. In vain do the latter assert that they are the followers of Bacon and reject innate ideas; with another starting point than the Cartesians they pursue the same path and, as with the Cartesians, after borrowing a little, they leave experience behind them. In this vast moral and social world, they only remove the superficial bark from the human tree with its innumerable roots and branches; they are unable to penetrate to or grasp at anything beyond it; their hands cannot contain more. They have no suspicion of anything outside of it; the classic spirit, with limited comprehension, is not far-reaching. To them the bark is the entire tree and, the operation once completed, they retire, bearing along with them the dry, dead epidermis, never returning to the trunk itself. Through intellectual incapacity and literary pride they omit the characteristic detail, the animating fact, the specific circumstance, the significant, convincing and complete example. Scarcely one of these is found in the *Logique* and in the *Traité des Sensations* by Condillac, in the *Idéologie* by Destutt de Tracy, or in the *Rapports du Physique et du Morale* by Cabanis. Never, with them, are we on the solid and visible ground of personal observation and narration, but always in the air, in the empty space of pure generalities. Condillac declares that the arithmetical method is adapted to psychology and that the elements of our ideas can be defined by a process analogous "to the rule of three." Sieyès holds history in profound contempt, and believes that he had "perfected the science of politics" at one stroke, through an effort of the brain, in the style of Descartes, who thus discovered analytic geometry. Destutt de Tracy, in undertaking to comment on Montesquieu, finds that the great historian has too servilely confined himself to history, and attempts to do the work over again by organizing society as it should be, instead of studying society as it is. Never were such systematic and superficial institutions built up with such a moderate extract of human nature. Condillac, employing sensation, animates a statue, and then, by a process of pure reasoning, following up its effects, as he supposes, on smell, taste, hearing, sight and touch, fashions a complete human soul. Rousseau, by means of a contract, founds political association, and, with this given idea, he deduces the constitution, government and laws of every system of social equity. In a book which serves as the philosophical testament of the century, Condorcet declares that this method is "the final step of philosophy, that which places a sort of eternal barrier between humanity and its ancient infantile errors." "In its application to morals, politics and political economy" we succeed in obtaining a foothold in the moral sciences "as certain as in the natural sciences; through it we have been able to discover the rights of man. . . ." This school is to subsist throughout the Revolution, the Empire and even into the Restoration. . . .

Combination of the Two Elements

Out of the scientific acquisitions thus set forth, elaborated by the spirit we have just described, is born a doctrine seemingly a revelation and which, under this title, assumes to regulate the government of human affairs. On the approach of 1789 it is generally admitted that man is living in "a century of light," in "the age of reason"; that, previously, the human species was in its infancy and that now it has attained to its "majority." Truth, finally, is made manifest and, for the first time, its reign on earth is apparent. Its right is supreme, since it is truth itself. Everybody must be ruled by it, for, in its nature, it is universal. The philosophy of the eighteenth century, in these two articles of faith, resembles a religion, the puritanism of the seventeenth century, and Mahometanism in the seventh century. We see the same outbursts of faith, hope and enthusiasm, the same spirit of propagandism and of dominion, the same rigidity and intolerance, the same ambition to recast man and to remodel human life according to a preconceived type. The new doctrine is also to have its doctors, its dogmas, its popular catechism, its fanatics, its inquisitors and its martyrs. It is to speak as loudly as those preceding it, as a legitimate authority to which dictatorship belongs by right of birth, and against which rebellion is criminal or insane. It differs, however, from the preceding religions in this respect, that instead of imposing itself in the name of God, it imposes itself in the name of reason.

The authority, indeed, was a new one. Up to this time, in the control of human actions and opinions, reason had played but a small and subordinate part. Both the motive and its direction were obtained elsewhere; faith and obedience were an inheritance; a man was a Christian and a subject because he was born Christian and subject. Surrounding this budding philosophy and the reason which enters upon its great investigation, is a system of recognized laws, an established power, a reigning religion; all the stones of this structure hold together and each story is supported by a preceding story. But what does the common cement consist of and what is its first foundation? Who authorizes all these civil regulations which control marriages, testaments, inheritances, contracts, property and persons, these fanciful and often contradictory regulations? In the first place immemorial custom, varying according to the province, according to the title to the soil, according to the quality and condition of the person; and next, the will of the king who caused the custom to be inscribed and who sanctioned it. Who authorizes this will, this sovereignty of the prince, this first of public powers? In the first place, eight centuries of possession, a hereditary right similar to that by which each one enjoys his own field and domain, a property established in a family and transmitted from one eldest son to another, from the first founder of the state to his last living successor; and, in addition to this, a religion directing men to submit to the constituted powers. And who, finally, authorizes this religion? At first, eighteen centuries of tradition, the immense series of anterior and concordant proofs, the steady belief of sixty preceding generations; and after this, at the beginning of it, the presence and teachings of Christ, then, farther back, the creation of the world, the command and the voice of God. Thus, throughout the moral and social order of things the past justifies the present; antiquity provides its title and if beneath all these supports which age has consolidated, the deep primitive rock is sought for in subterranean depths, we find it in the divine will. During the whole of the seventeenth century this theory still absorbs all souls in the shape of a fixed habit and of inward respect; it is not open to question. It is regarded in the same light as the heart of the living body; whoever would lay his hand upon it would instantly draw back, moved by a vague sentiment of its ceasing to beat in case it were touched. The most independent, with Descartes at the head, "would be grieved" at being confounded with those chimerical speculators who, instead of pursuing the beaten track of custom, dart blindly forward "across mountains and over precipices." In subjecting their belief to systematic investigation not only do they except and set aside "the truths of faith," but again the dogma they suppose to have been discarded remains in their mind latent and effective, to lead them on without their knowledge and to convert their philosophy into a preparation for, or a confirmation of, Christianity. Summing it all up, faith, the performance of religious duties, with religious and political institutions, provide the mother ideas of the seventeenth century. Reason, whether she admits it or is ignorant of it, is only a subaltern, an oratorical agency, a setter-in-motion, forced by religion and the monarchy to labor in their behalf. With the exception of La Fontaine, whom I regard as unique in this as in other matters, the greatest and most independent, Pascal, Descartes, Bossuet, La Bruyère, derive from the established system their first conception of nature, of man, of society, of right and of government. So long as reason is limited to this function its work is that of a councillor of state, an extra preacher which its superiors dispatch on a missionary tour in the departments of philosophy and of literature. Far from proving destructive it consolidates; in fine, even down to the Regency, its chief employment is to produce good Christians and loyal subjects.

But here the parts become inverted; tradition descends from the upper to the lower rank while reason ascends from the latter to the former. On the one hand religion and the monarchy, through their excesses and misdeeds under Louis XIV, and their laxity and incompetency under Louis XV, demolish piece by piece the basis of hereditary reverence and filial obedience so long serving them as a foundation and which maintained them aloft above all dispute and free of investigation; hence the authority of tradition insensibly declines and disappears. On the other hand science, through its imposing and multiplied discoveries, erects piece by piece a basis of universal trust and deference, raising itself up from an interesting subject of curiosity to the rank of a public power; hence the authority of reason augments and occupies its place. A time comes when, the latter authority having dispossessed the former, the mother ideas tradition had reserved to itself fall into the grasp of reason. Investigation penetrates into the forbidden sanctuary. Instead of deference there is verification, and religion, the state, the law, custom, all the organs, in short, of moral and practical life, become subject to analysis, to be preserved, restored or replaced, according to the prescriptions of the new doctrine.

Nothing could be better had the doctrine been complete and had reason, instructed by history and rendered critical, been qualified to comprehend the rival she replaced. For then, instead of regarding her as an usurper to be repelled she would have recognized in her an-elder sister whose part must be left to her. Hereditary prejudice is a sort of reason operating unconsciously. . . . Careful investigation shows that, like science, it issues from a long accumulation of experiences: men, after a multitude of gropings and efforts, have satisfied themselves that a certain way of living and thinking is the only one adapted to their situation, the most practical and the most salutary, the system or dogma now seeming arbitrary to us being at first a confirmed expedient of public safety. Frequently it is so still; in any event, in its leading features, it is indispensable; it may be stated with certainty that, if the leading prejudices of the community should suddenly disappear, man, deprived of the precious legacy transmitted to him by the wisdom of ages, would at once fall back into a savage condition and again become what he was at first, namely, a restless, famished, wandering, hunted brute. There was a time when this heritage was lacking; there are populations today with which it is still utterly lacking. To abstain from eating human flesh, from killing useless or burdensome aged people, from exposing, selling or killing children one does not know what to do with, to be the one husband of but one woman, to hold in horror incest and unnatural practices, to be the sole and recognized owner of a distinct field, to be mindful of the superior injunctions of modesty, humanity, honor and conscience, all these observances, formerly unknown and slowly established, compose the civilization of human beings. Because we accept them in full security they are not the less sacred, and they become only the more sacred when, submitted to investigation and traced through history, they are disclosed to us as the secret force which has converted a herd of brutes into a society of men. In general, the older and more universal a custom, the more it is based on profound motives, on physiological motives, on those of hygiene, and on the precautions taken by society. . . .

If there are valid reasons for legitimating custom there are reasons of higher import for the consecration of religion. Consider this point, not in general and according to a vague notion, but at the outset, at its birth in the texts, taking for an example one of the faiths which now rule in society, Christianity, Brahminism, the law of Mahomet or of Buddha. At certain critical moments in history, a few men, emerging from their narrow and daily routine of life, form some generalized conception of the infinite universe; the august face of nature is suddenly unveiled to them; in their sublime emotion they seem to have detected its first cause; they have at least detected some of its elements. Through a fortunate conjunction of circumstances these elements are just those which their century, their race, a group of races, a fragment of humanity, is in a state to comprehend. Their point of view is the only one at which the graduated multitudes below them are able to place themselves. For millions of men, for hundreds of generations, only through them is any access to divine things to be obtained. Theirs is the unique utterance, heroic or affecting, enthusiastic or tranquillizing; the only one which the hearts and minds around them and after them will heed; the only one adapted to profound cravings, to accumulated aspirations, to hereditary faculties, to a complete intellectual and moral organism. . . .

This is no barren formula. A sentiment of such grandeur, of such comprehensive and penetrating insight, an idea by which man, compassing the vastness and depth of things, so greatly oversteps the ordinary limits of his mortal condition, resembles an illumination; it is easily transformed into a vision; it is never remote from ecstasy; it can express itself only through symbols; it evokes divine figures. Religion in its nature is a metaphysical poem accompanied by faith. Under this title it is popular and efficacious; for, apart from an invisible select few, a pure abstract idea is only an empty term, and truth, to be apparent, must be clothed with a body. It requires a form of worship, a legend and ceremonies in order to address the people, women, children, the credulous, everyone absorbed by daily cares, any understanding in which ideas involuntarily translate themselves through imagery. Owing to this palpable form it is able to give its weighty support to the conscience, to counterbalance natural egoism, to curb the mad onset of brutal passions, to lead the will to abnegation and devotion, to tear man away from himself and place him wholly in the service of truth, or of his kind, to form ascetics, martyrs, sisters of charity and missionaries. Thus, throughout society, religion becomes at once a natural and precious instrumentality. On the one hand men require it for the contemplation of infinity and to live properly; if it were suddenly to be taken away from them their souls would be a mournful void and they would do greater injury to their neighbors. Besides, it would be vain to attempt to take it away from them; the hand raised against it would encounter only its envelope; it would be repelled after a sanguinary struggle, its germ lying too deeply to be extirpated.

And when, at length, after religion and habit, we regard the state, that is to say, the armed power possessing both physical force and moral authority, we find for it an almost equally noble origin. In Europe at least, from Russia to Portugal, and from Norway to the two Sicilies it is, in its origin and essence, a military foundation in which heroism constitutes itself the champion of right. Here and there, in the chaos of mixed races and of crumbling societies, some man has arisen who, through his ascendency, rallies around him a loyal band, driving out intruders, overcoming brigands, re-establishing order, reviving agriculture, founding a patrimony, and transmitting as property to his descendants his office of hereditary justiciary and born general. Through this permanent delegation a great public office is removed from competitors, fixed in one family, sequestered in safe hands; thenceforth the nation possesses a vital center and each right obtains a visible protector. If the sovereign confines himself to his attributions, is restrained in despotic tendencies, and avoids falling into egotism, he gives the country one of the best governments of which the world has any knowledge, not alone the most stable, the most capable of continuance, the most suitable for maintaining together a body of twenty or thirty thousand men, but, again, one of the best, because self-sacrifice dignifies both command and obedience and, through the prolongation of military tradition, fidelity and honor, from grade to grade, attaches the chieftain to his duty and the soldier to his chieftain.

Such are the valid claims of hereditary prejudice; like instinct, we see in it a blind form of reason. And what renders it completely legitimate, in order to make it serviceable, is that reason herself is obliged to borrow its forms. The inspiration of a doctrine is due to its blind activity. To enter into practice, to direct souls, to convert itself into a spring of action, it must lodge itself in minds in the shape of an accepted belief, enforced by habit, established by inclination, handed down by home traditions, and, descending from the stormy heights of the intellect, embed itself in the stagnant depths of the will; then only does it form part of the character and become a social force. But, through the same process, it ceases to be critical and clairvoyant; it no longer tolerates doubt or contradiction, it no longer allows restrictions or distinctions; its evidence is no longer comprehended or is misinterpreted. We, of the present day, believe in infinite progress about the same as people once believed in original sin; we still accept ready-made opinions from above, the Academy of Sciences taking the place, in many respects, of the ancient councils. Belief and obedience will, except with a few special savants, continue unreflecting, while reason would greatly err in resenting the leadership of prejudice in human affairs, since, to take this lead, she must herself become prejudice.

Unfortunately, in the eighteenth century, reason was classic; not only the aptitude but the documents which enable it to comprehend tradition, were absent. In the first place, there was no knowledge of history; there was a repugnance to erudition, because of its dullness and tediousness; learned compilations, vast collections of extracts and the slow work of criticism were held in disdain. Voltaire railed at the Benedictines. Montesquieu, to ensure the acceptance of his *Esprit des lois,* indulged in wit about laws. Raynal, to give an impetus to his history of commerce in the Indies, welded to it the declamation of Diderot. . . . The sympathetic imagination did not exist; people were incapable of going out of themselves, of betaking themselves to distant points of view, of conjecturing the peculiar and violent states of the human brain, the decisive and fruitful moments during which it gives birth to a vigorous creation, a religion destined to rule, a state that is sure to endure. . . .

Unable to comprehend the past, they were unable to comprehend the present. They had no accurate conception of the present, of the mechanic, of the provincial bourgeois, or even of the inferior rural noble; these were visible only at a distance, half-effaced, and wholly transformed through philosophic theories and sentimental mistiness. "Two or three thousand" polished and cultivated individuals formed the circle of honest folks, and they never went outside of this. If they obtained glimpses of the people from their chateaux and on their journeys, it was in passing, the same as of their post-horses, or of the cattle on their farms, showing compassion undoubtedly, but never divining their anxious thoughts and their obscure instincts. The structure of the still primitive mind of the people was never imagined, the paucity and tenacity of their ideas, the narrowness of their mechanical, routine existence, devoted to manual labor, absorbed with anxieties for daily bread, confined to the bounds of a visible horizon; their attachment to the local saint, to rites, to the priest, their deep-seated rancor, their inveterate distrust, their credulity growing out of the imagination, their lack of capacity for conceiving abstract right and of comprehending public events, the silent operation by which political novelties became transformed in their brain into nursery fables or into ghost stories, their contagious infatuations like those of sheep, their blind fury like that of bulls, and all those traits of character the Revolution was about to bring to light. . . . The classic reason declined to go so

MONTESQVIEV.

FIGURE 3. Montesquieu. A jurist and *philosophe*, Montesquieu satirized the social customs and political practices of his time and advocated extensive changes in the structure and policies of governments. (*Courtesy of the Fogg Art Museum, Harvard University*)

far as to laboriously study the ancient man and the actual man. . . .
Through this natural and conclusive state of blindness, it no longer
heeds the old and living roots of contemporary institutions; no longer
seeing them it denies that they exist. Hereditary prejudice to it
becomes pure prejudice; tradition has no further claim on us, and
royalty is an usurpation. Thenceforward reason arms itself against
its predecessor to wrest away the government of souls and to substitute the reign of truth for the reign of error.

In this great undertaking there are two halting-places; either
through good sense or through timidity many stop halfway. The
first campaign results in carrying the enemy's out-works and his
frontier fortresses, the philosophical army being led by Voltaire. To
combat hereditary prejudice, other prejudices are opposed to it
whose empire is as extensive and whose authority is not less recognized. Montesquieu looks at France through the eyes of a Persian,
and Voltaire, on his return from England, describes the English, an
unknown species. Confronting dogma and the prevailing system of
worship, accounts are given, either with open or with covert irony,
of the various Christian sects, the Anglicans, the Quakers, the Pres-
byterians, the Socinians, those of ancient or of remote people, the
Greeks, Romans, Egyptians, Mahometans and Guebers, of the wor-
shippers of Brahma, of the Chinese and of pure idolaters. In relation
to established laws and customs, expositions are made, with evident
intentions, of other constitutions and other social habits, of despotism, of limited monarchy, of a republic, here the church subject
to the state, there the church free of the state, in this country castes,
in another polygamy, and, from country to country, from century to
century, the diversity, contradiction and antagonism of fundamental
customs which, each on its own ground, are all equally consecrated
by tradition and legitimately forming the system of public rights.
From this time forth the charm is broken. Ancient institutions lose
their divine prestige; they are simply human works, the fruits of the
place and of the moment, and born out of convenience and a cove-
nant. Skepticism enters through all the breaches. With regard to
Christianity it at once changes into open hostility, into a bitter and
prolonged polemical warfare; for, under the title of a state religion
this occupies the ground, censuring free thought, burning writings,
exiling, imprisoning or disturbing authors and everywhere acting
as a natural and official adversary. Moreover, by virtue of being an

ascetic religion, it condemns not only the free and cheerful ways tolerated by the new philosophy but, again, the natural tendencies it sanctions, and the promises of terrestrial felicity with which it everywhere dazzles the eyes. Thus the heart and the head both agree in their opposition. Voltaire, with texts in hand, pursues it from one end to the other of its history, from the first biblical narration to the latest papal bulls, with unflagging animosity and energy, as critic, as historian, as geographer, as logician, as moralist, questioning its sources, opposing evidences, driving ridicule like a pick-axe into every weak spot where an outraged instinct beats against its mystic walls, and into all doubtful places where ulterior patchwork disfigures the primitive structure. He respects, however, the first foundation, and in this particular the greatest writers of the day follow the same course. Under positive religions that are false there is a natural religion that is true. This is the simple and authentic text of which the others are altered and amplified translations. On removing the ulterior and divergent surplusage the original remains and this common extract, with which all copies harmonize, is deism. The same operation ensues with civil and political laws. In France where so many institutions survive their utility, where privileges are no longer sanctioned by services, where rights are changed into abuses, how incoherent is the architecture of the old Gothic building! How poorly adapted to a modern nation! Of what use, in an unique and compact state, of all those feudal compartments separating orders, corporations and provinces? What a living paradox the archbishop lord of a semi-province, a chapter owning 12,000 serfs, a drawing-room abbé well supported by a monastery he never saw, a seignior liberally pensioned to figure in antechambers, a magistrate purchasing the right to administer justice, a colonel leaving college to take the command of his inherited regiment, a Parisian trader who, renting a house for one year in Franche-Comté, alienates the ownership of his property and of his person. Throughout Europe there are others of the same character. The best that can be said of "a polished nation" is that its laws, customs and practices are composed "one-half of abuses and one-half of tolerable usages." But, underneath these positive laws, which contradict each other, and of which each contradicts itself, a natural law exists, implied in the codes, applied socially, and written in all hearts. . . . "Justice and injustice is the same throughout the universe," and, as in the worst community force always, in some respects, is at the service of right so, in the worst religion, the extravagant dogma always in some fashion proclaims a supreme architect. Religions and communities, accordingly, disintegrated under the investigating process, disclose at the bottom of the crucible, some a residuum of truth, others a residuum of justice, a small but precious balance, a sort of gold ingot preserved by tradition, purified by reason, and which little by little, freed from its alloys, elaborated and devoted to all usages, must solely provide the substance of religion and all the threads of the social warp.

Here begins the second philosophic expedition. It consists of two armies, the first composed of the Encyclopedists, some of them sceptics like d'Alembert, others pantheists like Diderot and Lamarck, others open atheists and materialists like Holbach, Lamettrie and Helvétius, and later, Condorcet, Lalande and Volney, all differing and independent of each other, but all unanimous in regarding tradition as the common enemy. Such is the effect of prolonged hostilities: the duration of warfare begets exasperation; the desire to be master of everything, to push the adversary to the wall, to drive him out of all his positions. They refuse to admit that reason and tradition can occupy and defend the same citadel together; as soon as one enters the other must depart; henceforth one prejudice is established against another prejudice. . . . The first duty of a sound man is to get rid of it, to discard every superstition, every "fear of invisible powers." Then only can he establish a moral order of things and distinguish "the natural law." The sky consisting of empty space, we have no need to seek commands from on high. Let us look down to the ground; let us consider man in himself, as he appears in the eyes of the naturalist, namely, an organized body, a sensitive animal possessing wants, appetites and instincts. Not only are these indestructible but they are legitimate. Let us throw open the prison in which prejudice confines them; let us give them free air and space; let them be displayed in all their strength and all will go well. According to Diderot, a lasting marriage is an abuse, being "the tyranny of a man who has converted the possession of a woman into property." Purity is an invention and conventional, like a dress; happiness and morals go together only in countries where instinct is sanctioned. . . .

With Diderot, to say the least, these paradoxes have their correctives. In his pictures of modern ways and habits, he is the moralist. . . . But, associated with him, are others, cold and narrow, who form moral systems according to the mathematical methods of the ideologists, after the style of Hobbes. One motive alone satisfies these, the simplest and most palpable, utterly gross, almost mechanical, completely physiological, the natural animal tendency of avoiding pain and seeking pleasure. "Pain and pleasure," says Helvétius, "form the only springs of the moral universe; the sentiment of self-love is the only basis on which we can lay the foundations of practical morality. What motive but that of self-interest could lead a man to perform a generous action? He can as little love good for the sake of good as evil for the sake of evil." The principles of natural law, say the disciples, are reduced to one unique and fundamental principle, self-preservation. . . ." Virtue thus is simply egotism furnished with a spyglass; man has no other reason for doing good but the fear of doing himself harm, while self-devotion consists of self-interest. One goes fast and far on this road. When the sole law for each person is to be happy, each wishes to be so immediately and in his own way; the herd of appetites is let loose, rushing ahead and breaking down all barriers. And the more readily because it has been demonstrated to them that every barrier is an evil, invented by cunning and malicious shepherds, the better to milk and shear them. "The state of society is a state of warfare of the sovereign against all, and of each member against the rest. . . . We see on the face of the globe only incapable, unjust sovereigns, enervated by luxury, corrupted by flattery, depraved through unpunished license, and without talent, morals, or good qualities. . . . Man is wicked not because he is wicked, but because he has been made so." "Would you know the story, in brief, of almost all our wretchedness? Here it is. There existed the natural man, and into this man was introduced an artificial man, whereupon a civil war arose within him, lasting through life. . . . If you propose to become a tyrant over him, . . . do your best to poison him with a theory of morals against nature; impose every kind of fetter on him; embarrass his movements with a thousand obstacles; place phantoms around him to frighten him. . . . Would you see him happy and free? Do not meddle with his affairs. . . . Remain convinced of this, that these wise legislators have formed and shaped you as they have done, not for your benefit, but for their own. I appeal to every civil, religious, and political institution; examine these closely, and, if I am not mistaken, you will find the human species, century after century, subject to a yoke which a mere handful of knaves chose to impose on it. . . . Be wary of him who seeks to establish order; to order is to obtain the mastery of others by giving them trouble." All this must come to an end; the passions are proper, and if the herd would eat freely, its first care must be to trample under its *sabots* the mitred and crowned animals who keep it in the fold for their own advantage.

A return to nature, meaning by this the abolition of society, is the war-cry of the whole Encyclopedic battalion. The same shout is heard in another quarter, coming from the Rousseau battalion and that of the socialists who, in their turn, march up to the assault of the established régime. The mining and sapping of the walls practiced by the latter seems less extensive, but only the more efficacious, while the distinctive machinery it employs consists likewise of a new conception of human nature. Rousseau derived this conception wholly from the spectacle he contemplated in his own breast: a strange, original and superior man, who, from his infancy, harbored within him a germ of insanity and who finally became wholly insane; a wonderful, ill-balanced mind in which sensations, emotions and images are too powerful: at once blind and perspicacious, a veritable poet and a morbid poet, who, instead of objects beheld reveries, living in a romance and dying in a nightmare of his own creation. . . . Rousseau generalizes; occupied with himself, even to infatuation, and regarding no one in the world but himself he imagines man accordingly and "describes him as he feels him within. . . ." His contaminations all come to him from without; his vices and his baseness must be attributed to circumstances: "If I had fallen into the hands of a better master . . . I should have been a good Christian, a good father, a good friend, a good workman, a good man in all things." The wrong is thus all on the side of society. In like manner nature, with man in general, is good. "His first impulses are always right. . . . The fundamental principles of all moral questions, on which I have argued in all my writings, is that *man is naturally good and loving justice and order. . . .*" "Nature made man to be happy and good, while society has made him depraved and miserable." Divest him, in thought, of his factitious habits, of his superadded necessities, of his false prejudices; put aside systems, study your own heart, listen to the inward dictates of feeling, let yourself be guided by the light of instinct and of conscience, and you will again find the first Adam, like an incorruptible marble statue that has fallen into a marsh, a long time lost under a crust of slime and mud, but which, released from its foul covering, may be replaced on its pedestal in the completeness of its form and in the perfect purity of its whiteness. . . . Civilization, which boasts of its splendor, is simply the restlessness of over-excited, servile monkeys each imitating the other, and each corrupting the other to attain to super-refinement, discomfort and ennui. Human culture, accordingly, is in itself bad, while the fruit it produces is merely excrescence and poison. . . .

If civilization is bad, society is worse. For this could not have been established except by destroying primitive equality, while its two principal institutions, property and government, are usurpations. "He who first enclosed a plot of ground, and who took it into his head to say *this belongs to me,* and who found people simple enough to believe him, was the true founder of civil society. What crimes, what wars, what murders, what misery and what horrors would have been spared the human race if he who, pulling up the landmark and filling up the ditch, had cried out to his fellows: Be wary of that impostor; you are lost if you forget that no one has a right to the ground and that its fruits are the property of all!" The first property right was a robbery by which an individual abstracted from the community a portion of the public domain. Nothing could justify the outrage, nothing added by him to the soil, neither his industry, nor his trouble, nor his valor. . . . "Let us sum up in few words the social pact of the two estates: *You need me because I am rich and you are poor: let us then make an agreement together. I will allow you the honor of serving me on condition that you give me the little that remains to you for the trouble I have in governing you.*"

This shows the spirit, the object and the effect of political society. At the start, according to Rousseau, it consisted of an iniquitous bargain, made by an adroit rich man with a poor dupe, "providing new fetters for the weak and fresh power for the rich," and, under the title of legitimate property, hallowing the usurpation of the soil. Today the contract is still more iniquitous "as a child may govern an old man, a fool lead the wise, and a handful of people burst with superfluities whilst a famished multitude lack the necessaries of life." It is the nature of inequality to grow; hence the authority of some increases along with the dependence of the rest, so that the two conditions, having at last reached their extremes, the hereditary and perpetual subjection of the people seems to be a divine right equally with the hereditary and perpetual despotism of the king. . . .

We stop here. It is not worth while to follow the forlorn hope of the party, . . . the fanatics that erected atheism into an obligatory dogma and into a superior duty; the socialists who, to suppress egoism, propose a community of goods and who found a republic in which any man that proposes to reestablish "detestable owner-ship" shall be declared an enemy of humanity, treated as a "raging maniac" and shut up in a dungeon for life. It is sufficient to have studied the operations of large armies and of great campaigns. With different resources and contrary tactics, the various attacks are all directed to the same end. Every institution is undermined at its foun-dations. The dominant philosophy withdraws all authority from cus-tom, from religion, from the State. Not only is it admitted that tradition in itself is false, but again that it is baneful through its works, that it builds up injustice on error and that by rendering man blind it leads to subjection. Henceforth it is proscribed. Let this "infamous thing" with its upholders be crushed out. It is the great wrong of the human species, and, when suppressed, only the right will rémain. "The time will then come when the sun will shine only on free men recognizing no other master than reason; when tyrants and slaves, and priests with their senseless or hypocritical instruments, will exist only in history and on the stage; when attention will no longer be bestowed on them except to pity their victims and their dupes, we remaining vigilant and useful through horror of their excesses, and able to recognize and extinguish by the force of reason the first germs of superstition and of tyranny, should they ever venture to re-appear." The millennium is approaching and reason must again reor-ganize. We are thus to owe everything to its salutary authority, the foundation of the new order of things as well as the destruction of the old one.

The Organization of the Society of the Future

Consider future society as it appears at this moment to our legisla-tors of the closet and bear in mind that it will soon appear under the same aspect to the legislators of the Assembly. In their eyes the decisive moment has come. Henceforth two histories are to exist; one, that of the past, the other, that of the future, formerly a history of man ill deprived of his reason, and at present the history of the rational man. At length the rule of right is to begin. Of all that the past has founded and transmitted nothing is legitimate. Overlaying the natural man it has created an artificial man, either ecclesiastic or laic, noble or plebeian, sovereign or subject, proprietor or proletary, ignorant or cultivated, peasant or citizen, slave or master, all being factitious qualities which we are not to heed, as their origin is tainted with violence and robbery. Strip off these superadded garments; let us take man in himself, the same under all conditions, in all situations, in all countries, in all ages, and strive to ascertain what sort of association is the best adapted to him. The problem thus stated the rest follows.

Conformably to the ways of the classic spirit, and to the precepts of the prevailing ideology, a political system is constructed after a mathematical model. A simple proposition is selected, and set apart, very general, familiar, readily apparent, and easily understood by the most ignorant and inattentive schoolboy. Reject every difference which separates one man from other men; retain of him only the portion common to him and to others. This remainder constitutes man in general, or in other words, "a sensitive and rational being who, thus endowed, avoids pain and seeks pleasure," and therefore aspiring to "happiness, namely, a stable condition in which one enjoys greater pleasure than pain," or, again, "a sensitive being capable of forming rational opinions and of acquiring moral ideas." The first comer is cognizant of this notion in his own experience, and can verify it at the first glance. Such is the social unit; let several of these be combined, a thousand, a hundred thousand, a million, twenty-six millions, and you have the French people. Men born at twenty-one years of age, without relations, without a past, without traditions, without a country, are supposed to be assembled for the first time and, for the first time, to treat with each other. In this position, at the moment of contracting together, all are equal: for, as the definition states, the extrinsic and spurious qualities through which alone all differ have been rejected. All are free, for, according to the definition, the unjust thraldom imposed on all by brute force and by hereditary prejudice, has been suppressed. But, if all men are equal, no reason exists why, in this contract, any special advantage should be conceded to one more than to another. Accordingly all shall be equal before the law; no person, or family, or class, shall be allowed any privilege; no one shall claim a right of which another might be deprived; no one shall be subject to any duty of which another is exempted. On the other hand, all being free, each enters with a free will along with the group of wills constituting the new community; it is necessary that in the common resolutions, he should fully concur. Only on these conditions does he bind himself; he is bound to respect laws only because he has assisted in making them, and to obey magistrates only because he has aided in electing them. Underneath all legitimate authority his consent or his vote must be apparent, while, in the humblest citizen, the most exalted of public powers must recognize a member of their own sovereignty. No one may alienate or lose this portion of his sovereignty; it is inseparable from his person, and, on delegating it to another, he reserves to himself full possession of it. The liberty, equality and sovereignty of the people constitute the first articles of the social contract. These are rigorously deduced from a primary definition; other rights of the citizen are to be no less rigorously deduced from it, the main features of the constitution, the most important civil and political laws, in short, the order, the form and the spirit of the new state.

Hence, two consequences. In the first place, a society thus organized is the only just one; for, the reverse of all others, it is not the result of a blind subjection to traditions, but of a contract concluded among equals, examined in open daylight, and assented to in full freedom. The social contract, composed of demonstrated theorems, has the authority of geometry; hence an equal value at all times, in every place, and for every people; it is accordingly rightfully established. Whatever interposes any obstacle thereto is inimical to the human race; whether a government, an aristocracy or a clergy, it must be overthrown. Revolt is simply just defense; in withdrawing ourselves from such hands we only recover what has been wrongfully retained and which legitimately belongs to us. In the second place, this social code, as just set forth, once promulgated, is applicable without misconception or resistance; for it is a species of moral geometry, simpler than any other, reduced to first principles, founded on the clearest and most popular notions, and, in four steps, leading to capital truths. The comprehension and application of these truths demand no preparatory study or profound reflection; good sense suffices, and even common sense. Prejudice and selfishness alone impair the testimony; but never will testimony be wanting in a sound brain and in an upright heart. Explain the rights of man to a laborer or to a peasant and at once he becomes an able politician; teach children the citizen's catechism and on leaving school they comprehend duties and rights as well as the four arithmetical principles. Thereupon hope spreads her wings to the fullest extent and all obstacles seem removed. It is admitted that of itself, and through its own force, the theory engenders its own application; it suffices for men to decree or accept the social compact to acquire under this same act, at once a capacity for comprehending it and the disposition to carry it out. . . .

It is a sad thing to fall asleep in a sheepcot and, on awakening, to find the sheep transformed into wolves. And yet, in case of a revolution this is what we may expect. What we call reason in man is not an innate endowment, primitive and enduring, but a tardy acquisition and a fragile composition. The slightest physiological knowledge suffices to show that it is a state of unstable equilibrium, dependent on the no less greater instability of the brain, nerves, circulation and digestion. . . . Properly speaking man is imbecile, as the body is morbid, by nature; the health of our mind, like the health of our organs, is simply a repeated achievement and a happy accident. If such happens to be the case with the coarse woof and canvas, with the large and approximatively strong threads of our intellect, what risks are imminent for the ulterior and superadded embroidery, the subtle and complicated netting forming reason properly so called and which is composed of general ideas? Formed by a slow and delicate process of weaving, through a long system of signs, amidst the agitations of pride, of enthusiasm and of dogmatic obstinacy, how many chances there are, even in the most perfect brain, of these ideas inadequately corresponding with outward things! . . . Not only is reason crippled in man, but it is rare in humanity. General ideas and accurate reasoning are found only in a select few. The comprehension of abstract terms and the habit of making accurate deductions requires previous and special preparation, a prolonged mental exercise and steady practice, and besides this, where political matters are concerned, a degree of composure which, affording every facility for reflection, enables a man to detach himself for a moment from himself for the consideration of his interests as a disinterested observer. If one of these conditions is wanting, reason, especially in relation to politics, is absent. . . .

Not only is reason not natural to man nor universal in humanity, but again, in the conduct of man and of humanity, its influence is small. . . . The place obtained by reason is always restricted; the office it fulfills is generally secondary. . . . The masters of man consist of physical temperament, bodily needs, animal instinct, hereditary prejudice, imagination, generally the dominant passion, and more particularly personal or family interest, also that of caste or party. We should labor under serious error were we to suppose ourselves naturally good, generous, sympathetic, or, even at the least, gentle, pliable, and ready to sacrifice ourselves to social interests or to those of others. There are several of them, and of the most powerful kind, and which, if left to themselves, would make only havoc. In the first place, if there is no certainty of man being a remote blood cousin of the monkey, it is at least certain that, in his structure, he is an animal closely related to the monkey, provided with canine teeth, carnivorous, formerly cannibal and, therefore, a hunter and bellicose. Hence there is in him a steady substratum of brutality and ferocity, and of violent and destructive instincts, to which must be added, if he is French, gaiety, laughter, and a strange propensity to gamble and act insanely in the havoc he makes; we shall see him at work. In the second place, at the outset, his condition casts him naked and destitute on an ungrateful soil on which subsistence is difficult, where, at the risk of death, he is obliged to save and to economize. Hence a constant preoccupation and the rooted idea of acquiring, accumulating, and possessing, rapacity and avarice, more particularly in the class which, tied to the glebe, fasts for sixty generations in order to support other classes and whose crooked fingers are always outstretched to clutch the soil whose fruits they cause to grow; we shall see this class at work. Finally, his more delicate mental organization makes of him from the earliest days an imaginative being in which swarming fancies develop themselves into monstrous chimeras to expand his hopes, fears and desires beyond all bounds. Hence an excess of sensibility, sudden outbursts of emotion, contagious transports; irresistible currents of passion, epidemics of credulity and suspicion, in short, enthusiasm and panic, especially if he is French, that is to say, excitable and communicative, easily thrown off his balance and prompt to accept foreign impulsion, deprived of the natural ballast which a phlegmatic temperament and the concentration of lonely meditations secure to his German or Latin neighbors—and all this we shall see at work. These constitute some of the brute forces that control human life. In ordinary times we pay no attention to them; being subordinated they do not seem to us formidable. We take it for granted that they are allayed and pacified; we flatter ourselves that the discipline imposed on them has made them natural, and that by dint of flowing between dikes they are settled down into their accustomed beds. The truth is that, like all brute forces, like a stream or a torrent, they only remain in these under constraint; it is the dike which, through its resistance, produces this moderation. Another force equal to their force had to be installed against their outbreaks and devastations, graduated according to their scale, all the firmer as they are more menacing, despotic if need be against their despotism, in any event constraining and repressive. . . . At the bottom of all these wheels ever appears the principal lever, the efficacious instrument, namely, the gendarme armed against the savage, brigand and madman each of us harbors, in repose or manacled, but always living, in the recesses of his own breast.

On the contrary, in the new theory, every principle promulgated, every precaution taken, every suspicion awakened is aimed at the gendarme. In the name of the sovereignty of the people all authority is withdrawn from the government, every prerogative, every initiative, its continuance and its force. The people being sovereign the government is simply its clerk, and less than its clerk, merely its domestic. Between them "no contract" indefinite or at least enduring, "and which may be cancelled only by mutual consent or the unfaithfulness of one of the two parties." "It is against the nature of a political body for the sovereign to impose a law on himself which he cannot set aside." There is no sacred and inviolable charter "binding a people to the forms of an established constitution." "The right to change these is the first guarantee of all rights." "There is not, and never can be, any fundamental, obligatory law for the entire body of a people, not even the social contract. . . ." "The deputies of the people are not, nor can they be, its representatives; they are simply its commissioners and can establish no final compact. Every law not ratified by the people themselves is null and is no law. . . ." "The moment the people are thus assembled the jurisdiction of the government is to cease and the executive power is to be suspended," society commencing anew, while citizens, restored to their primitive independence, may reconstitute at will, for any period they determine, the provisional contract to which they have assented only for a determined time. . . .

Practice, accordingly, accompanies the theory, and the dogma of the sovereignty of the people, interpreted by the mass, is to produce a perfect anarchy, up to the moment when, interpreted by its chiefs, it produces a perfect despotism.

For there are two sides to this theory; while one side leads to the perpetual demolition of government, the other terminates in the illimitable dictation of the state. The new contract is not a historic fact like the English Declaration of Rights in 1688 or the Dutch federation in 1579, entered into by actual and living individuals, admitting acquired situations, groups already formed, established positions, and drawn up to recognize, define, guarantee and complete an anterior right. Antecedent to the social contract no veritable right exists; for veritable rights are born solely out of the social contract, the only valid one, since it is the only one agreed upon between beings perfectly equal and perfectly free, so many abstract creatures, so many species of mathematical units, all of the same value, all playing the same part and whose inequality or constraint never disturbs the common understanding. Hence, at the moment of its completion, all other pacts are nullified. Property, family, church, no ancient institution may invoke any right against the new state. . . . In the place of the sovereignty of the king the *Contrat social* substitutes the sovereignty of the people. The latter, however, is much more absolute than the former, and, in the democratic convent which Rousseau constructs, on the Spartan and Roman model, the individual is nothing and the state everything. . . .

This being admitted, let us trace the consequences. In the first place, I enjoy my property only through tolerance and at secondhand; for, according to the social contract, I have surrendered it; "it now forms a portion of the national estate"; if I retain the use of it for the time being it is through a concession of the state which makes me a "depositary" of it. . . .

In the second place, this convent is a seminary. I have no right to bring up my children in my own house and in my own way. "As the reason of each man must not be the sole arbiter of his rights so much less should the education of children, which is of more consequence to the state than to fathers, be left to the intelligence and prejudices of their fathers. . . ." Thus, "public education, within laws prescribed by the government and under magistrates appointed by sovereign will, is one of the fundamental maxims of popular or legitimate government." Through this the citizen is formed in advance. . . .

Finally, our lay convent has its own religion, a lay religion. If I possess any other It is through its condescension and under restrictions. It is, by nature, hostile to other associations than its own. They are rivals, they annoy it, they absorb the will and pervert the votes of its members. . . . Therefore, if the future Republic allows me to remain a Christian, it must be on the understood condition that my doctrine shall be shut up in my mind, without even affecting my heart. If I am a Catholic, (and twenty-five out of twenty-six million Frenchmen are like me), my condition is worse. For the social pact does not tolerate an intolerant religion; any sect that condemns other sects is a public enemy; "whoever presumes to say that *there is no salvation out of the church,* must be driven out of the state." Should I be, finally, a free-thinker, a positivist or skeptic, my situation is little better. "There is a civil religion," a catechism, "a profession of faith, of which the sovereign has the right to dictate the articles, not exactly as religious dogmas but as sentiments of social import without which we cannot be a good citizen or a loyal subject." These articles embrace "the existence of a powerful, intelligent, beneficent, foreseeing and provident divinity, the future life, the happiness of the good, the punishment of the wicked, the sacredness of the social contract and of the laws. Without forcing anyone to believe in this creed, whoever does not believe in it must be expelled from the state. . . .

These articles are all necessary sequels of the social contract. The moment I enter the corporation I abandon my own personality; I abandon, by this step, my possessions, my children, my church, and my opinions. I cease to be proprietor, father, Christian and philosopher. The state is my substitute in all these functions. In place of my will, there is henceforth the public will, that is to say, in theory, the mutable absolutism of a majority counted by heads, while in fact, it is the rigid absolutism of the assembly, the faction, the individual who is custodian of the public authority. On this principle an outburst of boundless infatuation takes place. . . . In the name of reason, of which the state alone is the representative and interpreter, they undertake to unmake and make over, conformably to reason and to reason alone, all customs, festivals, ceremonies, and costumes, the era, the calendar, weights and measures, the names of the seasons, months, weeks and days, of places and monuments, family and baptismal names, complimentary titles, the tone of discourse, the mode of salutation, of greeting, of speaking and of writing, in such a fashion, that the Frenchman, as formerly with the Puritan or the Quaker, remodelled even in his inward substance, exposes, through the minutest details of his conduct and exterior, the dominance of the all-powerful principle which refashions his being and the inflexible logic which controls his thoughts. This constitutes the final result and complete triumph of the classic spirit. Installed in narrow brains, incapable of harboring more than one idea, it is to become a cold or furious monomania, . . . all with a view to substitute for the existing man, enduring and slowly formed by history, an improvised automaton that is to fall away through its own debility when the external and mechanical force that keeps it up will no longer sustain it.

Pierre Gaxotte

THE ENLIGHTENMENT AS DOCTRINAIRE, IRRELIGIOUS AND CONSPIRATORIAL

Pierre Gaxotte is well known in France as a prolific historian, and one who enjoys a considerable following in spite of the fact that his works are oriented against the predominant schools of historical interpretation. A member of the French Academy since 1953, Gaxotte has frankly adopted a strong anti-liberal view of French history and politics, and is one of the major spokesmen for the conservatives in such matters. Among the many analysts of the influence of the Enlightenment on the French Revolution, Gaxotte is remarkable in preserving in his works most, if not all, the criticisms which have been leveled against the Enlightenment since the time of Burke. These arguments he marshals and summarizes in the following selection.

The seventeenth century had been an age in which the French genius reached its full bloom. The aspect under which men at that time liked to conceive of man was that of a being alive to realities and prone to reflection, who curbs his appetites and his passions in obedience to a higher rule of order and harmony. Such a man distrusts individual caprice, the vagaries of sentiment, instinctive action, all that is confused and ill-defined, and those blind impulses which are apt to dull the clearest minds like the shadow of a cloud on the surface of a pool. Knowing his own weaknesses, he does not take his own desires as the basis of morality and knowledge. He has a taste for hierarchical organization and discipline. He glories in submitting to experience the force of logic and tradition, which is but accumulated experience. He is a Christian and a conservative. He has a horror of disturbances and revolutions. He loves what is universal and stable. He delights in discovering the same eternal and universal verities in all ages and in all countries, however greatly they may differ in superficial appearance. He has the gift of organization, an upright mind, a love of truth and a sense of reality.

For fifty years France admired her own reflection in Louis XIV, for he was reasonable, moderate, exact, methodical and master of himself, his sentiments were noble and his life glorious and well-ordered.

Reprinted with the permission of Charles Scribner's Sons from *The French Revolution* by Pierre Gaxotte, translated by Walter A. Phillips (New York, 1932).

This same ideal inspired the whole century, Colbert and Vauban expressing it as vividly as Racine, Poussin and Bossuet. A sermon of Bourdaloue's, a diplomatic despatch composed by Hugues de Lionne, bears the impress in the same sense as do the Louvre, Versailles and the comedies of Molière. It was this that gave France a royal supremacy over all the world, and, through her, carried on the wondrous work of Athens and of Rome.

The tragedy of the eighteenth century lies, indeed, not in its wars nor in the "days" (*journées*) of the Revolution, but in the dissolution and reversal of the ideas which had illumined and dominated the seventeenth. Riots and massacres were but the bloody and signal expression of this fact; for, long before these happened, the real harm had already been done.

The revolutionary spirit is as old as society itself, and the form which it assumed about the year 1750 was in itself nothing new. In all ages poets have delighted in drawing imaginary pictures of enchanted lands where men, perfect in goodness, should live without restraint, amid natural scenes of exquisite beauty; and moralists have used the same device in order to admonish their contemporaries and make them ashamed of their vices. This, however, was no more than a sport of the imagination or an exercise in rhetoric. To ripen these dreams into dogmas, to turn these playful fancies into hatred of authority and contempt for civilization, they had to become inflamed with religious passion.

The Reformation was a preliminary explosion of destructive individualism and republican sentimentality. Great intellectual and social questions, instead of being solved in common and on traditional lines, began to be interpreted by the secret light of the individual heart and in the isolation of the individual conscience. The vague aspirations of each individual became in his eyes truth and God. The concerted activity of natural groups of men, their habits of discipline in religion and in the arts, gave place to the separate initiative of each of their members. This was known as "liberation." Wherever the Reformation triumphed in its pure Lutheran form, it meant in reality nothing but anarchy; and, once the period of ferment was over, there remained an almost infinite subdivision of territories and an all but irremediable disintegration of morals.

The unity of France was preserved and with it the crown. The dominant classical spirit of the age, illustrated by writers and thinkers like Pascal, Descartes, Bossuet and La Bruyère, borrowed from the monarchy their conception of law and government. It seemed as though nothing could ever overset this balance or disturb this good understanding. Yet revolutionary mysticism was not dead. It inspired the tirades of the *libertins,* who denounced memory and reason for having corrupted nature and robbed man of the taste for art and for pure enjoyment. It produced the Protestant libellists who flooded France and Europe with their pamphlets from Holland and Germany. It corrupted by its chimerical ideas one of the subtlest and most brilliant intellects of the century: Fénelon.

Louis XIV had been at pains to write, for the benefit of his children, a sort of "Manual of the Perfect Sovereign," in which he sought to make them feel the majesty of their station in life, so that they should carry out the duties attached to it serenely and with affection. Fénelon, who was tutor to the heir to the throne, did his best to give him a disgust for the duties of a monarch. His *Télémaque* is an unctuous criticism of all monarchical principles. "The office of a king," Louis XIV had written, "is grand, noble, delightful." "What folly," said Fénelon, "to find one's happiness in governing men. . . . How mad is he who seeks to be a king! Happy is he who is content with a private and peaceable state of life, in which it is less difficult for him to be virtuous. . . . Fear, then, my son, fear so perilous a position. . . . It is a crushing servitude. . . ."

But Fénelon lived too soon. The sturdy good sense of Louis XIV, and a polemic of Bossuet's, admirable both in its reasoning and in its eloquence, sufficed to stifle the threatened conflagration. The few little flames that continued to flicker here and there kindled no blaze. It needed the visits of Montesquieu and Voltaire to London to breathe new life into the preaching of individualism and revolution, and this time in real earnest.

The picture of England which Montesquieu and Voltaire brought back with them astonishes us. They had not seen "the gloomy and turbulent island of the regicides," the intolerant, greedy and ambitious nation which had organized religious persecution in its coldest and most implacable form—the administrative form—but a liberal and enlightened "Salentum," peopled by men of learning and philosophers, and worthy to act as a model of civic sense and virtue to all the world.

This was the starting point for a detailed criticism amusing by reason of the charms with which it was graced, but disconcerting in its childishness and superficiality. Undoubted abuses and recognized injustices were upbraided by it no worse than those principles and institutions which are, and will always be, essential to the life of all societies. With a pun, with a smile, with an epigram, everything was condemned indiscriminately and without appeal. For the purpose of this summary execution a novel character was created, an imaginary savage, representing unspoilt nature, adorned with all the graces and subtleties of ancient civilizations. His function was to be in a perpetual state of wonderment and to use all the resources of a cultivated, polished and refined intelligence in order to make refinement, polish and culture appear absurd, ridiculous and harmful.

For forty years France was full of these very Parisian Iroquois, these highly civilized Persians, these *ingénus* who were anything but ingenuous. By their clever irony, their depreciatory comparisons and their studied expressions of naïve wonder they succeeded in troubling men's minds, in inspiring the steadiest of them with doubt and disquiet, and in causing the most ordinary rights to be regarded as infringements or usurpations, and old institutions, which for centuries past it had been an honor to respect and serve, to be resented as new, vexatious and illegitimate.

Thanks to these topsy-turvy ideas, Germanic literature, the influence of which had been checked since the Reformation, naturally found its way into France. . . .

While English works were introduced into France only through the agency of Frenchmen, the Abbé Prévost and Voltaire, the Germans organized their own propaganda, and it was one of them, Grimm, who assumed the task of revealing to the subjects of Louis XV the literary merits of his country. In October 1750, the *Mercure de France* published a first letter from him, which was followed in February 1751, by a second. With all sorts of obsequious bows and compliments Grimm ventured to proclaim that German literature was quite equal to that of France, and that, if it had not achieved the same reputation as that of its neighbor, this was because it had lacked a Paris and a Louis XIV. But its turn would certainly come. Nay, it was close at hand.

The breach was now made, and through it passed articles, grammars and translations. Another German, Michel Huber, was the guiding spirit of the invasion. Supple, conciliatory and amiable, using alternately the language of philosophy and that of religion, with his hand on his heart, and overflowing with edifying maxims, he shaped the destinies of Teutonic literature with a sure touch. Controlling the *Journal étranger* and author of a bulky collection of German poems in four volumes, he was clever enough to offer the French public only what they wanted: that is, idyllic, sentimental and moralizing themes. He gained the good will of Fréron and the pious clique, who were reassured by such a rich outpouring of virtuous pronouncements. He obtained the enthusiastic collaboration of the most active section of the philosophic party, grouped round Rousseau and Diderot. Rousseau was no doubt too capricious to allow himself to be enlisted in person, but he urged on his friends. How, indeed, could he have remained indifferent? It was his own naturalistic mysticism returning to France through another channel. . . .

The scientific and practical progress made during the century contributed to these aberrations. Not that science has ever lent any confirmation to the myth of a blissful state of nature corrupted by human laws: nor, apart from d'Alembert, did the men of learning and the inventors belong to the sect of the philosophers. But the sight of so many strange mechanisms, the revelation of such a wealth of new knowledge, intoxicated the profane and the men of letters, and to their dazzled eyes it appeared that they lived in an extraordinary age, that everything that had been said and done before them counted for nothing, and, consequently, that it was proof of the possession of an enlightened mind to display an all-embracing contempt for the achievements of the past.

It is vain that Taine has taken so much trouble to show that Voltaire, Diderot, Rousseau and their friends were true men of science. Voltaire had a genius for popularization, but his laboratory at Cirey was only a fancy of Madame du Châtelet's, who would have set up a chapel or a metal foundry on its ruins had piety or metallurgy been in fashion at the moment. The experiments of Montesquieu were laughable: the most important of them consisted in holding the head of a duck under water and seeing how long it took the bird to die. As for Diderot and Rousseau, the former was nothing but a self-taught busybody and the later knew mighty little. . . .

The fact is, that the philosophers took the scientific achievements of the day on trust, and, without knowing much about them, exaggerated their importance because it was from them that they could

FIGURE 4. Diderot. One of the most fertile minds of the Enlightenment, Diderot wrote on a great variety of subjects and edited the *Encyclopédie,* which was a monument of contemporary erudition and propaganda for reform. (*Courtesy of the Fogg Art Museum, Harvard University*)

draw their arguments against tradition, Catholicism, history and authority. They did not, however, devote any real and sustained attention to any but the more abstract sciences, pure mathematics and the mechanism of the heavens, the deductive method of which they transferred to the domain of politics and society, to which it was all the less applicable since, as the postulate from which all their deductions were drawn, they assumed the natural goodness of man, for which there is no basis of proof.

From 1751 to 1772 the *Encyclopédie* marshalled all these ideas and all these aspirations against the common enemy. Here was to be found criticism of the monarchy and of its intellectual supports; here were atheism, sensualism, laudation of the eighteenth century considered as the century of enlightenment and progress, economic liberalism, disparagement of civilization, and the justification of a state of nature in which all men would have equal rights and equal possessions. Finally, there were very detailed and comprehensive studies of machines, crafts and professions, to which were annexed eleven volumes of plates. This part of the work, which was the best and most useful, served as a screen for the rest.

Rousseau did not like the Encyclopedists; for they had wounded his vanity, and some of their doctrines were repugnant to him. Nonetheless, he was fundamentally in agreement with them, and, for the rest, it was his genius which gave its brilliancy and propagandist power to revolutionary mysticism.

Unhappy in his birth, without family or friends, utterly perverted by his early adventures with women, devoured by a frenzy of unrest that was to end in absolute madness, he came from Geneva, one of the strongholds of the Reformation, where "for two centuries past the products of decomposition had been eddying." To express his frenzy, his revolt, his restlessness and his itch for destruction he had at his command a literary style of astonishing richness and beauty. And this use of the most magnificent powers of language and poetry for the canonization of so sordid a soul is a thing horrible to contemplate.

But Rousseau did not confine himself to anathemas, regrets and invectives. He laid the foundations of that future society which was to secure to men the exercise of their natural rights. These foundations are: the complete equality of those associated, the alienation of the rights of the individual for the benefit of the community, and the subordination of those entering into the contract to the *general will*.

Let us understand clearly what is meant by this last expression. The *general will* is not the will of the majority, but the deep tones of the human conscience, as it ought to find a voice in each of us and as it finds utterance in the mouths of the most virtuous and enlightened citizens. In a word, the *general will* is defined in conformity with a philosophical system, namely, individualism. The republic is identified with a doctrine, and society is made subject to a dogma. To make this a reality, to translate it into action, and to reorganize the world in accordance with its assumptions: such is the revolutionary policy.

Its first, and, so to speak, its only task consisted in destroying, and preventing the revival of all those natural institutions which had hitherto encompassed and sustained the individual, but were henceforth to be considered oppressive and immoral. Property, the family, corporate bodies, the city, the province, country and Church were all so many obstacles to be torn down. And if it were objected that the majority of the citizens respected them, were content with them, and found in them happiness and peace of mind, this mattered but little, for there is no freedom from liberty. If the *general will* is not articulate in the majority, it is because it is perverted and degraded; and it is the duty of "conscious" citizens to emancipate them in spite of themselves.

Having become a religion, the republic had its own orthodoxy, its elect and its reprobates. Majorities, elections, votes, popular discussions: all these were a mere façade, a game for taking in simpletons, who found to their astonishment that its rules were always applied against themselves alone. Behind this bustle there was the little flock of the faithful and enlightened. These were the guardians of the truth, whose empire they had sworn to establish. They were the *general will*. As to their opponents, however numerous they might be, whatever respect they might have for universal suffrage or devotion to the republican form of government, they were never to be anything but aristocrats, reactionaries, heretics, and, as occasion served, usurpers; for just as there was a legitimate king, so too, there was a "legitimate" people. Against these opponents all means were permissible, whether electoral manipulations or the guillotine.

Such was the outcome of all the idylls and the lachrymose sentiment. Man is born good. Since rogues and evil people exist, it is civilization that has corrupted them. In order that society may be regenerated, then, it is necessary that it should reject the alleged benefits of civilization, which are in reality nothing but chains and injustices. If it hesitates to do so, it must be constrained by force, since its unwillingness is a crime, a crime against virtue. All were to be declared suspect who, though they had done nothing against the Revolution, had done nothing for it either.

It is, however, impossible to understand the formation of revolutionary mysticism, and above all, its almost mechanical and inevitable evolution into its most exaggerated form, without taking into account the very special characteristics of the environment in which it was received, fostered and propagated. This has never been studied methodically and completely, for M. Augustin Cochin, who had undertaken the task, died before he had completed it. The works which he has left behind are, however, numerous enough to enable us to survey without going astray the domain which he had made his own.

In the eighteenth century those who had a taste for new theories did not remain in isolation. They associated themselves in groups for the purpose of giving others the benefit of their knowledge and in order to clarify their ideas. This organization, of which there were signs in 1720, developed with great rapidity in 1750 and by the death of Louis XV it was complete. In all the towns these associations of wits and sceptics multiplied, as well as literary salons, academies, reading-rooms, patriotic societies, lyceums, museums, masonic lodges, or agricultural societies. Their sessions were regular and well attended. There was reading at them, and, above all, discussion. Thus a whole army of thinkers trained themselves in controversy and debated the questions of the day: the circulation of grain, the new taxes, the provincial assemblies; or theoretical questions such as the role of civilization, natural rights, or the foundations of society. . . .

All the societies were, in fact, bound together either by ties of affiliation, like Freemasons' lodges, or by an unceasing correspondence which brought the more remote and less active of them under the influence of those which were bolder and better informed. From one end of the realm to the other there was a perpetual exchange of opinions, addresses and motions which confirmed the union of principles, stifled all aspirations toward independence, and made everyone march in step. . . .

Thus, the writers reacting on the societies, and the societies on the writers, it came about that the unconscious band of brothers found themselves carried away by an increasingly rapid movement "towards the advent of a certain intellectual and moral type which no one had foreseen, of which everyone would disapprove, yet for which all were preparing the way": the socialistic Jacobin of 1793. . . .

III THE ENLIGHTENMENT AS THE SOURCE OF LIBERALISM AND PROGRESS

Jules Michelet

THE ENLIGHTENMENT AS THE FOUNTAIN
OF SOCIAL AND POLITICAL JUSTICE

Jules Michelet (1798–1874) was a very successful nineteenth-century historian whose works enjoyed wide popularity. A major representative of the romantic school of historical writing, he developed a highly personalized style which is at once picturesque and eloquent. Michelet adhered strongly to the liberal ideology of his age, and became one of the foremost defenders of the French Revolution. This event he regarded as the great watershed in French history, since it reestablished social and political justice in France after its long absence during the old regime. Michelet also believed that the inspiration which underlay this development was derived from the great writers of the Enlightenment, and he regarded them literally as crusaders for the cause of humanity. In this selection, Michelet communicates to the reader some of the conviction with which he approved of the philosophes' principles and their influence during the Revolution.

That dead man is ancient France, and that bier, the coffin of the ancient monarchy. Therein let us bury, and forever, the dreams in which we once fondly trusted: paternal royalty, the government of grace, the clemency of the monarch, and the charity of the priest; filial confidence, implicit belief in the gods here below.

That fiction of the old world—that deceitful legend, which was ever on its tongue—was to substitute *love in the place of law.*

If that world, almost annihilated under the title of love, wounded by charity, and heart-broken by grace, can revive, it will revive by the means of law, justice, and equity.

O blasphemy! They had opposed grace to law, love to justice. As if unjust grace could still be grace: as if those things which our weakness divides, were not two aspects of the same truth—the right and the left hand of God.

They have made justice a negative thing, which forbids, prohibits, excludes—an obstacle to impede, and a knife to slaughter. They do not know that justice is the eye of providence. Love, blind among us, clear sighted in God, sees by justice—a vital absorbing glance. A

From Jules Michelet, *Historical View of the French Revolution*, translated by C. Cocks (London, 1896).

prolific power is in the justice of God; whenever it touches the earth, the latter is blest, and brings forth. The sun and the dew are not enough, it must have justice. Let her but appear, and the harvests come. Harvests of men and nations will spring up, put forth, and flourish in the sunshine of equity.

A day of justice, one single day, which is called the Revolution, produced ten millions of men.

But how far off? Did it appear, in the middle of the eighteenth century, remote and impossible? Of what materials shall I compose it? All is perishing around me. To build, I should want stones, lime, and cement; and I am empty-handed. The two saviours of this people —the priest and the king—have destroyed them, beyond the possibility of restoration. Feudal life and municipal life are no more— both swallowed up in royalty. Religious life became extinct with the clergy. Alas! not even a local legend or national tradition remains: no more of those happy prejudices which constitute the life of an infant people. They have destroyed everything, even popular delusions. Behold them now stripped and empty, *tabula rasa;* the future must write as best it may.

O, pure spirit, last inhabitant of that destroyed world; universal heir of all those extinct powers, how wilt thou guide us to the only bestower of life? How wilt thou restore to us justice and the idea of right?

Here, thou beholdest nothing but stumbling-blocks, old ruins, that one must pull down, crumble to powder, and neglect. Nothing is standing, nothing living. Do what thou wilt, thou wilt have at least the consolation of having destroyed only that which was already dead. . . .

Behold two ages of the young world—two days of the creation. Order is wanting, and so is unity. Let us make man, the unity of the world, and with him let order come, and with her, the Divinity whose advent we expect, the long-desired majesty of divine justice.

Man appears under three figures: Montesquieu, Voltaire, and Rousseau, three interpreters of the just and right.

Let us note law; let us seek law; perhaps we may yet find it in some corner of the globe. There may perhaps be some clime favorable for justice—some better land which naturally yields the fruit of equity. The traveller, the inquirer, who pursues it through the earth, is the calm, majestic Montesquieu. But justice flies before him;

it remains relative and moveable; law, in his estimation, is a relation, merely abstract, and inanimate; it is not endowed with vitality.

Montesquieu may be resigned to this result; but not so Voltaire. Voltaire is the one who suffers, who has taken upon him all the agony of mankind, who feels and hunts out every iniquity. All the ills that fanaticism and tyranny have ever inflicted upon the world, have been inflicted upon Voltaire. It was he, the martyr, the universal victim, whom they slaughtered in their Saint Bartholomew, whom they buried in the mines of the new world, whom they burned at Seville, whom the parlement of Toulouse broke on the wheel with Calas. He weeps, he laughs, in his agony—a terrible laugh, at which the bastilles of tyrants and the temples of the Pharisees fall to the ground.

And down fell at the same time all those petty barriers within which every church intrenched itself, calling itself universal, and wishing to destroy all others. They fall before Voltaire, to make room for the *human* church, for that catholic church which will receive and contain them all in justice and in peace.

Voltaire is the witness of right, its apostle and its martyr. He has settled the old question put from the origin of the world: Is there religion without justice, without humanity?

Montesquieu is the writer, the interpreter of right; Voltaire weeps and clamors for it; and Rousseau founds it. . . .

What was the resting-point whereon that strong man, finding a footing, stopped, held fast, and everything stood firm?

What footing did he find? O feeble world, O ye of little faith, degenerate sons, forgetful of Rousseau and the Revolution?

He found it in what has grown too faint among you—in his heart. In the depths of his suffering he read, and read distinctly, what the Middle Ages were never able to read: *A just God.* And what was said by a glorious child of Rousseau? *"Right is the sovereign of the world."*

That splendid motto was uttered only at the end of the century; it is its revelation—its profound and sublime formula.

Rousseau spoke by the mouth of another, by Mirabeau; yet it is no less the soul of Rousseau's genius. When once he severed himself from the false science of the time, and from a no less false society, you behold in his writings the dawn of a celestial effulgence —duty, right!

Its sweet and prolific power shines forth in all its brilliancy in the profession of faith of the Vicar of Savoy. God himself subject to justice, subject to right! Let us say rather that God and right are identical.

If Rousseau had spoken in the terms of Mirabeau, his language would not have taken effect. Necessities change with the times. To a world ready to act, on the very day of action, Mirabeau said: "Right is the sovereign of the world," you are the subjects of right. To a world still slumbering, inert, feeble, and devoid of energy, Rousseau said, and said well: "The general will is right and reason." Your will is right. Then arouse yourselves, ye slaves!

"Your collective will is reason herself." In other words, Ye are Gods!

And who, indeed, without believing himself God, could ever do anything great? Then it is that you may fearlessly cross the bridge of Arcola; then it is, that, in the name of duty, you sever yourself from your dearest affections, your heart.

Let us be God! The impossible becomes possible and easy. Then, to overthrow a world is a mere trifle; why, one creates a world.

This it is which explains how a feeble breath from a manly breast, a simple melody arising from the heart of the poor musician, raised the dead.

France is moved in her inmost soul. All Europe is changed by it. The vast massy German empire rocks on her old foundations. They criticize, but obey. "Mere sentimentality," say they, with an attempt to smile. And yet these dreamers follow it. The very philosophers, the abstractors of quintessence, take, in spite of themselves, the simple path of the poor Vicar of Savoy.

What, then, has happened? What divine light has shone, to produce so great a change? Is it the power of an idea, of a new inspiration, of a revelation from above? Yes, there has been a revelation. But the novelty of the doctrine is not what affects us most. We have here a more strange, a more mysterious phenomenon—an influence felt even by those who do not read, and could never comprehend. Nobody knows why, but since that glowing language impregnated the air, the temperature has changed; it seems as though a breath of life has been wafted over the world; the earth begins to bear fruits that she would never else have borne. . . .

That miracle he shares in common with his rival, Voltaire. His rival? No. Enemy? No. Let them be forever upon the same pedestal, those two apostles of humanity.

Voltaire, nearly octogenarian, buried among the snows of the Alps, broken down by age and labor, nevertheless rises also from the dead. The grand thought of the century, inaugurated by him, is also to be closed by him; he who was the first to open, is also to resume and finish the chorus. Glorious century! Well does it deserve to be called forever the heroic age of the mind. An old man on the verge of the grave; he has seen the others, Montesquieu, Diderot, and Buffon pass away; he has witnessed the extraordinary success of Rousseau—three books in three years. "And the earth was silent." Voltaire is not discouraged; behold him entering, lively and young, upon a new career. Where, then, is the old Voltaire? He was dead. But a voice has roused him all alive from the tomb, that voice which had ever given him life—the voice of humanity.

Ancient champion, to thee the crown! Here thou art again, conqueror of conquerors. Throughout a century, in every kind of warfare, with every weapon and doctrine, opposite, contrary, no matter what, thou hast pursued, without ever deviating, one interest, one cause—holy humanity. And yet they have called thee a skeptic! And they have termed thee changeable! They thought to surprise thee in the seeming contradictions of a flexible language ever serving the selfsame thought!

Thy faith shall be crowned by the very work of faith. Others have spoken of justice, but thou shalt perform it; thy words are acts, realities. Thou defendest Calas and La Barre, thou savest Sirven, and dost annihilate the scaffold of the Protestants. Thou hast conquered for religious liberty, and moreover, for civil freedom, as advocate of the last serfs, for the reform of our barbarous legislation and criminal laws, which themselves were crimes.

Behold in all this the dawn of the Revolution. Thou dost make it, and see it. Look for thy reward, look, behold it yonder! Now thou mayest die; thy firm faith deserved that thou shouldst not take thy flight before thou hadst seen the holy land.

When those two men have passed, the Revolution is accomplished in the intellectual world.

Now it becomes the duty of their sons, legitimate and illegitimate, to expound and diffuse it in a hundred ways: some in eloquence and fiery satire, others will strike bronze medals to transmit

it from hand to hand; Mirabeau, Beaumarchais, Raynal, Mably, and
Sieyès, are now to do their work.

The Revolution is on her march, with Rousseau and Voltaire still
in front. . . .

Alphonse Aulard

THE SOURCES OF THE DEMOCRATIC AND REPUBLICAN IDEALS OF THE REVOLUTION

*Alphonse Aulard (1849–1928) was one of the earliest French historians to
apply modern techniques of historical research to the French Revolution.
Working from the primary sources, he published a large number of studies
in the Revolutionary period and edited many collections of documents.
Rapidly he became an acknowledged master in the field, and exercised extensive influence upon many others who were working in this area of French
history. Aulard was distinctly liberal in his political ideas, and found genuine
greatness in the French Revolution. He firmly believed that the influence of
the Enlightenment in the eighteenth century was good, since it provided the
republican and democratic ideology of the Revolution and the groundwork
of modern liberalism. The exact manner in which the ideas of the philosophes,
who never advocated violent change, evolved into the principles of the
Revolution Aulard examines in the present selection.*

On August 10, 1792, the Legislative Assembly, in establishing universal suffrage, constituted France a democratic state, and the Convention, in establishing the Republic, on the following September
22nd, gave to this democracy the form of government which, in the
eyes of the Convention, was logically expedient.

Can we say that by these two acts a preconceived system was
brought into being? Many have thought so; many of our teachers and
writers, with much eloquence, have advanced the theory that democracy and the Republic sprang, fully fledged, from the eighteenth-

Reprinted with the permission of Charles Scribner's Sons from *The French Revolution* by A. Aulard, translated by Bernard Miall (New York, 1910).

century philosophy, from the works of the Encyclopedists, from the doctrine of the precursors of the Revolution. Let us see if the facts, and the written word, justify these assertions.

One prime and important fact is this: that in 1789, at the time of the convocation of the Estates General, there was no republican party in France.

Now the best testimony to be found as to contemporary French opinion is contained in the *cahiers* in which the people embodied their grievances and their desires. Of these we have many, different in origin and in kind, and in none is a republic demanded, nor even a change of dynasty; and I think my study of these justifies the assertion that in none is there found any criticism, even indirect, of the king's conduct. It would seem that none of the petitioners dream of attributing their stated grievances to the monarchy, nor even to the king. In all these documents the French are seen imbued with an ardent royalism, a warm devotion to the person of Louis XVI. Above all, in documents of the more humble kind, petitions from parishes, and the like, there is a note of confidence, love, and gratitude. "Our good king! The king our father!"—so the peasants and the workers address him. The nobles and the clergy, less ingenuously enthusiastic, appear equally loyal.

There were few Frenchmen, even among the enlightened, the critics, and the philosophers, who did not, in approaching the king, experience some emotion; who were not dazzled by the sight of the royal person. We may the better judge of the intensity of this feeling when we have noted how powerful it still was, and how general, in the early days of the Revolution, when the people had already tasted victory, and when the ill-will displayed by Louis must have diminished his popularity. On July 15, 1789, when the king repaired to the hall of the National Assembly, his presence excited a delirious enthusiasm, an enthusiasm which an eye-witness, the future member of Convention Thibaudeau, describes as follows: "All self-possession was lost. The delirium was at its height. A fellow-countryman of mine, Choquin, sitting hard by, stood up, stretched out his arms, his eyes full of tears, ejaculating his pent up emotion, then suddenly collapsed, struck all of a heap, babbling 'Long live the king!' He was not the only one to be seized by such a paroxysm. Even I myself, although I withstood the contagion, could not defend myself from a certain degree of emotion. After the President's reply, the king left the hall; the deputies flung after him, surrounded him, bustled about him, and escorted him back to the chateau, through a crowd as amazed as their representatives and stricken with the same vertigo." One deputy, a certain Blanc, suffocated by excitement, fell dead in the hall.

Even in Paris, where the populace had the reputation of having nothing to learn in the matter of insolence, no one, whether of the *bourgeoisie,* the artisans, or the poorest of wage-earners, offered to raise this cry of "The Republic!" which the Cardinal de Retz had heard in 1649 (as he says in his memoirs) at the time when England was a republic.

If we allow that in 1789 the people were not republicans, yet it will hardly be believed that no republican party was to be met with in the clubs, salons, lodges, and academies—in the higher intellectual circles in which the mind of France renewed itself so boldly. Nonetheless, there is no testimony, no indication, of any concerted, nor even of any individual design, at that time, to establish the republic in France.

For example, the Freemasons, according to all our authentic knowledge of their political ideas, were monarchists, frankly monarchists. They wished to reform the monarchy, not to destroy it.

And the writers of the time, the philosophers, the encyclopedists? Their boldness in every form of speculation has hardly been excelled. But was a single one of them in favor of constituting France a republic?

Among those who were, indeed, dead before 1789, but of whom we may truly say that they were the leaders of the living, who can be named as having counselled the substitution of a republic for the monarchy?

Montesquieu? His preference was for a monarchy after the English pattern.

Voltaire? His ideal—intermittently at least—was a benevolent reforming despot.

D'Argenson? He praises the abstract republic, but only in order to infuse into the monarchy what was good in the republic.

Diderot, d'Holbach, Helvétius? They declaim against kings, but, explicitly or implicitly, they do not mention the idea of establishing a republic in France.

Jean-Jacques Rousseau? A theorist of popular sovereignty, an admirer of the Genevan Republic, he held that republicanism was suited only to a small country, and the hypothesis of a French Republic seemed to him absurd.

Mably, the Mably of whom the men of 1789 were so full—was he the prophet and adviser of the Revolution? He declares himself a royalist: in royalty he sees the sole efficacious means of preventing class or party tyranny.

As for Turgot, he concerned himself only with the organization of the monarchy.

Not one of all these illustrious dead, living still so vital a life in the minds of men, had upheld, for Frenchmen and for France, the Republic, even as a remote ideal. On the contrary, for them the monarchy was the essential instrument of progress in the future, as it had been in the past.

And again, those thinkers and writers who in 1789 were still living agreed in ignoring the idea of a French Republic.

A very famous man, greatly admired, one to whom all men inclined their ears, was the Abbé Raynal. He, in his *Histoire philosophique des deux Indes* (1770), had put forth all manner of aspirations, raised all manner of questions, excepting that of establishing a republic in France. Is he more of a republican under Louis XVI than he was under Louis XV? By no means. In 1781, in a famous work on the American Revolution, he puts Frenchmen on their guard against the enthusiasm which that revolution had evoked in their hearts, and he gives voice to prophecies, pessimistic enough, concerning the future of the young Republic.

Condorcet, the greatest thinker of the day (if not the most influential): he who, in 1791, was to become the theorist of the Republic —Condorcet, whom one may set among the fathers, the founders of the French Republic, did not, before the Revolution, regard the republican form of government as one either possible or desirable in France. He was not even willing, in 1788, that the royal despotism should be censured, and in the establishment (could it be perfected) of the provincial assemblies he saw the regeneration of France.

As for the multitude of pamphleteers who, on the eve of the institution of the Estates General, and even afterwards, expressed, with courageous frankness, their social and political ideas: who among them cried out for a republic? Not Mirabeau, who was always so resolute a royalist. Not Sieyès; who, in his theories of national rights, the rights of the Third Estate, proved himself a monarchist, and remained a monarchist as long as the monarchy survived, and even after a republican party was in existence. Cérutti desired a thoroughly liberal monarchy. I am well aware that a few lampooners managed to get themselves accused of republicanism—for example, d'Antraigues, whose well-known *Mémoire sur les États Généraux* began with these words: "It was doubtless in order to afford the most heroic of virtues a mother-country worthy of them that Heaven willed that there should be republics, and it was perhaps to punish the ambition of men that Heaven has permitted them to erect great empires, to raise up for themselves kings and masters." But this goodly beginning was followed by the most royalistic conclusions, and the next performance of the author was to turn his coat, becoming a rigid aristocrat. Another and anonymous pamphlet, entitled *Le Bon sens,* which was known to be the work of Kersaint, a future member of the Convention, appeared to be of a republican character. But here is the boldest phrase it contains: "Could a king exist in a good government? Yes; but if men were more virtuous they would need no king." Is not this as good as saying that the French were not, in 1789, ripe for a republic?

Even the men whom we shall see, in 1792, as founders and organizers of the Republic—Robespierre, Saint-Just, Vergniaud, Danton, Brissot, Collot d'Herbois, the most famous of the future members of the Convention—were at this time monarchists.

Lafayette is cited as the type of French republican before the Revolution. Certainly the American Revolution had "republicanized" him, and he vaguely hoped, without saying so in public, that at some time in the future France would adopt the political system of the United States. But in 1789, as in 1830, he was an upholder of royalty, and we shall find him helping, perhaps more than any other Frenchman, to delay the advent of a republic in France.

And Camille Desmoulins? "There were perhaps ten of us republicans in Paris on July 12, 1789." So he writes in 1793. This is as much as to say, "I was a republican before the taking of the Bastille, and almost alone in my opinions." Ah, well! Camille Desmoulins, during the elections of the Estates General, wrote an ode comparing Louis XVI to Trajan; that is to say, he put aside his dream of a republic in 1789.

Is it, then, an exaggeration to say that, on the eve of and even during the commencement of the Revolution, not only was there no republican party in France, not only was there no concerted scheme to suppress the monarchy from that time forward, but also that not a single individual is known to have expressed in public any such purpose or desire? Hardly. And why is this the case?

Because the power of royalty had been, or had seemed to be, at one and the same time the cementing bond of that national unity then in sight of formation, and the historical instrument of all reform for the general good; because the king had been regarded as the adversary of feudalism and of local tyranny, and the protector of peasant communities against all forms of aristocracy. This idea is expressed in a hundred different forms: for example, we shall find Mounier, on July 9, 1789, saying to the Constituent Assembly, in the name of the Committee of Constitution: "Men have never ceased to appeal to it [the power of the sovereign] against injustice, and even in periods of the darkest ignorance, in all parts of the Empire, the oppressed and weak have always turned towards the throne, as to the protector entrusted with their defence." Who should dream of a republic at the time when the king, by convening the Estates General, appeared to be taking the initiative in the desired revolution?

An insane hypothesis truly, that a sudden attack could then, in 1789, have overturned the throne! The estrangement of the provinces which formed the French kingdom; the resurrection of feudalism; the omnipotence of local petty tyrants; a war, perhaps, foreign or civil—these might have done so. Almost one might say, without paradox, that in 1789 the more of a revolutionary a man was, so he was also a more rigid monarchist, because it seemed that the eventual unification of France, which was one of the ends and one of the means of the Revolution, could only be brought about under the auspices of the hereditary leader of the nation.

How is it, in spite of so many documents, so many undoubted facts, that there was ever a retrospective belief in the existence of a republican party in France before the year 1789, in a deliberate scheme to put an end to the monarchy?

The fact is that there arose, among such of the French as did not wish for the Republic, a republican state of mind, which was expressed by republican words and attitudes.

If all Frenchmen were at one in wishing to maintain the monarchy, they were not agreed as to the manner of regulating the royal authority, and we may go so far as to say that they did not all see the throne with the same eyes.

The masses of the people, in their unreasoned loyalty, did not, it would appear, discern the excesses of the royal prerogative. No doubt the commissaries were unpopular. But complaints of "ministerial despotism," as they preferred to call it, came from the nobles, the *bourgeoisie,* the rich and enlightened classes, rather than from the peasantry. The latter more especially lamented a "feudal despotism," because, in fact, they were the greatest sufferers from it.

Far from regarding the king as responsible for the conduct of his agents, the people would say that his agents deceived the king, that they annulled or hampered his power of doing good. The popular idea was to deliver the king from these unjust stewards in order that he might be enlightened, the better to direct his omnipotent power, to the profit of the nation, against the remnants of feudalism. The masses were beginning to have a certain idea of their rights, yet, so far were they from thinking to restrain his royal omnipotence, that it was precisely on that omnipotence that all their hopes were based. One petition said that, in order that all should go well, it was only necessary for the king to cry: *"To me, my people."*

Enlightened Frenchmen, on the other hand, knowing well what manner of men Louis XIV and XV had been, feared the abuse of the royal power, and were not all reassured by the paternal character of Louis XVI's despotism. They wished to restrain, by means of political institutions, this fantastic and capricious power, so that it should no longer be dangerous to liberty, while leaving it sufficient force to destroy the aristocracy and what remained of the feudal system, thus making France a nation. To ensure that the king should govern according to the laws—this was what they called "organizing the monarchy."

The way to this organization of the monarchy was prepared by the writers of the eighteenth century.

They, with the logical spirit natural to the French, did not attempt merely to prevent abuses and to regulate the exercise of sovereign power; they discussed the very essence of this power, of the pretended right divine; they sapped the Catholic faith by which the throne was propped, sought publicly for the origins of sovereignty and authority, in history, in the assent of subjects, and in the national will.

Thus, without desiring to establish a republic, and solely with a view to "organizing" the monarchy, they attacked the monarchical principle, and put in circulation republican ideals of such a nature that, although in 1789 no one wished for a republic, yet whoever thought at all was impregnated with these republican ideas; and this is why, in 1792, when circumstances made the Republic necessary, there was a sufficient number of thinking men prepared to accept, and to force on others, a form of government of which they had already adopted the principles.

A few examples will show the diffusion and elaboration of republican ideas before the Revolution.

Perhaps the republican frame of mind has always existed in France, in one form or another, since the beginning of the Renaissance. But one may say that in its modern form It dates from the period of the Regency, from the time of the anti-absolutist reaction which followed the death of Louis XIV; it was then that this spirit began to manifest itself among educated Frenchmen, to last, not for a time only, but during the whole century.

In 1694 the French Academy, in its Dictionary, after having defined the word *républicain,* was moved to add: "It is sometimes employed in an evil sense, when it signifies 'mutinous,' seditious'; one who holds opinions in opposition to the monarchical state in which he lives." In the edition of 1718, this phrase, so ill-disposed to republicans, is suppressed; and the edition of 1740 gives honorable examples of the usage of the word, such as "republican mind, spirit, republican system, republican maxims," and also, "He is a true, an eminent republican."

And what was the then current idea of a republic?

The French Academy defined a republic as "a state governed by many"—a state, in fact, precisely the opposite of that they desired to maintain, since all were unanimous in desiring to live under a monarch.

But Montesquieu, in 1748, in his *l'Esprit des Lois,* defined a republic otherwise: "The republican form of government," he says, "is that in which the people as a whole, or one party only of the people, exercises the sovereign power." This definition became classic. In 1765 it was reproduced in the article on "Republics" in the *Encyclopédie* (vol. xiv.), which consists entirely of quotations from Montesquieu.

Could not such a republic exist under a king? Montesquieu does not think so; but Mably does—when, for instance, he dreams of a "republican monarchy"; and the same idea is held by those whom we shall find, in 1789, speaking of a "monarchical democracy."

Montesquieu undoubtedly pronounces against a republic, and is of opinion that in a republic "the laws are evaded with greater danger than they can be violated by a prince, who, being always the chief citizen of the state, has the greatest interest in its conservation." Nonetheless, we see how he elsewhere commends the republican form of government, as when he says that virtue is its very mainspring, while a monarchy is founded upon respect and honor; or when, in approval of the popular elections, he writes: "It is an admirable thing that the people should select those to whom they are bound to confide some part of their authority."

It was after reading Montesquieu that Frenchmen became accustomed to regard the republican form of government—which they did not desire to see in France—as a theoretically noble and interesting form.

This theorist of the monarchy thus found that he had deprived monarchical government of some of its prestige; and, by his views upon the separation of the three forms of authority, he touched royalty itself to the quick—that royalty which pretended, by divine right, to concentrate all authority in itself.

In this manner did Montesquieu, so admired, so widely read, contribute towards the development of republican ideas and the formation of the republican spirit.

As for Voltaire, he assuredly is no republican; he does not even accept Montesquieu's theory that a republic is founded on virtue; we find him writing in 1752: "A republic is by no means founded on virtue; it is founded on the ambition of each and all; upon pride, which seeks to curb pride; upon the desire of domination, which will not suffer the domination of others. Hence are derived laws which as far as possible conserve equality; we have a society in which the members, of equal appetites, eat at the same table, until the advent of one more powerful and more voracious, who takes all for himself and leaves the crumbs of the feast to the others." But, with his usual openness of mind, Voltaire examines the question from every side; and in the same year (1752) he speaks very favorably indeed of republics. "A republican," he says, "is always more deeply attached to his country than a subject can be to his; for the reason that one desires one's own welfare before that of one's master." In his article on "Democracy" in the *Dictionnaire philosophique,* he weighs the evidence on either side (to Voltaire "republic" and "democracy" are apparently synonymous), but inclines to favor the republican as being practically "the most natural form of government." He ends by saying: "The question is heard every day, whether a republican government is preferable to a monarchy. The discussion always ends with the admission that the government of human beings is a very difficult business." Elsewhere he states that "he has it in his mind that offensive wars made the first kings, defensive wars the first republics." Truly enough, a defensive war made the Republic of 1792.

We must not overlook the fact that *Brutus (*1730) is a republican tragedy, nor that it was revived as such, with enthusiasm, under the French Republic. As firm a monarchist as Montesquieu, Voltaire no less than he does honor to the republican system which he did not wish to see in France. His attacks upon the Christian faith, his militant rationalism, his influence on the polite society of his time—an influence so powerful as to turn it, to a great extent, against religion —herein lies his principal contribution to the elaboration of republican ideals. At the sound of his irony the Church tottered, and with it the throne.

He was no democrat. It is likely enough that he would have regarded the advent of democracy with horror. No one, however, has done more than he to popularize the idea that man should be guided by reason, not by a mystical authority; and this idea is the very essence of republicanism. Jean-Jacques Rousseau, in his *Contrat social,* had written that "in general, government by democracy was suited to small states, government by aristocracy to those of medium size, and government by monarchy to large states." He further stated that "there is no form of government so liable to civil wars and internecine tumult as the democratic or popular," and that "if there existed a nation of gods, they would govern themselves by a democracy: so perfect a government is unsuited to mankind." But he was preparing for the ruin of the monarchical system when he said that "the two principal objects of every system of legislation should be liberty and equality." Prudent and reserved though he was in theory, he preached revolt by his conduct, in his speeches, and in his romantic writings

—revolt, in the name of nature, against the vicious and artificial social system of his time; and, although fundamentally a Christian, he replaced the mystical ideals of charity and humility by the republican ideal of fraternity.

If Mably is a supporter of monarchies, it is because the sovereign power "prevents the tyranny of class or party." At the same time, in his eyes the chief constituent principle of society is equality, and to his thinking the passion for equality is the one human sentiment that must never be outraged. The sovereign is the people of France. He believes he can find proof in history to the effect that the French formerly had legislative assemblies whose will the monarchs merely put into execution. This "republican monarchy," as he calls it, was realized by Charlemagne!—and this extraordinary historian finds that there existed, under Charlemagne, a Constituent Assembly. "Princes," he says, "are the administrators, not the masters, of the nation." If he accepts, in theory, the separation of the executive and legislative powers, it is not in order to balance them the one against the other, but to establish the subordination of the executive to the legislative power. The executive power he wishes to enfeeble; for which reason he would divide it into several departments, and have all magistrates elected by the people. He would have the king a mere phantom, and, although he labels it a monarchy, the state he organizes on paper is in reality a republic, and even so he wished to make it a communistic republic.

As for Diderot, Holbach, and Helvétius, if they did not demand a republic, they nonetheless enfeebled and discredited sovereignty, whether by abusing it or by undermining Christianity.

From the writings of these philosophers one idea stands out, an idea that quickly became almost general: that the nation is above the king; and is not this a republican idea? Although these writers wish to maintain the monarchy, they habitually speak of the republican system in honorable terms. A posthumous work of d'Argenson's, *Considérations sur le Gouvernement,* published in 1765, recommends the fortification of the monarchy by an "infusion" of republican institutions; and d'Argenson praises the government which he does not desire for his own country in terms so sympathetic as to invite misconception, so greatly does this work of royalist tendencies, which was much read at the time, do honor to the republican idea. As for writers who were living and were read in 1789, such as Raynal, Condorcet, Mirabeau, Sieyès, d'Antraigues, Cérutti, Mounier, it is enough to say of these also, monarchists though they were, that they indirectly undermined the principle of monarchy; and thus, without wishing it or realizing it, prepared the way for the Republic, since the greater number of their readers found in their writings, or derived from them, at all events, the idea that the law can only be the expression of the general will.

The idea that the king should be only a citizen subject to the law, causing the law to be executed, had gradually become popularized; of its popularity there is endless proof. When Voltaire wrote, in his tragedy of *Don Pédre* (1775):

> *A king is but a man with namo august,*
> *First subject of the laws: and, by law, just.*

he knew well that he would win applause. And if it be objected that this tragedy was not presented, that these lines were not actually heard by the theatre-going public, I will cite the line borrowed by Favart from a poem by Louis Racine, published in 1744, which drew applause in the *Trois Sultanes,* at the *Théâtre des Italiens,* on April 9, 1761:

> *Each citizen a king, under a citizen king.*

That such maxims were applauded in the theatre, nearly thirty years before the Revolution, that the government was obliged to tolerate them: does not this prove that public opinion had already, so to say, despoiled the king and his kingship of the mystical principle of sovereignty? And is not this idea of the "citizen king," so unanimously applauded, one of the most startling signs of the republicanization of the general mind . . . ?

To sum up: no one on the eve of the Revolution had ever dreamed of the establishment of a republic in France: it was a form of government that seemed impossible in a great state in course of unification. It was through the king that men sought to establish a free government. Men wished to organize the monarchy, not to destroy it. No one dreamed of calling the ignorant mass of the people to political life; the necessary revolution was to be brought about by the better class of the nation, the educated, property-owning class. It was believed that the people, blind and inconstant as they were thought, could only prove an instrument of reaction in the hands of the privileged. However, the future date of democracy was announced in the proclamation of the principle of the sovereignty of the people: and the republic, the logical form of democracy, was prepared by the diffusion of republican ideas—for example, from America; by the sight of an impotent monarchy, and by the continual proclamation of the necessity of a violent revolution, which, undertaken in order to reform the monarchy, was to expose its very existence to the dangers of a general upheaval. The ruling classes of society were steeped in republicanism. Such a state of mind was so prevalent that if the king, in whom men saw the historically indispensable guide to a new France, were to fail in his mission, or discard, for example, his authority as hereditary defender of French independence, a republic would be accepted without dislike and without enthusiasm, first by the better class, and then by the mass of the nation.

Daniel Mornet

THE INTELLECTUAL ORIGINS OF THE FRENCH REVOLUTION

Daniel Mornet (1878–1954) is well known as a very prolific author in the fields of intellectual history and literary criticism. He strongly believed that an author's works should be studied in the context of the period of history in which they were written, and that they provide valuable keys to the essential psychology of the age. Mornet's studies of the intellectual background of the French Revolution represent an unparalleled effort to examine in depth the extremely varied materials of intellectual history during the eighteenth century. With his findings he successfully demonstrated the wide diffusion of the new ideas and, by implication, their extensive influence. Mornet did not believe that intellectual currents were the most important cause of the Revolution. Rather, it was the political and social evils of the old regime and massive hatred of them, as exemplified by endemic popular revolts. However, he felt that the philosophes' influence was crucial in shaping revolutionary opinion, and that it provided the decisive element in initiating the Revolution.

The deliberate shaking of religious foundations was evidently dangerous to the State. The critical spirit shown in destroying the respect for religion was lessening the respect for every other type of institution, and particularly the respect for the monarchy. The French monarchy was really definitely doomed only when an important part of the population no longer thought it beneficent or inevitable. A revolution took place in men's minds, or at least in the minds of many, before the Revolution of 1789 actually broke out. And it is possible to follow very clearly the progress of this revolution in public opinion.

It was not general by any means. In 1789 a great number of Frenchmen who were neither dunces nor simpletons believed in the king and awaited the remedy for their misfortunes only from his kindness and wisdom. Until about 1750 this attachment of the nation to its king was general and profound. The illness which in 1744

From Daniel Mornet, *French Thought in the Eighteenth Century,* translated by Lawrence M. Levin. Copyright © 1929, Prentice-Hall, Inc., Englewood Cliffs, N. J. Reprinted by permission. The second part of this selection is from Daniel Mornet, *Les Origines intellectuelles de la Révolution française* (Paris, 1933). Reproduced with permission of Librairie Armand Colin. [Editor's translation] imperiled the life of Louis XV while he was at Metz caused universal sorrow, and his recovery caused as much rejoicing as a veritable resurrection. This love was already far less deep at the time of the criminal attempt of Damiens. Then quite rapidly it became indifference and even disdain. But until the very end there were still some who were obstinately faithful to the monarchical idea. Hardy detests Maupeou and all those who dismissed the Parlements, but he attests his love "for the sacred person of the king," and he would not abandon it "for an income of a hundred thousand crowns." Barbier, who has no sense of respect, has a genuine hatred and horror for anything resembling "a detestable scheme of revolt." More generally speaking, when one reads the hundreds of memoirs, journals, and diaries of the eighteenth century one observes how little concern there is about problems of general politics, except in the case of a few great names. People live as their fathers lived before them and they do not appear to believe that they could live otherwise. The disputes that interest them are local affairs and concern aldermen: for example, the construction of a fountain, the question of precedence in a procession.

Yet even those who do not reason are suffering. Even if one does not discuss the prevalent abuses and the necessity for reform in the state, one must needs feel the weight of these abuses and one must see that the state is not perfect. "There is here," writes Barbier in 1760, "a great agitation in men's minds with respect to the government. One must admit in very truth that famine and the scarcity of money, the misery in the country districts, and the multiplicity of taxes make one suspect that depredation is going on in the administration of the finances and that apparently nothing can be done about the matter." Let us add to that statement another that Barbier makes about "the pilfering of the court people" and the pilfering and the insolence of practically all those belonging to the privileged classes. Inevitably there will be a feeling of anger and a desire for vengeance. Even respectful and timid men like Hardy are impelled to avow that "one groans at seeing unpunished" crimes like that of the duc de Fronsac, who is guilty of kidnapping and rape, or the first public crime of the Marquis de Sade, and that "one is indignant when a young servant girl of twenty-two is hanged for a trivial domestic theft." The consequence of all this is that even if one may continue to respect and venerate the king himself when he has virtues like those of Louis XVI, nobody now respects the nobility.

The nobility of the higher rank makes a public display of its vices, its adulteries, its mistresses, its insolent luxury, its booty in the form of pensions and benefices, whereas the nobility of the provinces very often is ruined, degenerates, is a prey to utter misery, and is compelled to perform the most menial tasks. One may indeed resign oneself to the existence of privileges; but there is no one, if one excepts those who enjoy these privileges, who believes that they constitute a recompense and a right.

Above all, one cannot resign oneself to famine and to revolt. There had always been famines and revolts in France, even in the most flourishing period of monarchical unity and order. There were riots in the streets of Paris in the reign of Louis XIV because of the kidnapping of children by the police or because of the high cost of bread. But toward 1750 famines and the revolts caused by famine multiply. Perhaps the people were no more wretched than before. The really careful investigations of the subject that have been carried on hitherto have all been local and at times mutually contradictory. But certainly people were less resigned, more inclined to snatch up axes and scythes, and to pillage. From one year to another, from one month to another, the price of bread was subject to the most violent fluctuations, ranging in price from a *sou* and a half a pound to five *sous.* At times a half or even two thirds of the population were reduced to beggary. The sufferers ate grass; then they gathered in bands and violently attacked flour mills, bakeries, shops in the town or city. Everywhere, at Paris, Versailles, Caen, Valenciennes, Strasbourg, Toulouse, Clermont, Dijon, Nancy, Arles, Agen, Tours, Cherbourg, Rouen, Grenoble, Cette, and so on, diaries are full of frightened accounts of these popular uprisings. And these are not transitory outbursts of wrath, caused by empty stomachs and quite forgotten as soon as the insurgents are no longer hungry. The diarists are particularly frightened at the placards that the rebels post and at the principles that these placards proclaim. There is no mere repetition of those innumerable couplets, ballads, and ironical and insolent epigrams which multiply in the eighteenth century and which have caused it to be said that in France every tumult ends peaceably with song or verse. These placards, on the contrary, are really challenges and the announcement of a deliberate and concerted revolt. The authorities have to tear them down everywhere, in Paris, even in the Louvre itself, from the doors of churches, in the Luxembourg, at

Versailles, "in the very chamber of the king," at Caen, at Grenoble, at Troyes. At Grenoble the following truculent appeal is posted: "O, enslaved and servile people of France! Scorning the laws, one deprives you of your property in order to forge chains for you. Will you endure it all?" And at Troyes one may read: "We demand our daily bread. . . . It is better to live without law than without bread. No one can deny that!"

The dismissal of the Parlements clearly manifested the prevalent state of unrest. The Parlements were neither revolutionary nor republican nor even in favor of reform. At bottom they were merely defending their own privileges and their prestige. But they were menaced by the ministers of the king; they resisted; they suffered. The meetings of the Parlement of Paris were suspended in 1753, and the members of the Parlement were exiled or imprisoned. Then, after alternate triumph and defeat for the royal will, Maupeou suppressed all the Parlements in 1771 and replaced them by superior councils. Throughout all France, or very nearly so, the old Parlements are regretted; the councilors of Maupeou are scoffed at; there is determined resistance against their authority. When the old Parlements return, at the death of Louis XV, there is universal rejoicing; there are solemn celebrations, parades, fireworks.

In all this unrest, turmoil, and revolt there is really nothing that is directly philosophical. Neither the discontented, nor the seditious, nor their placards invoke the authority of Montesquieu, Voltaire, the *Encyclopedia,* or J.-J. Rousseau. As we have shown, not one of the philosophers could be considered a revolutionist, and they all profoundly distrusted popular government and even liberty. It seems quite certain that the Revolution was in one respect the unreasoning protest against misery and the spontaneous revolt against suffering. Yet philosophy did play a very definite role. It taught neither revolution, nor democracy. But it transformed men's minds; it made them lose the habit of respect for tradition; it made them apt to reflect upon revolution and democracy. It cleared the soil in which the seeds of new harvests could germinate.

A characteristic example is furnished by the violent uprising of the Norman nobility in 1771. The nobles were certainly not revolutionists nor were they reformers; they merely refused to pay a certain tax (the Third Estate had nothing to do with the movement). Nor was the uprising very audacious. As soon as the authorities became stern and imprisoned the leaders, the rank and file vied in proffering the most humble supplications. Yet these nobles claimed that they were supported by the people, whose misery at that time was very great. They printed pamphlets that a Morelly or a Sylvain Maréchal might well have signed: "Let us now hear the monarch, that is, the agent of the nation, say to those men from whom he holds his authority: 'I want no resistance; that is to say, I do not want you to think. . . . I do not want you to be men; far less, citizens, but I do want you to be perfectly servile.' "

The reception accorded the American Revolution also curiously reflects the half-conscious evolution of men's minds and the penetration of philosophical ideas into politics. At the outset, French public opinion is by no means won over to the cause of the American Revolution; moreover, it is powerfully influenced by English propaganda. It is men of influence (and particularly Vergennes) who shape public opinion and partly at least orient it, while calculating the political benefits accruing in the event of an American victory. But the moment that public opinion has definitely come to a decision, it sympathizes not merely with one people in its struggle with another but with ideas, with a political philosophy. The philosopher, Morellet, did not understand this enthusiasm; but he noted that everybody "wishes to drink a toast to the liberty of the Americans, to liberty of conscience, to freedom of commerce." The success of Franklin, who is the hero of the *salons,* is due to the fact that he appears to be a "philosopher" who unites the wit of Voltaire with the simplicity of Rousseau. The "sentimental souls," the disciples of Rousseau, find themselves for once in perfect agreement with the "dialecticians of liberty." One is touched by the evangelical life of the Quakers and by the happiness and the industry of the clearers of virgin forests. And this enthusiasm, in which are blended the love for ideas and the unreasoning impulses of the heart, soon wins the entire nation. All the younger nobility wish to depart with Lafayette to fight for a people that knows nothing of nobility and that proclaims equality. The students of the colleges take a passionate interest in the American cause. At the college of Plessis, Lafayette is the hero of the hour. At the college of Juilly, Father Petit deals as much with "the American war and the exploits of Washington and Lafayette as he does with the odes of Horace and the orations of Cicero." "At the convent," says Mme de Fars-Fausselandry, "the cause of the Americans seemed ours; we were proud of their victories." Neither the middle classes nor the lower classes are in ignorance of these victories. At Clermont-Ferrand the Declaration of Independence is celebrated by public rejoicings. A peasant of Provence, Gargaz by name, comes to Paris on foot, to cast himself at the feet of Franklin. And one of the first societies in which revolutionary ideas are adopted is the Society of the Friends of the Negroes, an organization obviously inspired by the doctrines of the Quakers.

Other evidence shows that little by little people are acquiring the habit of associating reforms, liberty, and philosophy. That is evident in the case of the "philosophical" *salons* in which one listens to Franklin, Raynal, Turgot, Necker, Mably, and Condorcet. It is certain, even in the case of those nobles who hasten to be present at the private readings of the *Marriage of Figaro,* at M. de Vaudreuil's, at M. de Liancourt's, at Mme de Vaines', at M. d'Anzely's, and so on. It is certain in the case of the provinces, where people seem to know all about what the philosophers do and publish. Very daring pamphlets in manuscript circulate at Bordeaux, Lectoure, and elsewhere. Those which the governor of Normandy receives and which he does not keep for his own use indicate the success of the *Observations on the History of France* by Mably, the *Ingenuous Man* by Voltaire, *Belisarius,* the *Philosophical History* by Raynal, the *Friend of the Laws,* the *Catechism of the Citizen,* the *Disadvantages of Feudal Rights,* in short, all those works which in demanding reforms develop ideas and speak in the name of principles.

"I will confess to you," writes Mably in June, 1789, "that I find the Third Estate, whose defender I have been and still am, a trifle radical in its views and its principles." Even before 1789 the Third Estate and the nobility itself certainly had very definite views in politics. And if these views were not revolutionary, they were in part at least philosophical.

Our conclusions will be more clearly delineated if we contrast them with those in Taine's *Ancien régime.*

For Taine, there was undoubtedly a growth or evolution of the public mentality between 1715 and 1789. The revolutionary spirit was sketchy at first, then became more definite; it was actually formulated only when one reaches a badly determined date which seems to be 1760 or 1770. This spirit was at once worldly-minded and academic.

It borrowed from Rousseau's *Contrat social,* from Mably, from Holbach's *Système de la nature* and *Politique naturelle,* and from one or two dozen abstract, speculative formulas. Man is a slave and yet has a right to liberty. Since all men are by nature equal, they enjoy the same rights; equality must be achieved. Men are naturally good and noble; if they had not been corrupted by badly organized society, they might live together happily as brothers. In both the present and the past experiences of France, there is nothing that resembles this liberty, equality, fraternity. It is even very difficult to see how the French political tradition can be adapted to this ideal. But such matters little. There is no need to be in the least concerned about a tradition that is merely a succession of accidents, violences and injustices. Let us abolish all in order to rebuild all. We shall rebuild very well, for we shall appeal to our reason which never deceives. When utilized properly, reason teaches us how to rediscover the permanent and eternal principles which provide the foundation of a happy, free, equal and fraternal society, and how to deduce logically, that is, infallibly, the corollaries which instruct us concerning all aspects of this type of society. Such was the dream primarily of society people, an educated minority who isolated themselves in an artificial social setting where they loved nothing more than endless reasoning and where their sole concern was flawless logic. Later the bourgeoisie followed their example. Thus the Revolution was preceded by a revolutionary spirit which was the more fearful because it was predicated on the false idea that one may destroy and rebuild a society as one destroys and rebuilds a system of ideas in a doctoral dissertation or a discussion in a salon. "Never any facts; nothing but abstractions, strings of maxims concerning nature, reason, the people, tyrants, liberty, like inflated balloons jostling each other uselessly in space."

In support of this interpretation, Taine borrowed some dozens of texts from as many works and a similar number of facts from memoirs, correspondence, etc. It would be easy to criticize endlessly these texts, facts and quotations with which he supports his position. How may we agree with Taine that Mably insisted on atheism as a compulsory dogma, that it was geometrical reason which accounts for Rousseau's Savoyard Vicar and Buffon's *Epoques de la nature,* that purist classical language was that of the eighteenth century, that almost all important works were produced in a salon, etc., etc.? But it matters little. Even if all the cited works were well understood and all the facts correct, Taine's interpretation, and more or less those of all other studies on the intellectual origins of the Revolution, would be worthless. How can one claim to reconstruct the ideas of millions or at least hundreds of thousands of Frenchmen with so little evidence? How can one claim that d'Argenson was correct when he said in 1753, "Hatred against the priests has reached the final extremity," when everything proves that this would have been very exaggerated in 1787 and was entirely false in 1753? How can one base an argument on a text where Brissot, in his *Essai sur la propriété et sur le vol,* seems to say that property is theft, when he is merely saying that as a matter of pure logic nature gives men the right to take what will prevent their dying of hunger, when his *Essai* passed entirely unnoticed, when Brissot himself later disavowed this youthful piece, and when the entire limited number of works with communist leanings remained all but unknown?

It has not been my intention to discuss Taine's general principle that reason is incapable of guiding the world. I have not sought to determine whether it was for good or for bad that things happened as they did. I have merely sought to show how they happened. They happened very differently than Taine contended.

First of all, one cannot analyze the origins of the Revolution while one is constantly preoccupied with the course of the Revolution. Without realizing it, Taine actually inferred what the French must have thought in 1787–1789 from what Robespierre and Saint-Just probably thought later. He might just as well have written that part of his *Ancien régime* by deducing French opinion before the Revolution from the ideas of the Jacobins; the earlier texts and facts which he utilized were so to speak superadded. He took his stand, and in the mass of texts and facts he could always find many to justify it. But it must be repeated that the direction taken by the Revolution was not necessarily that which men were thinking of when in 1787–1789 they sought to reform France. A Lenin or a Trotsky desired a certain type of revolution; they prepared it, initiated it and directed it. There was nothing similar in France. The origins of the Revolution constitute one history; that of the Revolution another. Having made this point, here is how things happened:

The spirit that first proposed and then demanded a fundamental reform of the state was at first directed against religion. Before about 1750, the writers who attacked the basic principle of religion, the faith, were fairly numerous, but their works more often than not remained in manuscript and had only limited circulation. On the other hand, as early as mid-century the policies of the church were violently condemned. Intolerance was openly abhorred; the church was denied the right to impose its doctrines by force; and every past and present instance of punishing bodies under the pretext of savings souls was denounced as a crime of fanaticism. From 1770 onward, one may say that opinion was unanimous on this score. The church did not officially renounce the use of force, but liberty of conscience and even of cult were regarded by all as indefeasible. In all discussions of these matters, the secular authority was intimately associated with the interests and position of the church. Before the Edict of Toleration (1787), the government never opposed the clergy's demands either in principle or in practice. Because it feared opinion, it contented itself with inaction and failure to apply its decrees. Thus the war against fanaticism necessarily became a war against political authority, the state. It was the state that seemed fanatical. Men became incensed against it, and the defeat of fanaticism partially shook the foundations of the state.

At the same time, incredulity proper made advances, but much less rapidly. Between 1750 and 1770, the proponents of incredulity had said almost everything that could be said. They dragged before the "tribunal of reason" the dogmas of the church, its sacred books, its history and its rites. They claimed to demonstrate their falsity, absurdity and ferocity. They subjected them to sarcasm and anger. In spite of an inept, passive or even collusive administration, they printed everything that was in manuscript; and all that they printed was circulated if not freely and easily, at least widely and practically without risks. All these books did not "dechristianize" France. But it is certain that they spread incredulity or at least indifference among the greater part of the aristocracy, that this indifference extensively pervaded the clergy, and that it made rapid strides among the middle class, the young people and in the schools. A good part of the nation was, if not impious or hostile to religion, at least sufficiently separated from the church and its priests to be indisposed to follow them. This progress of incredulity continued from 1770 to 1787, but everything essential had been said and the decisive blow had fallen as early as 1770. In the final period, it was chiefly politics that occupied men's minds.

They hardly thought of it before 1748. Everything that had been said or published concerning politics before that date was, with a few exceptions, merely academic. Whenever writers sought specific, practical remedies for evils and abuses, they did not for an instant consider changing the principles of government. It was a question of cleaning the house or furnishing it more comfortably, not rebuilding it. From 1748 to 1770, discussions became much more numerous, less abstract and much bolder. But all that might seem revolutionary were merely utopian or witty pieces which had small circulation and practically no influence, even when they were sincere. On the other hand, although writers did not seek fundamental political reforms, they were already proposing important social reforms. In justice, administration and poor relief, they were severely criticizing traditional procedures; they sought not only change but general upheaval. And they boldly committed themselves to financial reforms which necessarily clashed with one of the fundamental principles of the state, the privileged orders' exemption from taxation.

After 1770, works appeared which even questioned the order of the state, sometimes savagely. But these works were not numerous. Their number diminishes even further when instead of isolating certain sentences and formulas, one examines them as wholes. Very often their revolutionary statements were merely theoretical concepts, presented as theories and explicitly corrected when the author set forth his practical views. Not only did almost no one consider a revolution in the state; practically no one believed revolution to be near at hand or even possible. One may enumerate the predictions of revolution as I have done, but these were drowned in a sea of opinions where the idea of revolution seemed impossible or did not appear at all.

On the contrary, after 1770 there is evidence of widespread apprehension or at least anxiety concerning social and political problems. It appeared not only in literary circles and among the aristocracy who saw it merely as a pleasant pastime but among the middle and lower bourgeoisie, the young people and in the schools. Since time immemorial, affairs of state had been the preserve of the state. It had done everything possible to surround them with an awful mystery and to punish all who profaned them. But the seven seals had been broken, and by 1780 anyone might enter the sanctuary. Although few sought to drive out the gods and their priests, anyone who wished might presume to give them advice. Men were still willing to obey but began to think that they should place conditions.

Besides, whatever may have been the diffusion of incredulity and political unrest, this seems less important than the more widespread and definite evolution of opinion. All France was beginning to think. In other periods, the sixteenth century for example, one may find many works which are shot through with incredulity and political insubordination. But these found an audience only among a limited elite. The great majority were fully occupied with the painful struggle for life. During the second half of the eighteenth century, on the contrary, modern France was developing. The people were no longer content with mere living but wished to learn and think. Everywhere the most reliable evidence of this transformation appears in abundance. Not only indirect evidence such as the growing number of works of discussion, their popularity, the instances given in memoirs, correspondence, etc., but all sorts of direct evidence: fundamental changes in teaching, provincial academies, literary societies, circulating book collections, libraries and provincial journals. And the nature of this intellectual curiosity was as important as its extent. According to Taine's thesis, men were merely reading the *Contrat social,* the *Code de la nature* and the *Système de la nature* plus two or three dozen treatises in which the authors were abstractly constructing a philosophical or utopian city. There was nothing of the sort. Curiosity was derived from a thousand sources and flowed in a thousand channels. What would remain of the programs, memoranda and discussions of all those academies and reading groups, of all the intellectual activity of those whose lives we know, if we were to retain only what was derived from Rousseau, Voltaire, Mably and the others? For many, very little; for most, nothing. Undoubtedly, Frenchmen were very frequently interested in "philosophy," but it was philosophy as they conceived it and not as Taine deformed it. It was love of knowledge, the desire to learn and think, and to think not only about natural rights and the "contract" but about all knowledge, nature and life. Men wished to learn geography, foreign languages, physics, chemistry and natural history, and not merely deism and republicanism. Generally they did not seek "systems"—almost the entire century after 1750 was directed against systems—nor the laws of the mind, but realities, experimental laws, practical and usable knowledge. There was only one physics, chemistry and natural history that counted, and this was the physics, chemistry and natural history of observation and experiment. In economics, there was of course the "system" of the Physiocrats. But what place did it occupy in the discussions of all those academies and societies? Hardly any. What was actually discussed was the ills that were suffered locally at the moment, reforms that were immediately applicable to the province, diseases of cattle and crops, methods of cultivation, the best mills, etc. In the social sciences, men discussed similarly practical problems and sought workable solutions. Why did justice function so badly in France? Why were there everywhere so many poor people and how might their number be diminished? Why was the teaching in the schools so mediocre? Should the children of the poor be encouraged to improve their minds, etc., etc.?

Moreover, this realistic and practical scrutiny was just as danger-ous to the established order as the speculation that frightened Taine. As long as one is a Plato or a Platonist and composes or reads the *Laws* or the *Republic* in the clouds, one does not endanger the estab-lished state. Such is the abyss between the reality and the vision! The authorities knew and sensed this very well. They did not seriously persecute the *Contrat social* nor did they confuse Holbach's *Politique naturelle* with his *Système de la nature*. But when one adopts the habit of observation and experiment; when one insists that the sciences continually put their principles into practice; when instead of seeking abstract ideas about agriculture one asks what grows best and how much it costs to raise it, one simultaneously develops the habit of believing that politics should be no different from physics, chemistry or raising wheat, that there should be no mysteries, secrets or rea-sons of state, and that everyone has the right to observe, discuss and demand practical, effective reforms in the same way that one might analyze the air or the cultivation of mulberry-trees. If the dreamers alone had been against the old regime, it would not have collapsed —if it did collapse—so rapidly nor in the same manner.

This vast, vigorous and spirited awakening of intellectual interests was not limited to Paris or a few great cities. It belonged to all France, that is, the French middle classes since we have no means of penetrating the minds of the workers and peasants for whom the struggle to live was too great to permit them to speculate or even to read. The France that had ideas or sought new ideas no longer resembled d'Argenson's description of it: a spider with a great head and long, thin legs! Everywhere on the eve of the Revolution there were thinking minds or at least those that sought to think. This is one of the reasons why the Revolution was not a violent blow in which Paris dragged after her a frightened, passive countryside but fulfilled instead the aspirations of the whole nation.

One gains the same impression when one considers the role of the great writers. Certainly it was considerable. Voltaire and Rousseau more or less dominated the entire history of thought during the century. Editions of their works grew in number. Even in the mere posters in the provinces, it was these writers who were appealed to and cited. Voltaire was "king;" Rousseau was "the master." However, our entire study has shown that they were not genuine innovators in most of the matters that concern us. In religion, all the arguments of the skeptics had been written or published before Voltaire; his were not the most systematic and violent refutations of Christianity. In politics, neither Voltaire, Montesquieu, Rousseau nor Diderot was a revolutionary nor even the boldest reformer. All the daring and ruthless arguments were stated by third or tenth rate writers. Besides, popular opinion was frequently unable to distinguish between men of talent and mere prattlers. Raynal and Delisle de Sales were probably as famous and certainly more widely read than Diderot. Whatever problems may have been discussed by the great writers, we have seen that there existed before and after them a swarm of works which had the same intellectual curiosity and critical spirit, and upheld the same solutions or even more subversive ones. Rousseau's influence, while not directly revolutionary (since the *Contrat social* was given scant attention), was certainly immediate, powerful and creative. But even his optimism, that naive confidence in men's good will when they are not victims of bad society, did not stem strictly from him. It was the dream of all the travellers, moralists and novelists who pitied the noble savage before and after Rousseau, quite without his assistance. It is vain to speculate on what might have happened to France and the Revolution if Montesquieu, Voltaire, Diderot and Rousseau had written nothing, yet it seems certain that currents of opinion would merely have been less intense, enthusiastic

and dynamic but not very different. The great *philosophes* did not discover any unknown land; they merely replaced its thousands of paths
where innumerable travellers had gone astray with wide, commodious
and attractive roads which rendered the journey across it more direct and secure.

It is not mine to judge this journey. Whether it was good or bad
matters little for the subject that I have sought to discuss. I have attempted to analyze the role of ideas in the origins of the Revolution
and not to prosecute a case. The inquiry seems quite conclusive.
Surely if the old regime had been threatened only by ideas, it would
have run no risk. Ideas needed a fulcrum, the people's misery and
political unrest, in order to be effective. But these political causes
would not have sufficed to bring about the Revolution as rapidly as it
came. It was ideas that demonstrated and systematized the consequences of political unrest and gradually initiated the movement for
the Estates General. And it was from the Estates General, without,
however, denying the role of ideas, that the Revolution came.

Georges Lefebvre

THE *DECLARATION OF THE RIGHTS OF MAN* AS THE ESSENCE OF THE ENLIGHTENMENT

Georges Lefebvre (1874–1959) has probably been the most outstanding historian of the French Revolution during the twentieth century. His extensive influence on historical study of the period and his leadership in the field resulted both from his many excellent publications and his large following among students of the age. Although Lefebvre's personal political views were definitely liberal, he was not primarily concerned with the thought of the Enlightenment, and believed that the Revolution resulted chiefly from the more practical problems of the old regime. Nevertheless, his view of the period was sufficiently broad to include recognition of the role of ideas in the historical experience of the century. He believed that the guiding principles of the Revolution stemmed from the ideas of the philosophes *and were epitomized in the* Declaration of the Rights of Man, *the "incarnation" of the Revolution. In this sense, Lefebvre recognized the distinctive importance of the intellectual factor during the revolutionary period.*

The Revolution of 1789 consisted first of all in the fall of absolute monarchy and advent of a liberty henceforth guaranteed by constitutional government; nor on this score can it be doubted that it was a national revolution, since the privileged orders as well as the Third Estate demanded a constitution and a regime in which individual rights would be respected.

But it was also the advent of equality before the law, without which liberty would be but another privilege of the powerful. For the French of 1789 liberty and equality were inseparable, almost two words for the same thing; but had they been obliged to choose, it is equality that they would have chosen; and when the peasants, who formed the overwhelming majority, cheered the conquest of liberty they were in fact thinking of the disappearance of the authority of the manorial lord, and his reduction to the status of a mere citizen. They were thinking, that is, of equality.

Thus made free and equal in rights, the French founded the nation anew, one and indivisible, by voluntary consent, in the movements called federations and especially in the Federation of July 14, 1790. This third characteristic of the Revolution of 1789 was one of its most original features, and the assertion that a people has the right to dispose of itself, and cannot be annexed to another without its own adherence freely expressed, has exerted an influence by no means yet exhausted in the world.

Moreover, the men of 1789 never entertained the idea that the rights of man and citizen were reserved for Frenchmen only. Christianity drew no distinction among men; it called on them all to meet as brothers in the divine city. In the same way the revolutionaries thought of liberty and equality as the common birthright of mankind. Imagining that all peoples would emulate their example, they even dreamed for an instant that the nations, in becoming free, would be reconciled forever in universal peace.

In the view of the lawyers, who represented and guided the bourgeoisie, the Revolution was to be a peaceful readjustment, imposed by opinion and translated rather simply into new juridical formulations. And in fact the essential work of the Revolution of 1789 may be found registered in the resolutions of August 4 and in the Declaration of the Rights of Man and the Citizen. But it would be childish to emphasize only these legislative enactments, throwing into the background the events which gave them birth; childish likewise, and indeed more so, to select from among these events certain ones to compose a legend. The Estates General skillfully and boldly defended the cause of the Third Estate which was the cause of the nation, but as even Buchez admitted, a peace-loving and Catholic democrat of 1848, "The Assembly would have achieved nothing without the insurrections." The old regime did not bend before the juridical revolution. Having taken to force, it was destroyed by force, which the people, descending into the street, put at the service of what they regarded as right, though even their own representatives had not dared to ask such assistance from them.

Whether the resort to violence was *in principle* necessary or unnecessary the historian cannot know. He observes simply that in the spring of 1789 the French people still had no thought of it, and that two years earlier they did not even suspect the regime to be nearing its end. It was the aristocracy that precipitated the Revolution by forcing the king to call the Estates General. Once the Third Estate obtained the right to express itself, the possibility of concessions which would have satisfied it for a time depended on the nobles and on the king. The issue was not so much political in character as social; for the transformation of the monarchy into a constitutional government was a reform on which nobles and bourgeois agreed, and by which Louis XVI would have lost little authority; but the great majority of the nobles, while prepared to make concessions in the direction of fiscal equality, were determined, more from pride than from material interest, to preserve their other privileges and remain a nation within the nation. One wonders whether the year 1789 might not have become the first phase of an evolutionary movement, during which the nobles would have gradually come to accept the status of more citizens. It is possible, and, if one likes, even probable; but, since we cannot run history over like an experiment in a laboratory, opinions on this question will always be divided. In any case, what actually happened is that the necessary decisions were not made in time, that the court turned to force to protect the aristocracy and that the problem was therefore presented in all its fullness. The Third Estate, driven to the wall, had to choose between resistance and surrender, so that in fact insurrection became inevitable, considering that fundamentally the Third was resolved to stand its ground. . . .

Still it need hardly be said that many motives combined to bring the French people to their supreme dilemma. We have attempted to single them out. Class interests and personal interests, humbled pride, mass suffering, philosophical propaganda all made their contribution, in proportions different for each individual, but with the net effect of producing in the Third Estate a collective mentality that was strangely complex, but which in summary expressed itself as a belief in an aristocratic conspiracy, a belief which in turn aroused passionate feelings, the fear, the frenzy for fighting, the thirst for revenge that characterized the days of July. . . .

Yet it is no less clear that on August 26, 1789, the bourgeoisie laid the definitive foundations of the new society. Though the Revolution of 1789 was only the first act in the French Revolution, those that followed it in protracted series down to 1830 were in essence a long conflict over this basic charter. The Declaration of the Rights of Man and the Citizen stands as the incarnation of the Revolution as a whole.

Much labor has been spent in contesting the originality of the Declaration, in deducing its substance, for example, from the bills of rights adopted by the American colonists in the struggle that won their independence. The men of the Constituent Assembly were undoubtedly familiar with these documents, especially the one issued by Virginia on May 10, 1776. The inspiration and content of the American and French declarations were the same. It was in fact with Jefferson, as early as January 1789, that Lafayette discussed his project; the text that he presented to the Assembly on July 11, with the accompanying letter, has been found in the papers of the ambassador of the United States, annotated by his own hand. The influence of America is beyond question. But this is not to say that without America the French declaration would not have seen the light. The whole philosophic movement in France in the eighteenth century pointed to such an act; Montesquieu, Voltaire and Rousseau had collaborated in its making. In reality, America and France, like England before them, were alike tributaries to a great stream of ideas, which, while expressing the ascendancy of the bourgeoisie, constituted a common ideal that summarized the evolution of Western civilization.

Through the course of centuries our Western world, formed by Christianity yet inheriting ancient thought, has directed its effort through a thousand vicissitudes toward the liberation of the human person. The Church upheld the freedom of the individual so that he might work in peace for his salvation and entrance into heaven. From the sixteenth to the eighteenth centuries philosophers proposed that man also throw off the fetters that held down his rise on earth; they urged him to become the master of nature and make his kind the true ruler of creation. Different though such doctrine seemed from that of the Church, the two were at one in recognizing the eminent dignity of the human person and commanding respect for it, in attributing to man certain natural and imprescriptible rights and in assigning to the authority of the state no other purpose than to protect these rights and to help the individual make himself worthy of them.

The West, inspired by the same masters, continued also to acknowledge the unity of mankind. The Church promised salvation to all without distinction of race, language or nation. To this universalism the new thinkers remained faithful. They secularized the idea of the Christian community, but they kept it alive.

Both these principles are preserved in the Declaration, for which the free and autonomous individual is the supreme end of social organization and of the state, and which has no knowledge of chosen or pariah races. It appeals throughout the earth to men of good will who cry with Victor Hugo:

"Je hais l'oppression d'une haine profonde."

Many objections have been made to the Declaration. Some have already been mentioned because they apply to the circumstances in which it was debated in the Assembly. Others of more general bearing merit a moment's further attention.

The Declaration, it has been said, is a mere abstraction from real life. Some men may be worthy of the rights it proclaims; some are less so; some, indeed, are hardly human. For cannibals, for example, the rights of man can have no real application; and if it be argued that even cannibals are human beings, still they are scarcely human in our sense. Nor, it is alleged, does the Declaration allow for circumstances. If war or economic crisis endanger a nation's existence, are the rights of its citizens to have the same free scope as in times of prosperity? And if individual rights are not inherently limited, will not the government be granted the power to limit them?

There is no force in this criticism except when the Declaration is confused with a legal code, whereas its nature is that of moral principle, not of positive legislation. We are bound by moral principle, for example—as well as by the Declaration—not to do to another what we should not wish him to do to us. Moral principle does not specify what our conduct should be in each particular case; it leaves this task to the moralist or the casuist. Similarly the Declaration proclaims the rights of man, but leaves to the law, which may vary with circumstances, the task of determining the extent, which may also vary with circumstances, to which these rights may be exercised, always providing that the law is the true expression of the general will, i.e., of the majority of the community. That the members of the National Assembly considered this to be the character of the Declaration is clear from the debates in which, a month before its adoption, they discussed the operations of counter-revolutionaries and considered setting up a special court: governing in wartime is not like governing in peacetime, observed Gouy d'Arsy, anticipating Robespierre. Again, when the question of slavery arose, the relativism in the Declaration became apparent; it was judged impossible to transfer the Negroes abruptly; without apprenticeship in freedom, from slavery to the full status of citizenship. And the Assembly reached by implication the same conclusion for France, when it made the right to vote depend on degree of economic well-being, and the right to be elected depend on the owning of real estate, because, rightly or wrongly, it regarded such economic well-being, and especially the ownership of land, as the only means of assuring the enlightenment and self-restraint thought necessary to the exercise of the rights of man and of citizenship. These rights then are relative to circumstances. The Declaration is an ideal to be realized. It is a *direction of intention.*

Another criticism, vehemently raised in our day, is that it favored one class at the expense of others, namely the bourgeoisie that drew it up, and that it thus provoked a disorder that threatens the community with disruption. The Declaration did indeed list property among the rights of man, and its authors meant property as it then existed and still does; moreover, economic liberty, though not mentioned, is very much in its spirit. This amounts to saying that the man who holds the land and the other instrumentalities of labor, i.e., capital, is in fact master of those who possess nothing but their muscles and their intelligence, because they depend on him for the opportunity to earn their living. The evil is made worse, it is added, by the inheritance of property, which endows certain children, irrespective of merit or capacity, with the *means* over and above the *rights* which are all that others receive. The Declaration, in short, is blamed for having allowed capitalism to develop without control and for having thus caused the proletariat to rise against it—to have had as a consequence a new class struggle of an always accelerating violence, all for want of some power of arbitration that can be granted only to the state. Contrariwise, those who deny such a power to the state have not failed to invoke the Declaration, elaborating upon it with ideas drawn from its own authors, who undoubtedly held to *laissez-faire* and unlimited competition as universal panaceas, and conceived of property as an absolute right to use or to abuse.

Here again, for a reply, we must appeal to the Constituents themselves. They had before their eyes a society in which modern capitalism was barely beginning, and in which the increase of productive capacity seemed the essential corrective to poverty and want. Even to those who gave thought to the poor it seemed not impossible that every man might own a few acres or a shop that would make him self-sufficient; and this ideal, which was that of the *sans-culottes,* remained alive well into the nineteenth century. Experience has not justified these hopes. Rousseau had already observed, long before 1789, that democracy is not compatible with an excessive inequality of wealth. It is for the community to examine whether the changes since 1789 in the economic and social structure of society do not justify intervention by the law, so that the excess of *means* in the hands of some may not reduce the *rights* of others to an empty show. By what procedure? That too is for the community to decide, in the spirit of the Declaration, which in proclaiming liberty did not mean an aristocratic liberty reserved for a few, such as Montalembert demanded in 1850, but which rather, confiding to the law the task of delimiting the rights of citizens, left it to take the measures that may be suitable to prevent social disruption.

Finally, according to other critics, the Declaration regards law as simply the will of the citizens; but what would become of the nation if the majority oppressed the minority, or if it refused to make the necessary sacrifices which in time of war may reach to life itself? The community, this school concludes, cannot be identified with the citizens who make it up at a given moment; extending beyond them in time, it is hierarchically above them, for without it they would not exist; it is really embodied in the state, which in consequence cannot depend on the will of ephemeral citizens, and for that reason has the right to coerce them. With this idea, it need hardly be said, we return to the personal absolutism of the old regime, for the state, whatever may be said, has itself no effective existence except in individual persons, who by and large would confer their mandates upon themselves. Still less need it be remarked that this system is in radical contradiction with the Declaration in reducing the individual to be a mere instrument in the hands of the state, depriving him of all liberty and all self-determination.

But these answers do not remove the difficulty, as too often we delude ourselves into believing. It is perfectly true that the Declaration carries with it a risk, as do absolutism and dictatorship, though the risk is of another kind. The citizens must be made to face their responsibilities. Invested with the rights of governing themselves, if they abuse their powers with respect to one another, above all if they refuse from personal selfishness to assure the welfare of the community, the community will perish, and with it their liberty, if not indeed their existence.

We come here to the deeper meaning of the Declaration. It is a direction of intention; it therefore requires of the citizens an integrity of purpose, which is to say a critical spirit, patriotism in the proper sense of the word, respect for the rights of others, reasoned devotion to the national community, "virtue" in the language of Montesquieu, Rousseau and Robespierre. "The soul of the Republic," wrote Robespierre in 1792, "is virtue, love of country, the generous devotion that fuses all interests into the general interest." The Declaration in proclaiming the rights of man appeals at the same time to discipline freely consented to, to sacrifice if need be, to cultivation of character *and to the mind.* Liberty is by no means an invitation to indifference or to irresponsible power; nor is it the promise of unlimited well-being without a counterpart of toil and effort. It supposes application, perpetual effort, strict government of self, sacrifice in contingencies, civic and private virtues. It is therefore more difficult to live as a free man than to live as a slave, and that is why men so often renounce their freedom; for freedom is in its way an invitation to a life of courage, and sometimes of heroism, as the freedom of the Christian is an invitation to a life of sainthood.

IV A SPECIAL STRAIN: ROUSSEAU'S INFLUENCE ON THE FRENCH REVOLUTION

Joan McDonald

THE REVOLUTIONARY CULT OF ROUSSEAU

This selection from Joan McDonald's authoritative study of Rousseau in relation to the French Revolution presents an unusual but significant interpretation of the problem of his influence upon the movement. While admitting that Rousseau's political writings had no extensive following before 1789 and that his ideas did not entirely parallel those of any faction during the subsequent upheaval, she argues that the cult of Rousseau was an important element of revolutionary ideology. This cult, as she presents it, was built upon Rousseau's concept of human perfectibility and social regeneration, and was therefore a liberal influence during the Revolution.

In the first part of this work an attempt was made to show that the influence of Rousseau's political theories was by no means a major factor in the history of the first three years of the Revolution. It would appear that the *Social Contract* was not widely read either before 1789, or between 1789 and 1791. The majority of speakers and writers who appealed to the authority of Rousseau did so in order to put forward not Rousseau's views but their own, with the result that his name was frequently associated with arguments which were in direct contradiction with those which he had formulated. It is not unusual to find that when revolutionary writers actually studied the *Social Contract* they were critical of some aspects of Rousseau's political theory, particularly his condemnation of representation. It has been shown that the most careful analysis of Rousseau's political theory is to be found not in the pamphlets of revolutionary writers, but in those of the aristocratic critics of the Revolution who protested against the use of Rousseau's name to justify the deeds of the revolutionaries.

These conclusions, however, raise an important question. If it is denied that the political theory of Rousseau was well known to the men who played leading roles in the successive acts of the Revolution, how is it possible to explain the stubborn persistence of the

From Joan McDonald, *Rousseau and the French Revolution, 1762–1791* (London: The Athlone Press of the University of London, 1965). Reproduced with permission. Footnotes omitted.

revolutionary cult of Rousseau? How can the importance attached to Rousseau's name, and the homage paid to his memory from 1789 onward be reconciled with the apparent ignorance, or where it was not ignored, the misinterpretation, of his political theories?

No one would deny the ardor, enthusiasm and spontaneity with which the Revolution honored Rousseau's memory in public demonstrations and official ceremonies, nor the constant association of his name with its achievements. I do not propose here to describe in detail all the manifestations of the cult of Rousseau, but these must be referred to briefly. Rousseau's name was associated with the Revolution from a very early date. According to Girardin, when the news of the fall of the Bastille reached Mans, where he was garrisoned at the time, the citizens offered him the "cocarde nationale," acclaiming him: "Élève de Jean-Jacques, ton patriotisme te rend digne de la porter!" Whether or not this account is true, it is certainly the case that Rousseau's name was associated with the victory of liberty and equality symbolized by the fall of the Bastille. A bust was sculptured in stone taken from the Bastille, with the words *Liberté, Égalité, Fraternité* inscribed at its base, and on subsequent celebrations of the 14th July, a bust of Rousseau was carried in procession round the ruins of the fortress.

A bust of Rousseau was also installed in the National Assembly in 1790, with copies of *Émile* and the *Social Contract* deposited at its base. The Assembly accepted the presentation of the complete works of Rousseau in 1791. Rousseau's bust was similarly installed in the assembly rooms of many popular societies between 1790 and 1791, including the Jacobins, the *Société des Indigens,* and the *Société du Cercle Social des Amis de la Vérité.* Busts of Rousseau and quotations from his works decorated the *Autels de la Patrie,* a section of Paris was named *"Contrat Social,"* and a street in Paris received his name in 1791.

Fêtes were held in Rousseau's honor, the most famous of which was held at Montmorency in September 1791. As early as 1789 a fête was celebrated in Angers in honor of Rousseau and Voltaire. Hymns and poems to Rousseau were a frequent feature in revolutionary and literary journals, and invocations to his name were regularly made by orators and pamphleteers. A number of plays on the subject of Rousseau's life enjoyed considerable success in Paris. One such play, performed in 1791, was particularly popular. It depicted the last

FIGURE 5. Rousseau in "natural" garb. Rousseau's writings were a prime source of the back-to-nature movement for which he was chiefly known before the Revolution. This combined with his ideals of equality and democracy to create a powerful cult of Rousseau during the Revolution, when his political concepts inspired many of the most radical French leaders. (*Courtesy of the Fogg Art Museum, Harvard University*)

days of Rousseau, spent in modest retirement, and his death. Pro-
tests, however, were aroused by the author's introduction of the
character of the Marquis de Girardin into the death-bed scene, since
some members of the audience regarded it as unseemly that an
aristocrat should be depicted as present at the sacred moment.

Before the National Assembly officially decreed a statue to Rousseau in December 1790, a number of private projects for this purpose had been set on foot. The journal *Révolutions de Paris* opened
a fund for the erection of a statue to Rousseau under the inspiration
of Sylvain Maréchal. Finally, in November and December 1790,
Rousseau's name was officially honored by the state. The National
Assembly decreed the erection of a statue in his honor, and granted
a pension to his widow. In August of the following year the Assembly
received two petitions demanding the transference of Rousseau's
remains from Ermenonville to the Panthéon. The first of these, in-
stigated by Ginguené, who also introduced a motion on the same
subject in the National Assembly, was supported by a large number
of well known admirers of Rousseau. The second petition was presented by the citizens of Montmorency. It has been suggested that
it was the opposition of Girardin which prevented the removal of
the remains of Rousseau to the Panthéon in 1791. There is, however,
some evidence that opposition was more widely spread. The sentimental association of Rousseau's memory with the Île des Peupliers
was too strong to be effaced without opposition in a generation
which had made pilgrimages to that romantic spot and indulged in
all the excesses of *sensibilité* over Rousseau's tomb. It was argued
that the solitude and beauty of Ermenonville made a more suitable
resting place for the friend of nature than the Panthéon. It was
not until 1794, when Voltaire's remains had already been transferred
to the Panthéon, that this final honor was paid to Rousseau.

The honors paid to Rousseau's memory during the Revolution
have been regarded by historians as evidence of the influence exercised by his political theory. This is a patent non sequitur. In order
to discover the precise nature of the cult of Rousseau, and its roots
in the revolutionary mind, it is necessary to examine not simply the
outward manifestations of the cult, such as those which have been
described above, but also the ideas which emerged in relation to it,
and the particular concepts which were associated with Rousseau's

name. How far, in fact, was the cult political and attributable to the influence of the *Social Contract*?

Certain general ideas were associated with the Rousseauist cult. Rousseau was hailed as the founder of the constitution on the ground that he had revealed to humanity the fundamental principles of justice and right which the revolutionaries claimed to be putting into effect. These were: the sovereignty of the people, liberty and equality. D'Eymar, in a speech in the National Assembly, proposing the erection of a statue to Rousseau, asserted:

> *Vous verriez dans Jean-Jacques Rousseau . . . le précurseur de cette grande Révolution; vous vous souviendriez qu'il vous apprenait à former des hommes pour la liberté, lorsque vous étioz à la veille de faire des Français un peuple libre. . . . Le Contrat Social a été pour vous la charte dans laquelle vous avez retrouvé les droits usurpés sur la nation, et surtout le droit imprescriptible de souveraineté.*

Ginguené admitted that in some details the revolutionaries were not in fact following Rousseau's theories, but this, he said, did not in any way affect Rousseau's title to be considered as the father of the constitution:

> *De quelle souveraineté fûtes-vous investis pour régénérer un grand empire, pour lui donner une constitution libre? De l'inaliénable et imprescriptible souveraineté du peuple. Sur quelle base avez-vous fondé cette constitution, qui deviendra le modèle de toutes les constitutions humaines? Sur l'égalité des droits. Or, Messieurs, l'égalité des droits entre les hommes et la souveraineté du peuple, Rousseau fut le premier à les établir en système, sous les yeux même du despotisme.*

Ginguené therefore concluded that Rousseau was the first founder of the constitution.

Other writers and orators made the same claims on Rousseau's behalf. The citizens of Montmorency called Rousseau "ce vengeur indomptable des droits de l'homme," who had shown the means whereby societies could be recalled to their true purpose. An anonymous pamphleteer, demanding the erection of a statue to Rousseau asserted: "C'est parce que sur les points essentiels . . . il a vu et publié le premier la vérité . . . c'est que si la révolution actuelle est un grand bien, elle est son ouvrage." The President of the National

Assembly, replying to the petitions for the transference of Rousseau's remains to the Panthéon referred to him as the philosopher who had restored to men their equality of rights and to peoples their sovereignty. More important, he had prepared in men's hearts the love of liberty. Collot d'Herbois, speaking in the Jacobin Club, hailed Rousseau as the patron of all peoples who loved liberty. One writer designated him "the father of liberty." At Montmorency the following inscription was carved on the base of the statue erected to Rousseau in 1791:

> *Philosophe doux et modeste,*
> *Il a connu les droits de l'humanité,*
> *C'est dans cette vallée*
> *En contemplant l'ouvrage de la Divinité,*
> *Il a fait son Contrat Social*
> *La base de notre constitution.*

The significance of these and many more invocations to Rousseau must not be misinterpreted. When he was termed the founder of the constitution it was not in the sense that he had provided a kind of political and constitutional blueprint, but in the sense that he had formulated those basic principles of justice and those human rights which the makers of the constitution sought to guarantee. Why were these general principles ascribed to Rousseau? They cannot be regarded as peculiar to his political thought. The ideas of liberty, equality and the sovereignty of the people were general concepts accepted by the majority of those who supported the Revolution, and even by some who opposed it. They were not culled from the works of any one particular writer but belonged to that general body of eighteenth-century political theory to which not only the great philosophers but also the plagiarists and pamphleteers of the revolutionary and immediately prerevolutionary period had contributed. The real problem therefore is why such widely accepted ideas were associated particularly with Rousseau. It is of course true that his name was frequently used in conjunction with those of Voltaire, Montesquieu, Raynal, Mably and others. Nevertheless, the revolutionaries gave official recognition to Rousseau as a prophet and patron of the Revolution before they accorded the same recognition to any other philosopher. It is probably fair to say that more than that of any of the great prerevolutionary writers, the memory of Rousseau captured the imagination of the revolutionary generation. It is in this last assertion that the true explanation of the Rousseauist cult will be found.

In order to understand the reasons why it was predominantly upon the name of Rousseau that these general revolutionary principles were fathered, it is necessary to take into account the fact that a cult of Rousseau already existed before the Revolution began, and that his name was already highly charged with ideas and emotions which, if not directly political, were nevertheless in a sense revolutionary. This cult the Revolution took over, but its transfiguration from a purely personal and literary to a political cult was possible only because the basic ideas which had been associated with Rousseau's name during the latter part of his life and after his death were as relevant to the revolutionaries as they had been to the preceding generation.

The prerevolutionary cult of Rousseau had nothing to do with Rousseau's political theory, nor, except indirectly, with any political ideas. It was a personal and literary cult which owed its existence to the appeal of the *Nouvelle Héloise* and the *Émile* but even more to the personal legend of Rousseau. In this legend he featured as a captivating genius, a man of charm and gentleness, whose sufferings had not prevented him from laying down those sublime truths which he had learned in solitary communion with Nature, nor from being hounded by a perverse authority and betrayed by false friends. Seen through the eyes of that *sensibilité* of which he was the greatest eighteenth-century exponent, Rousseau's own person appeared larger than life; he became for his admirers the prototype of the natural and virtuous man whose education he had planned in *Émile,* and a living exemplar of the complex humanity which he had described in the *Nouvelle Héloise,* and later in his own *Confessions,* and with which his readers could so easily identify themselves. Mornet has examined in detail the influence of the Rousseauist myth, both during Rousseau's own lifetime and after his death, on the manners and attitudes of mind of his contemporaries and of the generation which followed. In the works of Mornet, and in those of Buffenoir, and Girardin may be found many examples of the emotional ardor, and, after Rousseau's death, the religious fervor, which characterized the Rousseauist cult. Admirers of Rousseau visited him in a spirit of reverence, and later adherents of the Rousseauist cult made solemn pilgrimages to his tomb. The Prince de Ligne, describing his first visit to Rousseau, wrote:

Despite my wishes I set the limit myself, and after a reverent silence spent gazing into the eyes of the author of the Nouvelle Héloise, I left that hovel, which was the home of rats, and at the same time the sanctuary of genius.

The abbé Brizzard recorded his visits to Rousseau with exaggerated enthusiasm:

I have seen him; I have conversed with the wisest of men. He accepted my youth, and I never left one of his conversations without feeling my soul uplifted and my heart more virtuous.

After Rousseau's death, his tomb on the Île des Peupliers at Ermenonville took on the character of a national shrine, attracting many hundreds of pilgrims. For the better preparation of their minds in approaching this hallowed spot the Marquis de Girardin addressed the visitors in a guide book to the grounds of Ermenonville:

It is to you, friend of Rousseau, it is to you that I address myself; you alone are able to sense the affecting charm of such a site. In these solitary places, nothing can distract you from the object of your love; you see it; it is there, let your tears pour out; never will you have wept sweeter or more justifiable tears.

The most remarkable account of a pilgrimage to Rousseau's tomb is that given by the abbé Brizzard, who visited Ermenonville with a party of friends, all enthusiastic admirers of Rousseau. They first fell on their knees and kissed the tomb, after which each member of the party paid tribute to Rousseau's memory and laid flowers on the monument. Finally they tore out and burned ceremoniously those pages of Diderot's *Essai sur Sénèque* in which the author had attacked Rousseau. Brizzard described the sombreness of their surroundings as giving an impressively august setting to the scene which they enacted.

It was this moral and personal cult which the Revolution appropriated. Professor McNeil, in his study of the revolutionary cult of Rousseau, takes the view that the revolutionary adoption of the Rousseauist cult involved a certain dissociation of the cult from the mainsprings of its origins so that it became to some extent artificial in its revolutionary context. He writes: "There was practically none of the intensely personal and emotional loyalty to the 'bon Jean-Jacques' that there was in the literary cult." He concludes, moreover, that, "as an expression of first this, and then that faction, the political cult could never achieve an independent existence or a rationale of its own."

A study of the ideas which emerged in relation to the Rousseauist cult during the Revolution makes it difficult, however, to accept these conclusions. In the first place it is difficult to see why the revolutionaries should have continued to pay homage to Rousseau's memory unless it were generally felt that the ideas which had been associated with his name before the Revolution were also relevant to revolutionary aspirations. The aristocrats, of course, accused the revolutionaries of using Rousseau's name simply as a cloak to give respectability to what they regarded as nefarious schemes, and it is certainly true that there was more than an element of expediency in the way in which revolutionary orators and writers appealed to Rousseau's authority. It would be a mistake, however, to explain the revolutionary cult simply in terms of opportunism. The pre-revolutionary and the revolutionary cult had a common rationale in the basic and fundamental idea of the moral regeneration of mankind. Rousseau had addressed himself to the individual; he had however stipulated that while men were potentially virtuous, society was immoral and corrupt. The revolutionaries had accepted the view that the regeneration of the individual could be brought about by the regeneration of society; and because it was with the name of Rousseau that the idea of individual moral regeneration had become particularly associated, so, in carrying the idea into the wider sphere of social regeneration, it was with Rousseau's name that the practical devices of the Revolution were associated. Since Rousseau had stated the ends, then the means adopted by the Revolution were also regarded as having been approved by Rousseau. Moreover since Rousseau's political principles had been set forth in the *Social Contract,* then this work had to be made to conform to the preconceived notions as to its contents. Thus, while the general political ideas which were grafted on to the Rousseauist cult had little or nothing to do with the theories put forward by Rousseau in the *Social Contract,* they had a great deal to do with that concept of Rousseau as

a great moral teacher which was common both to the pre-revolutionary and the revolutionary Rousseauist cult.

This basic concept of Rousseau's moral role emerges continu-
ously and emphatically in revolutionary writings.

"Ce qui plaça J. J. Rousseau au-dessus de tous les écrivains de
son siècle," wrote Mercier, "c'est que son éloquence avait un
caractère moral." More than any other writer Rousseau's name was
associated with the idea of social regeneration. He was indeed regarded as having laid the necessary foundations of the Revolution
by rescuing the individual from the toils of corruption and recalling
him to the path of virtue. He was considered to have prepared the
way for the social regeneration which the revolutionaries believed
they were bringing about, by teaching the need for individual moral
regeneration. D'Escherny claimed that Rousseau's *First* and *Second
Discourses* had inaugurated a new examination of the moral nature
of man as the basis of a new science of society. Rousseau's authority was invoked to plead for the alliance of public and private
morality as the prerequisite of a regenerated state. Aubert de Vitry
wrote an imaginary conversation between the spirits of the great
philosophers of the eighteenth century on the subject of the Revolution. He gave Rousseau a leading role in this discussion, because it
was Rousseau who in his view had initiated that *restauration des
mœurs* which had been the necessary prelude to the Revolution.
He is made to say:

> . . . ce sont mes écrits; qui ayant d'abord opéré une révolution dans la
> vie privée, finiront par en opérer également une dans la vie publique.

The same aspects of Rousseau's role were emphasized in various
official pronouncements. D'Eymar argued that the National Assembly
was only completing the work of regeneration which Rousseau had
begun. Ginguené claimed that Rousseau had rescued the people
from frivolity and false conventions, and that he had brought about
the moral regeneration without which their own attempts to bring
about a regeneration of the laws would have been fruitless. On the
autel de la patrie at Rennes, Rousseau's own words were inscribed:

> *La patrie ne peut subsister sans la liberté; la liberté sans la vertu.*

It is not therefore possible to accept the view that the revolutionary cult of Rousseau lacked a rationale of its own. On the contrary, the personal legend of Rousseau acquired a new significance as a result of the Revolution. Rousseau became the symbol of the virtuous man who suffers at the hands of tyranny, pride and privilege, but who courageously fights back with the weapons of truth. The revolutionaries regarded Rousseau as their forerunner. Saint-Just, discussing the characteristics of the "revolutionary man," and reciting his innumerable virtues, concluded by asserting that Rousseau was the type of man he was describing. In an article in the *Bouche de Fer,* a writer described the "Caractère de ces hommes rares destinés par la nature, comme Jean-Jacques, à réveiller les nations." Such a man, the writer asserted, is destined by nature to suffer, but never to lose his love of humanity; to be surrounded by deceitfulness, but never to lose sight of truth. His struggle is that of a god of nature against the demons of tyranny. "Pauvre Jean-Jacques, tu as fourni les traits de l'homme extraordinaire et toujours méconnu, qui doit influer sur les destins de l'univers. Il a souffert pour la liberté, combattu pour la liberté, il vient de conquérir la divine liberté!"

Writing after the Revolution, Étienne Dumont pointed out that Rousseau's influence was especially strong among the bourgeoisie, because those who were discontented with their social status, or who suffered under the system of privilege and corruption which Rousseau attacked could identify themselves in Rousseau's "martyrdom." They embraced him as an "avenger," a "tribune of the people and of virtue." As Dumont recognized, however, Rousseau's appeal was not confined to any one section of the community. It was universal, because the main content of his writing was his moral message, his recall to simple natural virtue.

The idea of Rousseau as a great moral teacher assumed new significance as a result of the Revolution. It is not the case that the revolutionary cult did not give rise to the same "intensely personal and emotional loyalty" which characterized the prerevolutionary cult. On the contrary, Rousseau's memory excited the same religious fervor which was common to the prerevolutionary expressions of loyalty to his name. Again and again in revolutionary pamphlets the reader comes upon the highly emotional concept of Rousseau as a kind of Messiah who was persecuted, misunderstood and martyred, but whose theories were now, for the first time, being realized by his revolutionary disciples. Writers and speakers invoked the spirit of

Rousseau and called upon him to look down and bless their undertakings; they pictured themselves as carrying out their master's injunctions beneath his benevolent eyes, and congratulated themselves on finally bringing peace and satisfaction to the spirit of one who had suffered persecution and death in order that they might find liberty.

An example of this almost religious fervor is to be found in an account of the installation of the bust of Rousseau at the *Société des Indigens,* in 1791. The writer concluded his description of the ceremony with a passionately expressed eulogy of Rousseau. He prayed to the spirit of Rousseau, who, he asserted, could read their hearts and minds, and asked him to return amongst them, to guide their footsteps. He referred to Rousseau as the instrument of God, who had helped humanity to gain their liberty at the cost of his own life. Finally, in a delirious outburst, he announced that Rousseau had heard their prayer, and had returned to guide them to their goal.

An account of a visit of a party of young Rousseauist enthusiasts to Ermenonville, as extravagant as any description of the prerevolutionary pilgrimages to Rousseau's tomb, can be found in a pamphlet which was published in 1791. This describes how, on the evening of the 31st December of 1790, a society of friends of the "citoyen philosophe" were assembled to discuss ways and means of defeating aristocratic plots against the constitution, when one of their members rushed in with the news of the Assembly's decree honoring Rousseau's memory. On this subject the new arrival made a lengthy and apparently extempore speech, after which it was decided that the occasion should be celebrated by a visit to Ermenonville. It was proposed to carve the Assembly's decree upon stone and offer it at Rousseau's tomb as a "sacrifice" to his "fiery spirit." Six representatives were accordingly elected from their numbers and on the following day they set out for Ermenonville.

The author describes with much feeling their approach to the tomb, and how, as they drew near to the île des Peupliers, they appeared to have entered a new spiritual world. They had an overpowering sense of the personality of Rousseau brooding over the spot, and of a supernatural peace which nature herself forbade them to disturb. In this profound solitude and silence they performed their rites. They began by bathing the tomb with their tears, after which they laid an olive branch and a laurel crown upon it, and deposited the carved stone at its foot. Finally one of those present broke silence by pronouncing, with great emotion, an address to Rousseau, which began with the words "Rousseau, ombre chère et sacrée," and proceeded in similar vein at some length.

The ceremony being over, they settled down to meditate round the tomb, each at the foot of a poplar, and to seek inspiration from Rousseau's spiritual presence. One tried to compose music after the style of the *Devin du Village,* another sketched the tomb, a third simply "poured on to the paper the wonderful thoughts which came into his head." Suddenly, however, they felt themselves seized by some strange and unknown power. Their pens fell to the ground and a voice, which they immediately recognized as the voice of Rousseau, was heard from the depths of the tomb, distinctly pronouncing these words: "Nation généreuse et sensible! Braves Français! Citoyens compatriotes! Amis!" In a style remarkably adapted to the conventions of revolutionary oratory, Rousseau's voice continued to tell them that they had justified the confidence he had placed in them, and by doing so, had amply repaid him for the persecution he had endured on their account. He congratulated them on the constitution, which followed so closely the path he had traced for them; he instructed them to forgive his enemies, sent messages of congratulation to an assortment of members of the Assembly, and asked them to correct Mme. de Staël's erroneous statement that he had taken his own life. His disciples listened in wonder and terror, and returned to Paris in exalted spirits to tell the world of their experience.

Such expressions of the revolutionary cult of Rousseau indicate a very real feeling of being spiritually at one with Rousseau, a feeling which was nonetheless sincere for all their ignorance of Rousseau's political theory, and for all the misinterpretations of that political theory which the Revolution set on foot. The aristocratic accusation that the revolutionaries deliberately and consciously misinterpreted Rousseau's political ideas was an oversimplification. Their enthusiasm was based, not on his political writings, but on the Rousseauist myth which the Revolution took over from the prerevolutionary cult, and according to which Rousseau featured as a great moralist, whose work in directing the attention of the individual to his moral rights and duties was a necessary prerequisite to the achievements of 1789.

The third element in Professor McNeil's analysis is also, it seems to me, invalidated by more detailed study. He argues that the revolutionary cult of Rousseau was unable to achieve an independent existence because it was merely used to bolster up the views of first this, then that political faction. It would be more accurate to describe the Rousseauist cult as having so general, and at the same time so intensely personal a hold upon the minds of the revolutionary generation that the ideas associated with Rousseau's name retained their significance for each succeeding faction as well as for countless individuals, both revolutionary and antirevolutionary. The personal and moral appeal of the Rousseauist cult survived into the Revolution, and the general political principles which were grafted on to it were sufficiently general to be acceptable to all those who had set themselves the task of regenerating French society, and who regarded Rousseau's name as one of the most important symbols of their hopes. Thus the individual and at the same time universal character of the Rousseauist cult ensured its continued survival, and it is possible to find at every stage in the Revolution both an official cult of Rousseau and at the same time individuals who appealed to his name, whether they belonged to the predominant faction or whether they opposed it, whether they defended or whether they attacked the Revolution itself. Those who disagreed with the particular faction in power as to the methods which should be used to push forward or to conserve the Revolution, still accepted the common inspiration and the common purpose of the Revolution which they regarded Rousseau as having stated. Those who feared the Revolution and opposed it still appealed to the great thinker who had formed the minds of their generation.

In the course of this study something has already been shown of the loyalty felt to Rousseau's memory by opposing factions. During the very years when Rousseau's name was coming to be increasingly venerated as a revolutionary symbol, during the period which culminated in the National Assembly's decree of December 1790, when official recognition was given for Rousseau's supposed contribution to the Revolution, other writers and politicians were appealing passionately to the authority of Rousseau to condemn the very Revolution with which his name had become so closely associated. It has been shown that in fact these aristocratic writers were the most scholarly exponents of Rousseau's political theory, but this achievement on their part was very largely accidental. Adherents of the personal and literary cult of Rousseau, they were shocked to find the name of a man whose memory they held in such esteem, being used to justify political measures which they could not condone. As Lenormant and Ferrand explicitly admitted, they were drawn to examine the *Social Contract* in detail because of the way in which the revolutionaries had appropriated Rousseau's name to support policies of which they did not approve. The revolutionaries, on the contrary, being convinced of their spiritual alignment with one whom they had adopted as their great precursor, had less incentive to make an objective and critical study of Rousseau's political theory, and were obviously not inclined to emphasize those points at which Rousseau's theory parted company with the accepted conventions of the Revolution. Yet it is important to remember that both revolutionaries and aristocrats appealed to the authority of Rousseau in the first place not because of his political writings, but because the Rousseauist myth had become an integral part of the common intellectual background of the educated classes.

This study of the influence and interpretation of Rousseau's political theory extends only as far as 1791, but there are indications that the same pattern continued through the revolutionary period. There continued to be an official association between the group in power and the cult of Rousseau on the one hand, while on the other, individuals still continued to appeal to Rousseau's authority both to support and to oppose the ruling faction. For example, Robespierre has probably been credited with having been inspired by Rousseau's works more than any other revolutionary leader. Both he and Saint-Just were admirers of Rousseau, and the members of the Committee of Public Safety frequently quoted Rousseau's name. Yet we know that among the opponents of the Jacobins there were admirers of Rousseau as ardent and sincere as Robespierre and Saint-Just. Mme. Roland, we have seen, constantly expressed her admiration for him in her letters and claimed that the reading of the *Nouvelle Héloïse* was a turning point in her life. Buzot in flight from his enemies, regretted the time when he had wandered among the fields of Normandy with a volume of Rousseau's works in his hands. Louvet, hiding from his enemies in the Jura, wrote:

Alors, je me rappelle que ce fut ton sort, O mon maître, O mon soutien sublime et vertueux Rousseau. Toi aussi, pour avoir bien merité du genre humain, tu t'en vis persécuté. Toi aussi, pour avoir été l'ami du peuple. . . .

Similarly, when Robespierre was overthrown, the revolutionary cults, including that of Rousseau, were stronger under the Directory than at any time during the Revolution. The President of the Executive was La Revellière-Lépeaux, who has already been mentioned as an ardent admirer of Rousseau. At the same time, Babeuf, executed under the Directory, was also a fervent Rousseauist, who christened his son "Émile." Babeuf numbered among his associates Sylvain Maréchal, who has already been noted as a contributor to the Rousseauist journal *Révolutions de Paris,* and the instigator, in 1790, of a fund for the erection of a statue to Rousseau.

Thus it is possible to find at every stage in the Revolution individuals in practically every faction who appealed to Rousseau's authority, and who were familiar with and admired his works. For this reason the revolutionary cult cannot be regarded as an artificial phenomenon, officially cultivated by the successive factions which acquired transitory dominance. On the contrary, its continued existence and its personal attraction for so many of such diverse opinions is evidence of the power which the Rousseauist myth continued to exercise over the minds of the revolutionary generation. The diversity of viewpoint among those who appealed to Rousseau's authority helps to explain why historians have reached such a variety of conclusions about his political influence. Such general conclusions, however, ignore the distinction between individual loyalty to Rousseau's memory, which was the fundamental basis of the official cult, and the actual knowledge and application of Rousseau's political theory, as stated in the *Social Contract.* Of the men of the revolutionary generation one might say that all of them and at the same time none of them were Rousseauists, in that while the literary and personal cult of Rousseau had become an integral part of their intellectual equipment, those who read the *Social Contract* and accepted its specific theories were a mere handful. In every revolutionary faction there were admirers of Rousseau; in every argument between those in power and those in opposition, appeal was apt to be made at some stage and by individuals on both sides to Rousseau's authority. But this appeal to Rousseau's name had not necessarily any connection with his political writings, of which, at least during the period 1789–1791, the majority of the protagonists were very largely ignorant.

Since Rousseau's name had been most intimately associated with that gospel of regeneration which the revolutionaries were supposed to be putting into practice, it was natural, if illogical, on the part of the revolutionaries to suppose that Rousseau would have approved the means which they used to achieve the ends which he stated. It was equally natural, if also illogical, that they should have cherished a deep respect for the work in which Rousseau's political theory had been enshrined, particularly since its publication had played so important a part in the history of Rousseau's "martyrdom," an essential component of the Rousseauist cult. Thus the actual contents of the *Social Contract* were for a very large number of people immaterial; the *Social Contract* itself was part of the myth, and it was the myth of Rousseau rather than his political theory which was important in the mind of the revolutionary generation.

Lester G. Crocker

ROUSSEAU'S GENERAL WILL AND REVOLUTIONARY DICTATORSHIP

Lester G. Crocker is chairman of the Department of French Literature and General Linguistics at the University of Virginia. A recognized authority on many phases of eighteenth-century intellectual history, his publications include special studies of Diderot and Rousseau as well as two important works of synthesis on major currents in the Enlightenment. In this selection he argues that in spite of the complexities of Rousseau's thought and subsequent influence, the major thrust of the latter was toward totalitarian democracy.

While a complete study of the influence of Rousseau's political thought would require a large volume, or several volumes, it will be useful even to mark some of the highlights. In regard to a man who left so deep an imprint on intellectual and cultural history, it is unpersuasive and arbitrary to suggest that the fortunes of his ideas—what those who came after him did with them—are irrelevant. To explore the radiations and consequences of a set of ideas we may, it seems to me, seek to determine where they have taken root (influences) and to what the ideas may conceivably lead (analogues). Undoubtedly it is dangerous and unfair to judge Rousseau not by what he wrote, but by the light of history's nightmares. My intention, however, is not to judge Rousseau, but only to point to the implications and potentialities of what he wrote; any comparisons are based on the meaning of what he wrote. Critics also assert that it is wrong to judge Rousseau in the light of the misinterpretations of later statesmen. Certainly, he is not responsible for their misinterpretations, nor for their acts. Yet the fact that they turned to him is not devoid of significance, and that significance cannot be dismissed with a pat phrase. He is responsible for what he wrote. Some of what he wrote is unclear and ambiguous. Consequently, Rousseau's influence has been equally strong in opposite directions, and he has been interpreted (or misinterpreted) to support liberal democratic systems and institutions as well as their contraries. Obviously, he cannot be given the credit for one and be protected by his apologists from receiving the debt for the other. I do not think that anyone could have read Locke, Jefferson, or Diderot and been inspired to construct a totalitarian system or State from their ideas. In much of what follows we shall be speaking of relationships, then, rather than ascertainable influences. In some cases ideas may have come directly from him; in others they come from the mainstream of which his ideas were a part. We shall go beyond historical influences into the realm of constructive imagination—the realm in which Rousseau dwelt. By a study of certain interesting analogues, our final conclusions will be deepened and strengthened.

The *Social Contract* was little read during Rousseau's lifetime. In contrast with his other writings, it was arid and impersonal, and despite its temporary notoriety was too easily confused with the mass of speculative treatises. There was, to be sure, the first splash, augmented by the fuss over *Emile*. In 1762–63 no less than thirteen French editions were put out, as well as three English, one in German, and one in Russian. But interest in the work quickly faded. Not until the 1780's did the French public begin to read it more widely. In fact, there was only one new edition between 1763 and 1790. The Rousseau cult was literary and personal, and the times were not ready for his political thought. In 1790, however, four editions were published, and his cult fast became a political one. Three more editions appeared in 1791, and a total of twenty between 1789 and 1796.

It has long been argued whether Rousseau was an optimist or a pessimist. In an absolute sense, he was neither. If he had been a complete pessimist, he would not have outlined a utopian social system in several works, or attempted to show the "right road" to Corsica and Poland. Yet he had little or no hope for the advanced (i.e., "corrupt") societies of his day. In a century prompted by the nascent power of science to look forward to a better future for mankind, he looked backward to early Rome and Sparta, and to a rural, patriarchal mode of life. One scholar writes: "Paradoxically, this rebel, whose message will help to give birth to revolutions, is a reactionary out of spite." There is no paradox in this, for a reactionary may certainly be a revolutionary. But Rousseau was, even more, a conservative, fearful of any changes that might upset the prevailing order. Although he predicted revolution in both the *Social Contract* and *Emile,* he dreaded the horrors of such a cataclysm.

Just consider the danger of exciting the enormous masses that compose the French monarchy. Who will be able to halt their movement once it is started or anticipate its ultimate effects? Even if all the advantages of the new plan were indisputable, what sensible men would dare undertake to abolish old customs . . . and to give another form to the State. . .?

But if Rousseau was not himself a revolutionary, he was in revolt; and his work was revolutionary in character. True revolution lies not in violence of action or language, but in the will that rejects the traditional order. When Rousseau censured Montesquieu for concerning himself with what is, instead of with what ought to be, he was being revolutionary, thinking of abolishing the past, which Voltaire had termed a record of crimes and follies; in his mind he was setting up something based on abstract and absolute values— something that had never existed before. He was revolutionary when he wrote in *Emile* that reform of abuses is useless, and that "everything must be remedied at one blow." In the Preface he declared his refusal to write about "possible things," about "some good which can ally itself to the existing evil." He felt strongly that acceptance of reform only makes us a part of what we today call the "Establishment." This attitude was one important reason for Burke's bitter opposition.

There is no doubt that in some important respects Rousseau's thought was opposed to the trend of the Revolution. That matters little, historically; our task is only to examine the various understandings of what his thought was.

During the French Revolution Rousseau was called upon by partisans of both sides, or, more exactly, all sides. Usually they distorted his ideas to favor their own viewpoints. During the first years of the Revolution, the question of his relation to it was actually the subject of a continuing debate. A few examples from the voluminous literature are worthy of mention. One pamphleteer used the *Social Contract* to attack the National Assembly. Rousseau, he reminds his readers, said that the legislature is not sovereign, nor should it concern itself with "particular objects." In 1789 Isnard, the future Girondist, rejected Rousseau's theory that law is only the expression of the general will. Natural law, he maintained, exists apart from the will of the people.

But Aubert de Vitry, in *Jean-Jacques Rousseau à l'Assemblée Nationale,* pretending that Rousseau was an elected deputy, has him defend the representative assembly as the voice of popular sovereignty. The people are "too unenlightened." They must be "enlightened." "The unfortunate people, who are so easily misled, must be protected against the seduction of our enemies." The decrees of the Assembly are irreversible, he declares, and not subject to revision. "No one has the right to oppose them." Anyone who challenges this is "guilty of *lèse-nation* . . . [and is] a puppet of the aristocracy who is trying to weaken the public power by eternal contradictions and the veto of private interests. . . ." There is no such thing as defending the rights of the people against those who speak for the people. The example of the American republic, he insists, significantly, is deadly.

Charles-François Lenormant, author of *Jean-Jacques Rousseau, aristocrate,* approves of Rousseau's bust being placed on the right of the Assembly. In his judgment, it is unworthy of standing on the left, alongside those of Washington and Franklin, the defenders of liberty. The *Social Contract* shows that is where he belongs. "Far from being the author of the revolution of 1789, he would have been its adversary and scourge." Many quotations from Rousseau's political writings are offered to substantiate this view. The writer emphasizes the fact that the Assembly has assumed the popular sovereignty and has not submitted the constitution or the laws for the people's ratification. Again and again, he quotes Rousseau about the "stupid, brutish people" and their need for masters to contain them. Had not Rousseau warned that one can give new laws only to people who do not yet have any, that it is dangerous to disturb existing institutions or to agitate the masses? Had he not warned, in his plan for the Polish government, of "democratic tumult"?

A certain Father Gudin criticized Rousseau's *Social Contract* in 1791. He accused Rousseau of making liberty an impossible, disheartening goal, quoting his lines:

> *Proud and holy liberty, if those poor people . . . knew how your laws are more austere than the harsh yoke of tyrants, their weak souls, the slaves*

> *of the passions they would have to stifle, would fear your liberty a hundred times more than servitude; they would fly from you with fear as a burden ready to crush them.*

He blames Rousseau for praising Moses, who oppressed his people, for lauding Lycurgus because he imposed on the Spartans "an iron yoke such as no people has ever borne," for promoting nationalism with all its hatreds, and for exaggerating the worth of governments of times long past. He himself defends the alienation of sovereignty to an elected assembly, and demands the rights of petition, protest, and freedom of the press, which he finds to be excluded from Rousseau's system.

By the end of 1791 the conservatives had lost the argument, and Rousseau became a myth-figure, the idol of the masses. Many even thought that the articles of the Declaration of the Rights of Man were taken from the *Social Contract*!

His general will became a myth, "the will of the people." His bust had been placed in the Assembly in 1790. Borne on a tide of mass emotion, his body was interred in the newly established Pantheon in 1794. The masses, writes Albert Soboul, were impregnated with a vague Rousseauism in their social aspirations and political tendencies. They did not read him, but his ideas were diffused in the penny press, in popular "literature," and by oral means. His influence was deepest on the radical extremists, including the *sans-culottes* masses, who condemned luxury, demanded approximate equality of fortunes, and claimed a popular sovereignty that could not be delegated. Laws, they declared, must be sanctioned by the people, and representatives must be subject to recall. They also demanded censorship, and longed for a unanimous nation. Marat, Billaud-Varenne, Saint-Just, and Robespierre—authoritarian fanatics devoted to an absolute—were steeped in his thought, and there are frequent reminiscences of it in their speeches.

The relation between Rousseau and the Jacobins, as Albert Soboul has shown in an important article, was close but intricate and varying. Rousseau furnished a large part of their ideology, but he was "politically ineffective" in their time of triumph. The Jacobin rule was in many ways an attempt to realize the total, collectivist State of the *Social Contract,* in which "virtue-patriotism" would rule. It made clear the dangers of the absolute, including absolute sovereignty, and the fallacy of the general-will concept of liberty: an individual or a group always arrogates for itself the sole right to speak in the name of the general will, or of the people, and all dissidents become, by definition, enemies of the people, or of the State. Robespierre was to develop the collective idea "in terms of the State as a collective moral and political body, with absolute power over the individual." He condemned the separation of powers. In his theory of public safety and the repression and terror it involved, he based himself less, according to Soboul, on Rousseau's chapter on dictatorship than on the chapter "On the Right of Life and Death." The individual alienates his rights, the community keeps those it needs. "The social treaty's purpose is the preservation of the contractants," wrote Rousseau. "He who wants the ends, wants the means." Like Rousseau in "Political Economy" and in the two constitutional projects, Robespierre planned to shape a new kind of citizen "by exposing him from childhood to inspirational messages and behavioral models," utilizing every artistic and communication medium, as well as schools, sports, and public festivals. Both Rousseau and Robespierre blamed social inequality on property, and neither sought a logical remedy for it. Reasoning juridically, both were guided by purely political concepts, when an economic and social analysis was needed. Both turned their backs on the nascent capitalistic evolution. They had the same intellectual pride, the same rigid attachment to principles, the same certainty that they alone were right. The Jacobin spirit, like Rousseau's, was puritanical in both the superficial and the more profound senses of that word, and it was the puritanical spirit of the "sea-green Incorruptible" that directed the worst excesses of the French Revolution. Robespierre agreed with Rousseau's statement in "Political Economy" that "to be just, it is necessary to be severe"; and he agreed that from the political viewpoint pity is fatal to the establishment of the "reign of virtue" that both called for.

> To prevent pity from degenerating into weakness, it is necessary to generalize and extend it over the whole human kind [abstract love of man]. Then you give way to it only when it is in accord with justice, because, of all virtues, justice is the one that tends to the common good of men. We must, out of reason and self-love, have pity for our kind [i.e., man], even more than for our neighbor. And pity for the wicked is a very great cruelty toward men.

But even love of mankind, while it produces virtues like charity and indulgence, does not, according to Rousseau, inspire courage, or "that energy which [men] receive from love of country and which inspires them to heroism." (Ms. de Neuchâtel.) In both men, we recognize the archetype of the authoritarian mind.

Robespierre, according to one scholar, "was certainly a faithful disciple of Rousseau." He did not misinterpret his master's ideas, but made the error of applying them "to conditions they did not fit." Nevertheless, Rousseau's thought was subjected to many deviations as each party adapted it to its own purposes and deformed it in the act of applying general theories to real situations. This is an inevitable process of which Marx was to be another example. The question, as one historian, C. Mazauric, has put it, "is to know how, in a concrete historical situation, Rousseauism was able to redispose itself in a much vaster ideological field, and become the spring from which most political and social reform movements of the late eighteenth century and doubtless later times have drunk." Nowhere is this more striking than in the case of the communist conspirator Babeuf, who was executed in 1797 after a famous trial.

Like Robespierre, Babeuf started from a utopian Rousseauism and ended by a commitment to "the tyranny of liberty"—an excellent phrase to describe the commitment of all three men. But whereas Robespierre, a lawyer, had studied Rousseau closely, the peasant Babeuf had, until the Revolution and perhaps after, only vague and secondhand ideas about the man he idealized. Babeuf came to believe that if one has a part in the making of laws he is free. He thought, however, that Rousseau, like himself, wanted an egalitarian, communistic society. He too was convinced that the good society would not be brought about by enlightenment, and for a while he believed that Rousseau's Legislator was the answer—a new Lycurgus. In his mind, the Legislator was also a dictator. The course of events and disillusionment with Danton and Robespierre led him to replace this idea with those of popular insurrection and "the direct democracy preached by Rousseau." The voice of the people would be heard in the committees and sections—the popular assemblies Rousseau had planned, in a revised format. This "direct democracy" really amounted to a popular dictatorship—the means of realizing the general will. Babeuf at first followed the common utopian misinterpretation of Rousseau, according to which equal political rights and control of wealth would by themselves insure that the general will is that of the majority—an interpretation that ignored the real reliance on indoctrination and subtle coercion. But after Robespierre's overthrow on the ninth of Thermidor, Babeuf abandoned this idea, too, and decided that only a select group could be the voice of the people and the general will and that it would have to conspire to seize dictatorial power (the Conspiracy of the Equals). While going beyond Rousseau's system, the conspirators thought they were remaining faithful to his message. In doing this, they also became the precursors of "contemporary socialist [i.e., communist] parties"; for such a dictatorial party would become "the expression and guarantee of the *popular will,* that notion which was elaborated between 1789 and 1795 and which is in sum only the last incarnation of Rousseau's idea of the *general will.*" No longer is unanimity held to be possible; history has shown (writes Mazauric) that the dictatorship of a class and party is the way to realize the spirit of Rousseau.

V RECENT COMPREHENSIVE TREATMENTS OF THE PROBLEM

Henri Peyre

THE INFLUENCE OF EIGHTEENTH-CENTURY IDEAS ON THE FRENCH REVOLUTION

Henri Peyre is one of the outstanding authorities on French literary history in the United States. Although a native of France, he has spent the greater part of his career as a member of the French Department at Yale University. Professor Peyre is known especially for his many excellent publications in the history of French literature during the seventeenth and later centuries. True to the French tradition in the field, he has not limited himself to technical matters of literary criticism but has acquired great breadth of knowledge in the general field of intellectual history. The following article concerning the influence of the Enlightenment on the French Revolution is doubly valuable in that it not only summarizes the various elements of the controversy but states Professor Peyre's own views.

No question is likely to divide students of the past more sharply than that of the action of philosophical ideas and literary works upon political and social events. Our age has been powerfully impressed by the economic interpretation of history proposed by Marxists; but it has also witnessed the important role played by men of letters and men of thought in the Spanish Civil War and in the Resistance movement of World War II. The conscience of many writers is more obsessed today than it has ever been by the temptation—some call it the duty—of "engaged literature." The affinities of many of the leading authors in France and other countries link them with the men of the eighteenth century. Sartre, Camus, Giono, Breton are not unworthy descendants or reincarnations of Voltaire, Diderot, Rousseau.

It may thus be useful to attempt a restatement of an old, and ever present, problem, without any presumptuous claim to renovate its data or its solutions, but with an honest attempt to observe a few conditions which are obvious but all too seldom met. A summation of such an immense and thorny question should be clear, while respecting the complex nature of reality. It should be provocative, in the

From Henri Peyre, "The Influence of Eighteenth-Century Ideas on the French Revolution," *Journal of the History of Ideas,* Vol. X (1949). Reprinted by permission of the *Journal* and the author. Footnotes omitted.

sense that it should suggest that much remains to be said on these matters by young scholars determined to launch upon the study of ideas in relation to the Revolution. Above all, it should be impartial if that is humanly possible, concerning questions on which it is difficult not to take sides, and it should attempt to retain in these questions the life with which they are instinct, without on the other hand sacrificing objectivity or solidity.

The problem of the effect of the Philosophy of Enlightenment on the French Revolution is one of the most important problems that confront the pure historian as well as the historian of thought and of literature. It is without doubt the most complex of the thousand aspects involved in the study of the Revolution, that is to say the origins of the modern world. Together with investigation of the origins of Christianity and the end of the ancient world, this study concerns one of the two most important upheavals that the philosophically-minded historian can conceive: Taine and Renan, as well as Michelet and Tocqueville, the four most important French historians of the past century, had quite rightly realized its magnitude.. This problem is inevitable for every teacher of literature who lectures on Voltaire and Rousseau to his students, for every historian of the years 1789–1799 in France, and likewise for every historian of these same years and of the beginning of the nineteenth century in Germany, England, the United States and Latin America. It presents itself to every voter who reflects even a little about the things in his country's past that he would like to maintain and those that he desires to reform.

But because it presents itself so insistently to everyone, this problem has often been met with solutions that are crude or at the very least lacking in necessary overtones; because it closely parallels our present-day preoccupations, it has aroused the partisan spirit; because it concerns not only facts but ideas it has favored excessively dogmatic generalizations on the one hand and on the other, the voluntary blind timidity of chroniclers who have chosen to see in the events of the Revolution nothing but a series of improvisations and haphazard movements.

There is for one thing a long and devious current of ideas which first springing forth as a swift and turgid torrent in the sixteenth century, becoming a more or less tenuous water-course in the great period of the reign of Louis XIV, and finally like a river encircling the most obdurate islets of resistance within its multiple arms, seems to have engulfed the eighteenth century in the years 1750–1765. More and more clearly, those who set forth and develop these ideas take it upon themselves to influence the existing facts, to change man by education, to free him from outmoded superstitions, to increase his political liberty and his well-being. In no way do they dream of a general cataclysm and several of them are not insensitive to the re- fined amenity of the life that surrounds them or to the exquisite blend of intellectual boldness and voluptuous refinement that characterizes their era.

Suddenly, this pleasant eighteenth-century security, *Table d'un long festin qu'un échafaud termine*, as Hugo's beautiful image calls it, crumbles. The Revolution breaks out, and within a few years, rushes through peaceful reforms, produces a profusion of constitu- tions, sweeps aside the old regime, devours men, and causes heads to fall. This great movement is certainly confused, turbulent and irra- tional like everything that men accomplish by collective action. How- ever, lawyers, officers, priests, and journalists play a part in it that is often important. These men had grown up in an intellectual climate that had been established by Montesquieu, Voltaire, Rousseau, Raynal and Mably. May we accurately reach a conclusion of "Post hoc, ergo propter hoc"?

It would not have been so difficult to answer such a question if partisan quarrels had not needlessly clouded the issue. Frenchmen are Incapable of viewing their nation's past dispassionately or ac- cepting it as a whole. For a hundred and fifty years they have not ceased to be of different minds on their Revolution which is doubt- less a proof that it is still a live question among them, while in other countries the revolution of 1688 or the revolution of 1776 is calmly in- vested with the veneration accorded to a buried past. It is a curious fact that the great majority of their political writers from Joseph de Maistre, Louis de Bonald, and Auguste Comte himself, to Le Play, Tocqueville, Taine, at times Renan, Barrès, Bourget, Maurras and many others, has pronounced itself hostile to the "great principles of '89" or at least to that which was drawn from these principles. Three fundamental assertions are the basis of most of the anti-revolutionary arguments. A) The Revolution was harmful and anti-French; it could only be attributed to foreign influences that perverted the French genius of moderation, restrained devotion, and obedience to the hereditary monarch. It was caused by foreign influences that contaminated eighteenth-century thought: Locke, the English deists, the Protestants in general, the Swiss Rousseau, etc. . . . B) These corrupting ideas were introduced among the French people who had been sound and upright until then, by clubs called "Sociétés de Pensée" and by secret groups of conspiring intellectuals, the Freemasons for example and the "Philosophes" themselves, who formed an authentic subversive faction. (Augustin Cochin, *Les Sociétés de Pensée,* Plon, 1921.) C) The Revolutionary spirit is the logical outcome of the classical spirit strengthened by the scientific spirit. This spirit delights in abstraction, generalizes profusely, and considers man as a creature apart from his environment, isolated from his past; it lacks the subtle empiricism which characterizes the English reformists; it is ignorant of everything touching reality. Accordingly it sets out to make laws for universal man, without regard for France's age-old traditions or the local conditions of these provinces. This contention advanced with talent and a semblance of thorough documentation by Taine has beguiled a great number of excellent minds because of its specious clarity.

These contentions have not stood the test of serious scrutiny by literary historians trained in more rigid methods since the dawn of the twentieth century. The penetration with which Gustave Lanson has laid bare many of our prejudices concerning the eighteenth century forms one of his best-established claims upon our gratitude. Numerous investigators, Frenchmen and Americans especially, have since followed upon the path that he had pointed out. Lanson's ideas in their turn have become accepted opinion and doubtless it will be necessary to modify and complete them in the future by adopting new points of view. It is nonetheless true that it is thanks to him and to Daniel Mornet after him that we can state today that the three assertions summed up earlier are contradicted by the facts. The French revolution is truly of French origin. If certain foreigners, in particular Locke, whose name may be found at almost all the century's crossroads of ideas, did exert a real influence in France, this influence was assimilated and naturalized there. It had moreover implanted itself in a group of ideas going back to Bayle, Saint-Evremond, Le Vayer, Naudé and Montaigne, which were quite as indigenous and "French" as the absolutism of Bossuet. The philosophical Clubs and similar groups that made themselves felt in France around 1750 and played an active part after 1789 are not all revolutionary—far from it! Furthermore, the part that they played in preparing the Revolution is nowhere clearly ascertained. The role of a gigantic conspiracy attributed by some to Freemasonry is a myth.

Finally and above all, nothing justifies the assertion made with assurance by Taine that the writers of the eighteenth century were men of reason alone with no experience of the realities of life. In their time there was some use of empty rhetoric, as there is in every time; the Revolutionaries for their part will cherish a type of eloquence reminiscent of the ancients, and be occasionally intoxicated with words; they will also have an ambition to proclaim universal truths and formulate principles for all men. It is not certain that this ambition is not one of the finest qualities of the French Revolution. But it would be a mistake to forget that the eighteenth century is a great century in science, as much or more so in experimental science as in deductive and abstract disciplines. The works of M. Mornet have proved that eighteenth-century thinkers were on the contrary suspicious of scholastic generalizations and of systems in general: they made observations and conducted experiments. They introduced into education the taste for very detailed empiricism and for actual practice in the arts and trades. They praised techniques and described them with care. They traveled like Montesquieu in order to see at close hand constitutions and the way people lived by them. They cultivated the soil, in the case of the physiocrats; lived on their lands, as did Helvétius; or administered provinces, like Turgot. The most thoroughgoing Revolutionaries had not, like Marx or Lenin, spent years in reading-rooms; they were petty lawyers in contact with the people, like Robespierre at Arras, veterinaries like Marat; in short, provincial men who knew the lives of the peasant, the artisan and the humble country priest of France. Taine's abstraction existed chiefly in his mind, and perhaps in that of Descartes and in a few works of Rousseau. But the Revolution was hardly Cartesian and never put into practice as a complete doctrine the ideas of the *Contrat Social,* which are moreover as contradictory as they are logical.

So let us differ with those who claim a priori that the Revolution sprang from the teachings of the "Philosophes," only in order to justify their condemnation of both the Revolution and the teaching.

But in opposition to this group, the admirers of the "Philosophes" and even more the admirers of Rousseau, who was not exactly one of the "Philosophes," have taken up the cudgels in an attempt to deny the responsibility or even the guilt of the eighteenth-century political writers in the upheaval that ensued. Particularly notable among these efforts is Edme Champion's abstruse but well-informed book: *Rousseau et la Révolution française* (Colin, 1909). Bringing the concept of retroactive responsibility into these matters is a questionable method. "My God!" Karl Marx is said to have exclaimed on one of the rare occasions when he seems to have called upon Heaven, "preserve me from the Marxists!" Rousseau has accused himself of enough sins without our taxing his memory with the errors of his followers. Without inquiring whether the Revolution was good or bad, which would be entirely too naïve in this day, may we not be able to show how and in what way it absorbed, reflected or brought to fruition the ideas of thinkers who had prepared it without wishing for it?

Professional historians generally tend to limit the part played by ideas in world events: the best of them devote, apparently for the sake of form, one or two chapters to the literature, painting and music of the periods studied by their manuals. But the history of civilization and culture is still very clumsily related to general history. Historians prefer to emphasize the purely historical causes of the Revolution: financial disorder, ministerial blunders, or the hostility of parlements that had been alienated by encroachments upon their prerogatives, etc. Perhaps in doing so they are choosing the easiest way. Their history does grasp the events, the things that change, that is, the things that would be presented in today's newspapers as facts or news: a tax-measure, a famine, the dismissal of a minister, a change in the price of bread, or a treaty. But it often fails to apprehend the slow subterranean movements which minds inclined to be too matter-of-fact find intangible, until they one day make their appearance as acts that make news or usher in a historical era. Now there are cases in which they never appear as acts; and orthodox history gives scant consideration to abortive movements or history's side-roads into which the past has ventured briefly only to turn back.

The history of ideas has the advantage of being able to give leisurely consideration to elements of history that changed only slowly and did not necessarily express themselves in events which demand attention by virtue of their suddenness. It would gladly declare that ideas rule the world. This would doubtless be an over-optimistic creed, if one did not add immediately that these ideas often turn into those truths wrapped in the gilt paper of falsehood that our contemporaries call in France "mystiques," or that they crystallize into a few fetish-words which imprison or falsify them. The history of the idea of progress has been sketched, although insufficiently in our opinion, by J. Delvaille and the English writer J. M. Bury. History itself would owe much to the man who would attempt to write the story of the idea of evolution, or the idea of revolution, the idea of comfort, or the idea of efficiency and the myth of success in the United States, among many others. On occasion he would have to go beyond the texts or interpret them, but this should not be forbidden provided that it is done with intellectual honesty. One must also remember the fact that the history of ideas is not simply the exposition of theoretical views expressed in philosophical writings, but at the same time the history of the deformations undergone by these ideas when other men adopt them, and also the history of the half-conscious beliefs into which ideas first clearly conceived by the few promptly transform themselves. In his lectures published in Buenos Aires in 1940 under the title *Ideas y creencias* the Spanish philosopher Ortega y Gasset has rightly claimed for these half-formulated "beliefs" a position in historical works on a par with that of ideas.

The difficulties presented by such a history of ideas when they become beliefs, articles of faith, or emotional drives and impel men to action are enormous: they should, by this very fact, challenge research-men. Up to now, sociology has failed to make over the study of literature to any considerable degree because histories of the prevailing taste and the environment in which a writer lived and of the social and economic conditions in which he was placed while conceiving his work have little bearing on the creation and even the content of the original work. But a knowledge of the public that greeted a literary work or of the work's subsequent career might on the contrary prove extremely fruitful. Such knowledge requires painstaking inquiry into the work's success, based on a great number of facts; it also demands a qualitative interpretation of history and statistics and the occasional intervention of that much-feared "queen of the world" called imagination. For the most read book is not the one that exerts the greatest influence. A hundred thousand passive or half-attentive readers who bought and even leafed through the *Encyclopédie,* for example, count for less than five hundred passionate admirers of the *Contrat Social* if among the latter may be counted Robespierre, Saint-Just or Babeuf. A school-master or a lecturer heard with interest may pass on Marx or Nietzsche to generations of barely literate people who will never guess the source of a thought that has modified their whole lives. It is not even necessary to have understood a book or even to have read it through in order to be profoundly influenced by it. An isolated phrase quoted in some article or a page reproduced at some time in an anthology, may have done more to spread some of the opinions of Montesquieu, Proudhon, or Gobineau than thirty re-editions of their writings bought by private libraries and commented upon by ten provincial academies.

In 1933 Daniel Mornet published on the subject sketched here his work entitled *Les Origines intellectuelles de la Révolution française* (Colin), which is a study of the spread of ideas justly termed a model of intellectual probity and discretion. Henceforth no one can consider this historical and philosophical problem without owing much to this solid book. The author has avoided the error of so many other writers who make the Revolution inexplicable by drawing a rough contrast between 1789 and 1670 or even 1715. He has followed the slow progress of the spread of new ideas from 1715 to 1747, then from 1748 to 1770, the date when the philosophic spirit had won the day. He has made very searching inquiries into the degree of penetration of the reformist spirit among the more or less learned societies and academies, in the letters of private individuals, in provincial libraries and even in educational curricula. His conclusions are new in many respects because of the exact information they offer and because they show those who are misled by the perspective of a later day into the error of limiting the group of "Philosophes" to five or six names, that writers half-unknown to us (Toussaint, Delisle de Sales, Morellet, Mably) were among those most widely read in the eighteenth century. With fitting reserve they tend to show that the thought of the century, by itself, would never have caused the Revolution if there had not been misery among the people as well; and that misery which was not a new thing at the time would not have brought about the Revolution if it had not had the support of opinion that had long been discontented and desirous of reform. It is clear that the Revolution had various causes including historical causes, meaning economic, political and financial causes as well as intellectual ones. However, it would seem that Mornet has limited the role of the latter causes to an excessive degree and further work still needs to be done after his admirable effort.

The most obvious justification for further research lies in the fact that his investigation leaves off at 1787 because of the very purpose of his work. Now if a revolution was ready to break out at the time of the preparation of the *Cahiers de doléances* for the Estates General it was not the Revolution that actually developed. Neither the days of June 20th and August 10th 1792, nor the death of Louis XVI nor the Terror, nor the constructive work of the Convention was contained in germ in the convocation of the Estates General. In fact we know very little about the influence of Montesquieu, Voltaire and Rousseau himself on the different phases of the Revolution or the way in which they influenced certain actors in the great drama.

The special quality of the French Revolution, compared with other revolutionary movements in France or other countries, obviously lies in the titanic proportions of this upheaval but also in an ardent passion for thought, for embodying ideas in deeds, and for proposing universal laws. This accounts for the unparalleled world-wide influence of the work of destruction and construction which was accomplished between 1789 and 1795. An abstract passion for justice and liberty, the latter being sometimes conceived in strange fashion, inspired the men who made the Revolution and those who prepared it. The original tone that characterizes the Revolution and the verve that enlivens it, which are fundamental things although they elude the grasp of facts and figures, are due in part to the movement of thought and sensibility which goes from Montesquieu to Rousseau and from Bayle to the abbé Raynal.

If there is really one almost undisputed conclusion on the origins of the Revolution reached by historical studies coming from radically opposite factions, it is that pure historical materialism does not explain the Revolution. Certainly riots due to hunger were numerous in the eighteenth century and Mornet draws up the list of them; there was discontent and agitation among the masses. But such had also been the case under Louis XIV, such was the case under Louis-Philippe and deep discontent existed in France in 1920 and 1927 and 1934 without ending in revolution. No great event in history has been due to causes chiefly economic in nature and certainly not the

French Revolution. France was not happy in 1788, but she was happier than the other countries of Europe and enjoyed veritable economic prosperity. Her population had increased from 19 to 27 millions since the beginning of the century and was the most numerous in Europe. French roads and bridges were a source of admiration to foreigners. Her industries such as ship-fitting at Bordeaux, the silk-industry at Lyons and the textile-industry at Rouen, Sedan and Amiens were active while Dietrich's blast-furnaces and the Creusot were beginning to develop modern techniques in metallurgy. The peasants were little by little coming to be owners of the land. Foreign trade reached the sum of 1,153 million francs in 1787, a figure not to be attained again until 1825. The traffic in colonial spices and Santo Domingo sugar was a source of wealth. Banks were being founded and France owned half the specie existing in Europe. So misery in France was no more than relative. But truly wretched people such as the Egyptian fellah, the pariah of India or even the Balkan or Polish peasant or Bolivian miners for example rarely bring about revolutions. In order to revolt against one's lot, one must be aware of his wretched condition, which presupposes a certain intellectual and cultural level; one must have a clear conception of certain reforms that one would like to adopt; in short, one must be convinced (and it was on this point that the books of the eighteenth century produced their effect) that things are not going well, that they might be better and that they will be better if the measures proposed by the reformist thinkers are put into practice.

Eighteenth-century philosophy taught the Frenchman to find his condition wretched, or in any case, unjust and illogical and made him disinclined to the patient resignation to his troubles that had long characterized his ancestors. It had never called for a revolution nor desired a change of regime; it had never been republican and Camille Desmoulins was not wrong in stating: "In all France there were not ten of us who were republicans before 1789." Furthermore he himself was not one of those ten. But only an over-simplified conception of influence would indulge in the notion that political upheaval completely embodies in reality the theoretical design drawn up by some thinker. Even the Russian revolution imbued as it was with Marxian dialectic did not make a coherent application of Marxism or quickly found it inapplicable when tried. The reforms of limited scope advocated by *L'Esprit des Lois, L'Homme aux quarante écus,*

L'Encyclopédie and the more moderate writings of Rousseau struck none the less deeply at the foundations of the ancien régime, for they accustomed the Frenchman of the Third Estate to declaring privileges unjust, to finding the crying differences between the provinces illogical and finding famines outrageous. The propaganda of the "Philosophes" perhaps more than any other factor accounted for the fulfillment of the preliminary condition of the French Revolution, namely, discontent with the existing state of things.

In short, without enlarging upon what is already rather well known we may say that eighteenth-century writers prepared the way for the Revolution, without wishing for it, because:

a) They weakened the traditional religion, winning over to their side a great number of clerics, and taught disrespect for an institution which had been the ally of the monarchy for hundreds of years. At the same time they had increased the impatience of the non-privileged groups by uprooting from many minds the faith in a future life which had formerly made bearable the sojourn in this vale of tears that constituted life for many people of low estate. They wished to enjoy real advantages here on earth and without delay. The concept of well-being and then that of comfort slowly penetrated among them.

b) They taught a secular code of ethics, divorced from religious belief and independent of dogma, and made the ideal of conduct consist of observation of this system of ethics, which was presented as varying in accordance with climate and environment. Furthermore they gave first importance in this ethical code to the love of humanity, altruism and service due society or our fellowmen. The ideas of humanity, already present in the teaching of Christ, in Seneca and Montaigne but often dormant, suddenly exert fresh influence over people's minds.

c) They developed the critical spirit and the spirit of analysis and taught many men not to believe, or to suspend judgment rather than accept routine traditions. In D'Argenson, Chamfort, Morelly, Diderot, Voltaire of course, D'Holbach, Condillac and many others, and even in Laclos and Sade, we will find the effort to think courageously without regard for convention or tradition, that will henceforth characterize the French intellectual attitude. From this time on, inequality with respect to taxation, the tithe paid to the Church, and banishment or persecution for subversive opinions will shock profoundly the sense of logic and critical spirit of the readers of the "philosophes."

d) Lastly, these very thinkers who have often been depicted as builders of Utopias are the creators of history or the historical sense, or almost so. Montesquieu studiously examined the origins of law and constitutions and saw men "conditioned" by soil and climate in contrast with the absolute rationalists who were foreign jurists and not Frenchmen. Boulainvilliers and many others of lesser fame studied France's past. Voltaire's masterpiece is probably his work on general history. The result of this curiosity about history was two-fold: it encouraged faith in progress and convinced numbers of Frenchmen that it was their task to fulfill humanity's law, to endeavor to increase the sum of liberty, relative equality, "enlightenment" and happiness in the world; it also proved to many men of the law who examined old documents and the titles of nobility and property, that the privileges of nobility were based on a flimsy foundation. The respect that these bourgeois or sons of the people might have felt for the aristocrats was accordingly diminished, at the very moment when the bourgeois saw the nobles not only accept with admiration but take under their protection destructive writings produced by the pens of commoners: sons of tailors (Marmontel), vine-growers (Restif), cutlers (Diderot) and watch-makers (Rousseau). And the history of the origins of royal sovereignty itself seemed to them scarcely more edifying than that of the feudal privileges.

As for the means of dissemination of those ideas or new beliefs that the philosophes were spreading between the years 1715 and 1770 or 1789, it will suffice to enumerate them rapidly, for numerous studies have examined them: they were the salons, although very few of the future revolutionaries frequented society gatherings; the clubs, that more and more called for tolerance, preached deism, demanded the abolition of slavery (*Société des Amis des Noirs*) and dreamed of imitating the American Revolution (*Club Américain*); books or tracts which made their appearance as works of small format, easily carried or hidden, lively and sharp in style and prone to surprise and arouse the reader; periodicals; the theatre especially after the coming of the "drame bourgeois" and the "comédie larmoyante," and then with Beaumarchais; and the education given in the secondary schools. Mornet's book sums up the essential material on the subject that can be found in documents. The other means of spreading new ideas, such as conversation, which is doubtless the most effective means man has always used to borrow and pass on new views, elude documentary research.

It is among the actors in the great revolutionary drama that investigations of broader scope might show us which of the ideas of the eighteenth century exerted influence and how and why they did so. Sieyès, among others, has been the subject of an exhaustive intellectual biography which has established with precision what the young abbé coming to Paris from Fréjus to devise constitutions owed to Descartes, Locke, and Voltaire in particular (for the negative side of his ideas), to Rousseau (for his impassioned logic) and to Mably. (Paul Bastid, *Sieyès et sa pensée,* Hachette, 1939). Another recent book, by Gérard Walter, is a study of Babeuf (Payot, 1937). It would be instructive to know how the minds of many of the revolutionaries were developed and by what books and meditations they were influenced; such men range from Mirabeau and Danton to Marat, from Rabaut de Saint-Etienne to Hérault de Séchelles and from Desmoulins or Brissot to generals of the Convention who may have read Raynal and Rousseau with passionate interest, as Bonaparte did later. Only when many monographs have been written devoting at least as much if not more attention to the history of ideas and the psychology of the protagonists in the Revolution than to the facts of their lives of action, will we be able to make sure generalizations about the influence of Montesquieu or Rousseau on the France of '89 or '93.

Montesquieu and Rousseau are certainly the two great names worthy of consideration in some detail. The presiding judge of the High Court of Bordeaux obviously did not want the Revolution; had he lived to see it, he would not have approved of its reorganization of the judiciary, nor its audacity in reform, nor the Declaration of the Rights of Man, nor even the interpretation of certain principles he himself had enunciated. Still he is one of the spiritual fathers of the first two revolutionary assemblies. Like so many other men who have made history, he influenced the fateful years of 1789–1792 by what he did say almost involuntarily, by the thoughts other men read in his sentences and by the tone even more than by the content of his writings. His great work breathes a veritable hatred of despotism founded on fear; it shows no moral respect for monarchy, and so helped to alienate the most reasonable minds from it. The great principle of the separation of powers presumes the right to seize from the king the united powers that he believed he held as a whole by divine right. Finally, Montesquieu, however elevated his position as a citizen or as a magistrate may have been, uttered words which will assume a mystic authority in later times on the subject of the people's inherent good qualities and its ability to select its leaders: "The common people are admirable in choosing those to whom they must delegate some part of their authority," (II,ii) or "When the common people once have sound principles, they adhere to them longer than those we are wont to call respectable people. Rarely does corruption have its beginning among the people." (V,ii)

Finally, in his admirable eleventh book, Montesquieu had defined liberty in terms that were to remain etched in people's memories: this liberty required stable laws, which alone could establish and protect it. These laws were also to correct economic inequality. Certainly its historical examples adduced in great profusion, highly technical juridical considerations, certain generalizations that had been too cleverly made symmetrical and its lack of order made this voluminous treatise hard to read. But Montesquieu's influence was not one of those that can be gauged by the number of readers: it expressed itself in action thanks to a few thoughtful minds who found in it a sufficiently coherent overall plan capable of replacing the old order which obviously was crumbling. Montesquieu's influence inspired a more important group of revolutionaries who were familiar with only a few chapters of his work, but these chapters were filled with the love of freedom and the great feeling for humanity that condemned slavery and the iniquitous exploitation of some men by others.

Montesquieu's influence on the French Revolution began to decline at the time when Rousseau's was coming to the fore. Many studies have been devoted to the subject of Rousseau and the French Revolution; and the subject deserves still further study, for perhaps no more notable case of the effect of thought on life exists in the whole history of ideas and of dynamic ideas in particular. But this broad subject has too often been narrowed down by the most well-meaning historians. So many dogmatic and partisan statements had portrayed Rousseau as the great malefactor who was guilty of the excesses committed by the Terrorists and as the father of collectivism that, as a reaction, the best-disposed scholars set about proving by facts and texts that the author of the *Contrat Social* was guiltless of so many misdeeds. As a result they have belittled his influence. But there is some narrowness and naiveté in these scholarly arguments.

According to some, everything that Rousseau wrote already existed before his coming in the works of a number of writers and thinkers both at home and abroad and Jean-Jacques brought forth very little that was new. That is quite possible, and scholars have been able to make fruitful inquiries into the sources of the *Discours sur l'Inégalité* and the *Contrat.* But the fact remains that whatever Rousseau borrowed from others he made his own; he rethought it and above all felt it with a new intensity and set it off to advantage by his own passion and his own talent. What he owes to Plato or Locke suddenly "shook" the men of 1792 only because Rousseau had charged it with a new electric current.

Furthermore Rousseau is rife with contradictions and the most ingenious men of learning (Lanson, Höffding, Schinz and E. H. Wright) have not yet succeeded in convincing us of the unity of his thought. For Corsica and Poland he proposes finely adapted and moderate constitutions that do not seem to have sprung from the same brain as the *Contrat Social.* He writes a very conservative article on *l'Economie politique* for the fifth volume of the *Encyclopédie* while in his second *Discours* he had propounded anarchical theses burning with revolutionary ardor. "To expect one to be always consistent is beyond human possibility, I fear!" he himself had admitted in the second preface of the *Nouvelle Héloïse.* We will not go so far as to pay homage to Rousseau for his contradictions and may choose to reserve our unalloyed admiration for other systems of thought more dispassionate and logical than his. But an author's influence does not have much to do with the rigor and coherence of his philosophical system. In fact, it would not be hard to show that the thinkers who have contributed the most toward changing the face of the world exerted influence because of their contradictions, since very different periods and highly diverse individuals drew from them various messages of equal validity. Let us add with no ironic intention that because of this the ingenuity of the learned will never tire of seeking the impossible golden key to these disconcerting enigmas and that the hunger for systems, among those lacking the necessary imagination to construct new ones, will always exert itself to bring about a happy synthesis of the successive assertions of a Plato, a Montaigne, a Locke, Rousseau, Comte or Nietzsche.

After all, as the historians tell us quite correctly, the *Contrat Social* is only a part of Rousseau's political thought and not the most important part in the eyes of his contemporaries; the author himself attributed only a rather limited importance to this logical Utopian book. Rousseau never seriously contemplated a revolution in France; he did not think that a republic was viable, or perhaps even desirable for France. One might even make the assertion supported by texts that Jean-Jacques, that *bête noire* of the anti-revolutionaries from Burke to Maurras, Lasserre and Seillière, was a timid conservative. It is quite true (M. Mornet has proved this once again) that the influence of the *Contrat Social* was very weak between the years 1762 and 1789; the book caused so little disturbance that Rousseau was not even molested; and it is probable that Rousseau would have been frightened by certain inferences that were later drawn from his ideas. What he wrote in 1765 in no way justifies an assertion on our part that he would still have written the same thing in 1793 and so it is quite as conceivable that Rousseau might have violently changed his point of view and espoused the cause of the revolutionaries, had he lived long enough to receive their acclaim. And above all, without having consciously wanted the Revolution, Rousseau did a great deal, if not to cause it, at least to give it direction when it had broken out. The success of Rousseau's works and the reception accorded them in his lifetime have been investigated in sufficient detail. From now on groups of research men might well give their attention to the enormous influence Rousseau exerted on the men of the Convention and on those of the Empire or the Restoration or on the Romantics. Granted that Rousseau was neither a republican nor a revolutionary, he was in revolt and that is no less important. A. Aulard who was not inclined to over-estimate the influence of the intellectuals on the French Revolution nevertheless accurately described the paradoxical result of any fairly broad study of this subject: "All these men in revolt want to keep the monarchy and all of them blindly deal it mortal blows. The French, monarchists to a man, take on republicanism without their knowledge."

Not one of the men of the Revolution adopted Rousseau's philosophical system outright in order to put it into practice; that is only too plain. Not one of them understood Rousseau's thought in its subtleties, its contradictions and its alterations as the scholar of the present-day can understand it with the aid of much posthumous documentation: this is scarcely less obvious. Whatever chagrin it may cause minds devoted to strict methods, the unparalleled effect produced on the imagination of posterity by Montaigne, Rousseau or Nietzsche can be credited to quotations drawn from their contexts and probably perverted from their original sense. This influence is not so much an influence of ideas as it is an influence of *idées-forces,* to use Fouillée's expression, and exerts its power more by setting men's sensibilities aflame than by convincing their minds.

"Man is born free, and everywhere he is in chains." This peremptory formula from the first chapter of the *Contrat Social,* in conjunction with a few others which declared the sovereignty of the people inalienable and affirmed the right to revolt in the event of the usurpation of powers by the government, contributed immeasurably toward crystallizing in the general mind from 1789 on the resolve to make the king subject to the only true rights which were inherent in the people. On October 5th, 1789 Robespierre and Barrère contended that the sovereign could not oppose the constituent power which was superior to him. The passion for equality which wildly inspires the Revolutionaries and the modern world after them owes no less to Rousseau's fundamental idea that law should rectify natural inequality (which he was not foolish enough to overlook) by means of civic equality. The XIth chapter of the second book of the *Contrat Social* stated in striking terms: "For the very reason that the force of things always tends to destroy equality, the force of legislation must always tend to maintain it." The third book of the same work castigated the vices to which kings are prone, for if they are not narrow or evil on attaining the throne—"the throne will make them so." That does not make Rousseau a partisan of republicanism or a democrat; but had it not been for such aphorisms, Saint-Just never would have proclaimed in his fine *Discours concernant le jugement de Louis XVI* of November 13th, 1792: "Royalty is an eternal crime against which every man has the right to rise up and take arms . . . One can not reign in innocence."

The *Discours sur l'Inégalité* contained pages of impassioned rhetoric that were even more effective. The English writer C. E. Vaughan, who is a scrupulous commentator on the political writings of Rousseau, did not hesitate to state, after years of reflection of this subject: "Wherever, during the last century and a half, man has revolted against injustice and oppression, there we may be sure that the leaven of the second *Discours* has been working." (*Op. cit.,* i, 5) Doubtless Rousseau had never dreamed of the application of his declamations against property: but he had set forth the idea that inheritances ought to be whittled down by fiscal measures and that those who owned no lands ought to receive some, without necessarily advocating collectivism. He had also uttered against wealth words whose echoes will ring down the centuries: "It is the estate of the wealthy that steals from mine the bread of my children. . . . A bond-holder whom the State pays for doing nothing is scarcely different in my eyes from a highwayman who lives at the expense of the passers-by . . . , every idle citizen is a rogue."

The precautions with which Jean-Jacques had surrounded some of his bold affirmations quickly disappeared in the heat of action. The chapter called "Du Peuple," in the *Contrat Social* (ii, 8), was most cautious: but its author had nevertheless hinted in it that sometimes, in the life of peoples, "the State, set aflame by civil wars, is so to speak reborn from its ashes, and regains the vigor of youth in leaving the arms of death." People retained phrases from the *Emile* too—the prophetic phrases in which the educator had proclaimed to the people of his time that they were approaching the era of revolutions when men would be able to destroy what men had built. These few phrases, gaining added violence in tone from the fact that they were detached from contexts that often contradicted them, seemed charged with new meaning when the great upheaval had broken out. Such was also the case of the mystic system of happiness taught by the Genevan "philosophe's" entire work. Man is born good; he is made to be happy; he may become so if he reforms himself and if his governments are reformed. We know how the echo of these doctrines will resound in the noble formulas of Saint-Just, who was perhaps the revolutionary most deeply steeped in Rousseau's thought.

The aspect of Rousseau that Albert Schinz called "the Roman Rousseau" exerted no less influence on that other myth which prevailed or raged among the men of the Revolution (and among the women, too, as in the case of Madame Rolland), the myth of the ancients and their passion for liberty and virtue. "The world has been empty since the day of the Romans," cried Saint-Just; and he stated to the Convention of February 24th, 1793: "The Republic is not a Senate, it is virtue." The whole of Saint-Just's remarkable youthful work entitled: *Esprit de la Révolution et de la Constitution de la France* is imbued with Rousseauist themes and ends on this cry of regret: "France has only now conferred a statue upon J.-J. Rousseau. Ah! Why is that great man dead?"

Robespierre, whom Michelet maliciously called a "weak and pale bastard of Rousseau" because of his cult of the Supreme Being, was indebted to Rousseau to no lesser degree than Saint-Just, although he does not show the mark of the born writer that stamps the formulas of the terrorist guillotined at the age of twenty-seven. It was by assiduous reading of Rousseau that he formed his style: and his style served him as a powerful weapon. It seems that the young student from Arras met Rousseau in 1778, the year of his death, and never forgot it. "I saw thee in thy last days, and this memory is a source of proud joy for me," he declares later in his *Mémoires,* placed under the aegis of Rousseau, and promised to "remain constantly faithful to the inspiration that I have drawn from thy writings." Dozens of sentences which reiterate formulas from the *Contrat Social* might be extracted from his speeches. It was Rousseau who had helped to turn Robespierre away from Catholicism, and of course he was the man from whom Robespierre borrowed his cult of the Supreme Being; his *Observations sur le projet d'Instruction publique* presented to the Convention in 1793 are based on the Rousseauist faith: "If nature created man good, it is back to nature that we must bring him." His speech made at the Jacobin Club on January 2nd, 1792 against the war at that time desired by the Girondins rendered homage to Rousseau in impassioned terms: "No one has given us a more exact idea of the common people than Rousseau because no one loved them more." The secret of the enormous influence exerted by Rousseau lay less in the substance of his thought than in the burning tone of a man who had lived his ideas and had suffered (or thought he had) because he had sprung from the people and had known poverty. "According to the principles of your committee," declared Robespierre to the Constituent Assembly on August 11th, 1791, "we ought to blush at having erected a statue to J.-J. Rousseau, because he did not pay the property tax." The history of ideas and their influence on persons and things is full of elements that defy all possibility of quantitative or statistical measurement. How can one estimate all that the men of the Revolution owed Rousseau in the way of fervor, mystic hope, logic that was impassioned and even fierce on occasion and—what is not less important, even for history, as Danton, Saint-Just and Robespierre were aware—the imperious and incisive style that made their formulas resound in twenty countries and across one hundred and fifty years? "One does not make revolutions by halves" or "the French people are voting for liberty for the world"—these aphorisms or decrees of Saint-Just, like certain phrases of Mirabeau, or a multitude of orators of lesser stature, and of Bonaparte himself, would not have been uttered, and would not have had the resonance that has kept them alive, if these men had not been imbued with the spirit and the style of the Citizen of Geneva.

The history of the cult of Rousseau during the French Revolution is easier to trace than that of his deep influence on the revolutionaries. The former has been studied in part, and the manifestations of this idolatry of Rousseau are often amusing. The setting-up of the bust of Jean-Jacques in the Constituent Assembly on June 23, 1790, the consecration of a street of Paris named after him in the same year, the repeated edition of the *Contrat Social* (4 editions in 1790, 3 in 1791, etc.), the constitutional articles put under his aegis, the decree ordering that Rousseau's ashes be brought to the Pantheon in 1794 and the pious emotion of the crowd, and lastly, the invocation to "his generous soul" by the Incorruptible One in his speech of May 7th, 1794 on the religion of the Revolution and the pompous application of his declamations on the Supreme Being; all these things have been mentioned more than once and recently, too. But the way in which Rousseau's influence profoundly modified the men and women of the revolutionary and imperial era, and then the romantics great and small, and the continuators of the Revolution, in and out of France, in the nineteenth and twentieth centuries: these are the questions that intellectual history seems to have been reluctant to investigate.

Its timidity is regrettable and our knowledge of the past suffers twice over because of it: first, because history that devotes itself too exclusively to what we call material facts such as a military victory, the fall of a ministry or the opening-up of a railroad track, seriously falsifies our perspective of what took place. The development of the Napoleonic legend, the quietly working influence of Rousseau or

Voltaire, the growth of anticlericalism and the elaboration of socialist myths are phenomena which are partly literary or sentimental in nature, but are second to no other order of phenomena in importance and in the effects they had on the course of human affairs. Our knowledge of the past suffers additionally because historians, by turning aside from this history of ideas and sentiments with their vigorous influence on the lives of men, abandon these research subjects to men less trained than themselves in exact methods of study; the latter are disposed to write with the sole intent of finding in the past arguments to support their political views or their partisan claims. Meanwhile youth is tempted to reject history as it is officially presented, as an endless series of wars, diplomatic ruses, crimes, examples of intense selfishness and the impotent efforts of men to bring more reason into the world. It refuses to lend credence to those who advise it that man has remained a religious and ideological animal even more than an "economic" creature. Youth's awakening, when it is suddenly placed face to face with the terrible power of ideas, myths and fanaticisms in the world, is sometimes a rude shock, as we have seen recently.

The Frenchmen in particular who have thought fit in the past few years to deny their eighteenth-century thinkers as traitors to the classic and monarchical tradition of France have only to open their eyes in order to ascertain that no French tradition is more alive than that of the Century of Enlightenment. Pascal and Descartes are doubtless greater; Montaigne has more charm and Saint Thomas more logical power: but it is Voltaire and Rousseau, and sometimes Montesquieu and Condorcet, that one finds almost always behind the living influence of France on the masses and the ideologies of South America, of the United States itself, of central and eastern Europe and that one will find tomorrow in Africa and Asia. The world of today expects from postwar France, and France herself expects from her political thinkers who had lost the habit of expressing themselves in universal terms during the last fifty years, a renewal and modernization of her liberal ideas of the eighteenth century, boldly adapted to the social and economic problems of today, but still inspired by the same faith in man and his possibilities.

Students from other countries remind the French of this fact, lest they forget it too readily. Their studies on the influence of Voltaire and Rousseau on the French Revolution and the revolutions that ensued elsewhere in the world are becoming more numerous and sometimes more objective than the French ones. A Slavic scholar Milan Markovitch in a large and exhaustive book on *Rousseau et Tolstoi* (Champion, 1928) set forth in detail the Rousseauism of the Russian novelist, who in his adolescence carried the portrait of Jean-Jacques around his neck like a scapular and wrote the following message to the newly-founded Rousseau Club on March 7th, 1905: "Rousseau has been my teacher since the age of fifteen. Rousseau and the Gospel have been the two great influences for good in my life." The German thinker Ernst Cassirer devoted a little book written in 1945 to commemoration of the admiration for Rousseau expressed by Goethe and Fichte as well as Kant who declared: "Rousseau set me right. . . . I learned to respect human nature." Thoreau and D. H. Lawrence are indebted to the Genevan for a good half of their thinking. George Eliot, on meeting the philosopher Emerson in Coventry in 1848, found herself being asked by him what her favorite book was; Rousseau's *Confessions,* she answered; at which the American transcendentalist cried: "It is mine too." Shortly afterwards, on February 9th, 1849, she wrote Sara Hennel these extremely lucid sentences on the mechanism of intellectual influence:

> *I wish you thoroughly to understand that the writers who have most profoundly influenced me are not in the least oracles to me. . . . For instance, it would signify nothing to me if a very wise person were to stun me with proofs that Rousseau's views of life, religion, and government were miserably erroneous—that he was guilty of some of the worst bassesses that have degraded civilized man. I might admit all this; and it would be not the less true that Rousseau's genius has sent that electric thrill through my intellectual and moral frame which has awakened me to new perceptions; . . . and this not by teaching me any new belief. . . . The fire of his genius has so fused together old thoughts and prejudices, that I have been ready to make new combinations.*

In the face of such proofs of a fruitful and life-giving though possibly dangerous influence, an important English historian who was moreover an admirer of Burke and usually more adquate in his statements, but was conscious of the importance of ideas in the events of this world, Lord Acton, was impelled to exclaim: "Rousseau produced more effect with his pen than Aristotle, or Cicero, or St. Augustine, or St. Thomas Aquinas, or any other man who ever lived."

Alfred Cobban

THE ENLIGHTENMENT AND THE
FRENCH REVOLUTION

Alfred Cobban (1901–1968) was one of the ablest British historians of France in recent years. His extensive contributions to knowledge include many books and articles, especially on the eighteenth century, and his editorship of History *from 1957 to 1967. In this selection he makes use of his extensive familiarity with French history to reexamine the relationships between the Enlightenment and the Revolution. While recognizing that ideas were essential to the upheaval, he emphasizes the difficulties of relating intellectual currents to the various phases of the Revolution and to such vital developments as popular sovereignty and nationalism.*

The debate over the problem of the relation between the ideas of eighteenth-century France and the Revolution is not new. I have been aware of it ever since reading, as a schoolboy, what then seemed to me, and must still seem to many, the convincing explanation of Taine. "When," he wrote, "we see a man . . . apparently sound and of peaceful habits, drink eagerly of a new liquor, then suddenly fall to ground, foaming at the mouth, . . . we have no hesitation in supposing that in the pleasant draught there was some dangerous ingredient." The man, of course, was France, the liquor the Enlightenment, and the fit that overtook the unwise imbiber was the French Revolution. Similies are the camouflage of bad history, but Taine also put it more succinctly. "Millions of savages," he says, "were launched into action by a few thousand babblers."

Does anyone read Taine now? Some sixty years ago Aulard said that at the Sorbonne a candidate for the diploma in historical studies or the doctorate would disqualify himself if he quoted Taine as an authority on any historical question. Curiously enough, on the basic aspects of the problem under discussion here, Taine and his critic were in fundamental agreement. They both believed that a historian should be interested in causes, not as yet having learned from philosophers of history the impossibility of getting from one set of facts to another set of facts except by the interposition of a third set of

From Earl R. Wasserman, ed., *Aspects of the Eighteenth Century*, (Baltimore: Johns Hopkins Press, 1965). Reprinted with permission. Footnotes omitted.

facts, and so on ad infinitum; and they believed that ideas were the essential motive force in history. We should not be too critical of their interpretation of the relationship between the Enlightenment and the Revolution. The belief that the Revolution was caused by the spread of enlightened ideas is natural enough. It was put forward at the time by Burke and schematized by the Abbé Barruel in the form of a triple conspiracy—conspiracy being the easiest way of accounting for any great calamity of which one does not understand the origins. The three prongs of the conspiracy, as Barruel saw it, were (1) an anti-Christian conspiracy by the philosophers; (2) these sophists of impiety were joined by the sophists of rebellion in the occult lodges of the Freemasons; (3) impiety and anarchy became fused into a conspiracy against all religion, government, and property in the sect of the *Illuminés.* The heads of the conspiracy were Voltaire, d'Alembert, Frederick II, and Diderot, its chief weapon the *Encyclopédie,* and its active agent the club of the Jacobins.

The historians of the nineteenth century continued the same basic assumption, except that instead of regarding the Revolution as a disaster, they began to regard it as a good thing, and hence not the work of conspirators spreading dangerous ideas but of the people inspired by noble ones. Thus, for Lamartine the Revolution came into existence the day when printing was invented, for this made public opinion possible: eighteenth-century philosophy was the code of civil and religious liberty put into action in the Revolution by the people. Michelet is more specific. He says, "When these two men [Voltaire and Rousseau] had formed their ideas, the Revolution was accomplished in the high realm of the mind." But this was only because they expressed the thought of the masses, "the chief author was the people." Of course, the eighteenth century could not have seen the Revolution as the revolt of the masses, since the masses did not exist before the great growth of population and urbanization that characterized the nineteenth century. The eighteenth-century belief in the primacy of ideas, however, persisted, even when the newer conditions of the nineteenth century had brought economic motivation to the fore, as it was in the history of Louis Blanc. Writing, like Karl Marx, in that great incubator of revolutionary thought the British Museum, Louis Blanc used the Croker collection of pamphlets, from which, aided by his own experience of France under the July Monarchy, he discovered the contempt of the revolutionary

FIGURE 6. D'Alembert. An outstanding mathematician and *philosophe*, d'Alembert aided Diderot in editing the *Encyclopédie* in its initial stages and wrote the *Discours préliminaire* which traced the growth of rationalism and science and expressed great confidence in man's ability to improve the conditions of his life. (*Courtesy of the Fogg Art Museum, Harvard University*)

bourgeois for the people and the hatred of the people for the bourgeois. This, added to the struggle of the *Tiers Etat* against the privileged orders, could have been interpreted in terms of a class struggle
and conflict of economic interests, but Louis Blanc, for all his socialist ideology, still puts the revolutionary struggle as one of conflicting
principles—authority, individualism, and fraternity, corresponding
respectively to noblesse, bourgeoisie, and people. There were few
students of the revolutionary period who, like de Tocqueville, saw
social and political factors as more powerful than ideas. Even socialist historians, such as Jaurès, Mathiez, Lefebvre and Labrousse, for
all their awareness of economic factors, still seem to interpret the
Revolution as basically a conflict of principles, a struggle for the
hearts of men. "All historians agree on the influence of *lumières* on
the Revolution," wrote Professor Jacques Godechot recently, "but
disagree whether their influence is essential, or secondary to economic factors."

The problem adumbrated here is not one which is peculiar to the
French Revolution. The degree of influence to be attributed to ideas
is an unresolved question in respect of all great historical movements—Renaissance and Reformation, Industrial Revolution, benevolent despotism, as well as French Revolution. The attempt to
dispose of the difficulty by treating ideas as merely the ideologies
of social classes underestimates the elasticity of principles, what
Whitehead called the "adventures of ideas." They cannot be identified
with social forces; for once an idea has been let loose on the world,
no one knows where it will settle or what new movement it will start.
This is not a reason for abandoning the attempt to establish connections between changes in ideas and political and social developments, but it does suggest that these connections need to be
examined with as much care and criticism of the evidence as would
be applied to any other historical problem. Although contemporaries
and historians have agreed on the causal relation between the
thought of the eighteenth century, or more specifically the Enlightenment, and the Revolution, it has usually been on the basis of assumptions about both that have hardly survived more recent historical
analysis.

What do we now understand by the Enlightenment? Its enemies,
from the time of Burke and the Abbé Barruel, have condemned it
for dealing in abstractions, to which the real interests of actual men

and women are sacrificed. It can hardly be denied that the Enlightenment, though scientific and empirical on the one hand, was also a system of abstract, generalizing thought which tried to substitute impersonal for personal forces over a large range of human life: indeed the measure to which it succeeded in doing this is the measure of its success in changing much of the social ethic of Western civilization. If we look for rational, physical causes of misfortunes instead of attributing them to witchcraft, if we accept the impersonal wage system in place of personal slavery, if we reject the torture of individuals as a means of eliciting the truth and use instead the impersonal rules of the law, if we do not regard personal salvation as so important that we are prepared to burn people in order to achieve it for them as well as for ourselves, if we do not believe that the stars are concerned with our individual fortunes, and so on, we are tacitly acknowledging the influence of the Enlightenment over our assumptions and actions; for the opposite was in each case the normal view before what has so often been condemned as the abstract thought of the Enlightenment extended the scientific, generalizing approach from physical nature to human actions. The Enlightenment was the end of a spiritual world ruled by angels and demons, cherubim and seraphim, Beelzebub and Satan. "Farewell rewards and fairies." In religion, the Enlightenment substituted the impersonal god of deism for a personal deity, and skepticism about the dogmas of revealed religion was followed by toleration. Systems of ethics based on religious authority and sanctions were replaced by ideas of utilitarianism and humanitarianism and the search for a new ethic. There is a paradox by which the ages most condemned at the time for immorality are in fact those most concerned with morality. Such were fifth-century Athens and eighteenth-century Western Europe.

It is not my purpose, nor is it necessary here, to provide a detailed survey of the ideas of the Enlightenment; but any account, however brief, cannot fail to point out that one element is the strong current of political liberalism that runs through it. This is particularly important for the present argument, in that the Revolution, whatever else it may have been, was also a struggle for political power. In the course of this were revived many of the political concepts employed by the political writers of seventeenth-century England to justify the revolutions of that century. Locke's political ideas, in particular, were introduced into eighteenth-century France in the translations and commentaries of Burlamaqui and Barbeyrac. They were reproduced by the chevalier de Jaucourt in his contribution to the *Encyclopédie*. They appear in a modified form in the writings of Montesquieu, Rousseau, d'Holbach, or Mably, and are not absent from those of Voltaire and Diderot. However, the political content of the French Enlightenment must not be exaggerated. If we exclude Montesquieu and Rousseau, we are left for the most part with general sentiments about the desirability of liberty and the undesirability of despotism, with especial reference to freedom of thought and religion. The in-influence of Montesquieu's emphasis on the virtues of the English constitution did not outlast the third quarter of the century, and his famous *Esprit des lois* was often, though not quite correctly, interpreted merely as a defense of the claims of the French parlements. Rousseau's *Contrat social* had no ascertainable influence before the Revolution and only a very debatable one during its course. True, there is the oft-repeated story of Marat reading it to enthralled crowds at street corners, but anyone who could believe this could believe anything.

Alternatively, there has been the suggestion that the *philosophes* were the theorists of benevolent despotism. This view has been too effectively dealt with elsewhere to require any further demolition here. Insofar as it ever appeared to have any plausibility was due to the confusion of the *philosophes* with the small group of Physiocrats, and only with the first generation even of these.

It must be recognized that the French Enlightenment was on the whole lacking in systematic political theory; it was hardly to be expected in a country which had no active politics. Since the French Revolution was primarily a political revolution, this must cast doubt upon its supposed causal relationship with the Enlightenment. But we are left with the need to ask, if they did not come from the Enlightenment, what were the sources of the political theories of the Revolution, which if they did not cause it—and this would be difficult to prove in any case—at least were used to justify it. Framed in these terms, however, this is a problem that is not susceptible of a single answer. There is now general agreement that the picture of the French Revolution as a block with one inspiration, though used in the propaganda both of supporters and opponents of "the Revolution," is invalid. The historic reality is a series of revolutions, very different in their aims and therefore in any theoretical affiliations they may have had.

The revolutionary period opened, in 1787, with what has been termed the *révolte nobiliaire.* This was in effect an attempt on the part of sections of the privileged classes to take over the government of France. It was an aristocratic movement, using the term in its strictly political sense of government by those who believed in rule of an aristocracy. Thus one could have a "bourgeois aristocrat" or even a "peasant aristocrat," and on the other hand a patriot noble. The theoretical justification for such a polity evidently cannot be sought in the Enlightenment. There is an obvious ancestry—without venturing into any speculations about causal connections—in the political literature of the Fronde and of the so-called faction of the duke of Burgundy under Louis XIV.

A second revolution, the peasant revolt of 1789, which has been correctly singled out by Lefebvre as a separate and autonomous movement, was a practical revolt against practical grievances. It could have occurred at any time when circumstances were favorable, and no theory was needed to instigate or justify it. There had been a paper attack on "feudalism," it is true, running through the century, but this bore remarkably little relationship to the ills of the peasantry, and when it was employed on the famous night of the Fourth of August, it was used in an attempt to save what could be saved of the seigneurial rights and dues by limiting the definition of "feudal" rather than to promote the rising against them.

What made the peasant revolt possible, however, had been a third revolutionary movement, that of the *Tiers Etat,* which followed on the *révolte nobiliaire.* Here we certainly meet with political ideas in abundance, at least of expression. This is not the place for a detailed analysis of the ideology of *Tiers Etat.* It can hardly be questioned, however, that its central theme was the idea of popular sovereignty, which was given its fullest expression by the Abbé Sieyès in the most famous pamphlet of the Revolution, which, because it embodied the wishes of the Third Estate, obtained unprecedented circulation. In *Qu'est-ce que le tiers état?* Sieyes stated the new political ideology in uncompromising form. "The nation," he wrote, "is prior to everything. It is the source of everything. Its will is always legal. The manner in which a nation exercises its will does not matter; the point is that it does exercise it; any procedure is adequate, and its will is always the supreme law." The logical consequence of this extreme assertion of popular or national sovereignty, as I have suggested elsewhere, is to identify the people with the government, the rulers with the ruled. The result of apparently removing the need for any check on government must be something very like what Professor Talmon has called totalitarian democracy. It should be noted in qualification that the application of this idea in the French Revolution was nothing like as extreme as it has been subsequently, and that totalitarianism, even in an embryonic form, is more easily associated with the Napoleonic dictatorship than with the revolutionary assemblies.

For our present purpose, however, the problem is whether, or how far, the revolutionary idea of popular sovereignty can be derived from the thought of the Enlightenment; and the answer must be that it is not easily to be found in the writings of the *philosophes* or of their seventeenth-century predecessors. Locke, who summed up the political thinking of the seventeenth century and passed it on to the eighteenth, directed his whole argument to limiting sovereignty of any kind. The same can be said of Montesquieu, de Jaucourt, Voltaire, and d'Holbach. To Rousseau alone is it even plausible to attribute any conception of the sovereignty of the people; and it is not difficult to see that even in his case the attribution rests upon an elementary, though common, misunderstanding of his thought. Sovereignty for Rousseau resides in the General Will, and the General Will is an ideal will—what would be willed by the people if it were willing only in the common interest, enlightened and disinterested. Even so the General Will is restricted by him to the function of making general laws. Government, involving individual acts, does not enter into its scope.

Indeed any theory of absolute sovereignty is incompatible with the political liberalism of the Enlightenment. The supremacy of the interests of the people is another matter, and this indeed can be attributed to the thinkers of the Enlightenment, who were all more or less explicit utilitarian in their social philosophy. The revolutionary theory of popular sovereignty only appeared when the belief that government should be in the interests of the people was fused with the principle of sovereignty, deriving from quite a different source. Eighteenth-century France learned the idea and the practice of sovereignty from the absolute monarchy. It was not difficult, when the leaders of the *Tiers Etat* made their bid for power to envisage their aims as the transference of the sovereignty from the monarchy to the people. That this was so was tacitly acknowledged when they substituted *lèze-nation* for *lèze-majesté*.

The Revolution, thus, was inaugurated not by the application of an old political idea but by the invention of a new one. Even this might not have been so decisive if it had not been applied also in a new political and social situation, for in the last quarter of the eighteenth century romanticism and the religious revival were creating new political conditions. They gave emotional content and organic unity to the idea of the people, and so made possible the rise of what might loosely be called totalitarian thought. It is significant that even in the contemporary world, totalitarian regimes have only been successfully established in countries with strong religious orthodoxies, such as Italy, Germany and Russia.

The end of the eighteenth century may truly be said to have witnessed a partial transition from an individualist to a collectivist view of society; but this was not a continuation of, but a break away from, the ideas of the Enlightenment. For Locke and his followers a state had been a society of individuals associated together by voluntary choice for the pursuit of common interests and ideals. Rousseau's people was a *corps moral,* that is to say an artificial body, a collection of individuals. With the romantic movement the idea of the people gained historic dimensions and organic unity. It became the nation. In Lockian and enlightened thought the state had existed for the sake of the individual. Now the view began to grow that the individual existed for the sake of the nation. It was a sign of the new age when, in the first revolutionary constitution, the king of France became the *roi des Français.* The Revolution ends the age of individualism and opens that of nationalism. At the same time, politics became more emotional, now that it had to appeal to large numbers. Journalism assumed its modern role of whipping up popular passions and lowering the level of political discussion. Wars became national and therefore much more bitter. In all this can be seen not the fulfillment but the frustration of the Enlightenment. It has always been difficult to believe that the liberal political ideas of the Enlightenment were the source of revolutionary terrorism, oligarchy, and military dictatorship. It ceases to be a problem if we realize that such developments were indeed not the result of the Enlightenment but of the new social and political trends that appeared in the last quarter of the eighteenth century.

The revolutionary period, which in the past has been most often linked with Enlightenment, cannot be understood unless we realize that it was also the period of the romantic and conservative reaction. In the Revolution itself, historians have in recent years discovered the presence of conservative and even reactionary trends, and this has involved much rethinking and rewriting of its history. Now, being invited to think in new ways about subjects which one had thought were safely docketed and pigeonholed can be very distressing, as is shown in an article by Mr. Franklin L. Ford. A lecture I gave some ten years ago suggesting the need for revisionism in revolutionary history seemed to him to cast doubt on the fundamental reality of the Revolution, and in his article Mr. Ford set out to reassert that there *was* a revolutionary age. The article is hardly likely to have a major influence on historical thought, and I would not have troubled with it if it did not also illustrate a common form of confusion which is relevant to the present discussion. To prove that there really was a French Revolution that effected revolutionary changes throughout the whole gamut of European society, Mr. Ford lists the developments of the turn of the century in literature, music, the visual arts, administration and institutions, social structure, the strategy of war, and so on. That there were these and many more changes is undeniable: they can be found in any textbook. But Mr. Ford's anxiety to rehabilitate the French Revolution led him into making the assumption that all these changes—revolutionary, counterrevolutionary, nonrevolutionary—were identified with, or resulted from, the French Revolution. Therefore, the conclusion is, "In 1789, after long, confused preliminaries, the old Europe began a transformation, convulsive, bewildering, to some of the participants wildly exhilarating, to others bitterly tragic."

The history of a period that is full of such a variety of currents and cross-currents is more complicated and requires a more sophisticated analysis than this simple approach allows for. For the same reason, any attempt to link the Revolution—or to be more exact any of the successive revolutions—with the Enlightenment, as a single case of cause and effect, is unacceptable. To do this would be to distort the ideas of the Enlightenment and to reduce the history of the Revolution to a myth. It does not follow from this that we must write off the Enlightenment completely as an influence in the Revolution. Agreed that the Enlightenment had no identifiable part in causing any of the successive revolutions between 1787 and 1795, and that the revolutionary ideology of popular sovereignty ran counter to its basic political ideas, even so there was a great deal more in the Revolution than this.

To see only the principle of sovereignty in the political ideology of the revolutionaries is to ignore the strong elements of liberalism, derived from the Lockian tradition of the Enlightenment, in it. It would also be a willful disregard of patent facts to pretend that when the members of the *Etats Généraux* and the subsequent revolutionary assemblies came to Versailles, they did not bring along the effects of their education and their reading in the literature of the eighteenth century. They were inevitably the children of the Enlightenment, and if, as I have suggested, they could get little in the way of specific political theory from the *philosophes,* they could get much in the way of humanitarian ideas and legal reform. Thus, torture as an element in judicial procedure, which reached its height between the fifteenth and seventeenth centuries, was eliminated from the law and very largely from practice. Despite the opposition of powerful vested interests, the Revolution saw the inauguration of a campaign for the abolition of both slavery and the slave trade, though it only achieved success in France in 1848. Religious toleration and the extension of civil rights to non-Catholics had made some progress before the Revolution: it was carried through to completion in the course of the revolutionary secularization of the state. The codification of the laws, which the revolutionary assemblies set in hand and Napoleon completed, represents the fulfillment of an ideal of Voltaire. And, not to go into further detail, the positive creed of the Enlightenment, the search for happiness *(bonheur)* was also one end of the Revolution. "Un peuple," declared St. Just on November 29, 1792, "qui n'est pas heureux, n'a pas de patrie."

But in reaching this utilitarian ideal we have also reached the point at which the Revolution broke away from the Enlightenment. Here, Bentham and utilitarianism carried forward its true inheritance. The Revolution, meanwhile, strayed from the primrose path of enlightened happiness to the strait and narrow road of Jacobin virtue, from the principle of representative and constitutional government to the rule of an authoritarian élite, from the *philosophes'* ideal of peace to the revolutionaries' crusading war and the Napoleonic dream of conquest. Nothing could have been more alien to the Enlightenment than this transition from the ideals of democracy and peace to a policy of dictatorship and war. It has been said that the principles of the *lumières* light up the Revolution intermittently, like the beam of a lighthouse swinging round brilliantly and then disappearing. The influence of the Enlightenment cannot be disregarded in any history of the French Revolution; but the revolutionaries did not set their course by its light in the beginning, nor did they steer the ship of state into the haven of the Enlightenment in the end.

Norman Hampson
THE REVOLUTIONARY CLIMACTERIC

Norman Hampson is professor of modern history at the University of New-castle upon Tyne and the author of several books on eighteenth-century France. In this selection, which is taken from a very successful work of historical synthesis, he traces the general thrust of the late Enlightenment, particularly its emphasis upon equality, through its various vicissitudes at the hands of successive regimes, showing that libertarian ideas were essential to the achievements of the Revolution but were gradually lost as France became involved in wars and conquest beyond her borders.

To ask what relationship, if any, linked the Enlightenment and the French Revolution, is a legitimate question—provided one does not expect the answer to be either scientific or simple. The difficulty is not merely that we predetermine the result by the terms in which we define the two movements. Each was extremely complex and composed of apparently self-contradictory elements. The relationship between them appears to vary as we concentrate on different aspects of either. The more nuances we introduce into our awareness of these movements the more difficult it becomes to think in terms of any simple causal relationship between them. As always in history, cause and effect are to some extent reversible: what some men did as a result of ideas they had received from the Enlightenment influenced the picture of the Enlightenment which they and others transmitted to posterity. Stumbling amidst this *embarras de richesses,* the historian is in permanent danger of being buried beneath his own treasure trove. As facts, ideas and shadowy intuitions cascade about him, he is overwhelmed, like Prince Andrew in *War and Peace,* when he listens to Natasha singing, by the contrast between the splendor of which he has at least a dim perception and the little that he can hope to define for himself or communicate to others. His most rewarding insights are liable to be the most elusive and the most easily misunderstood. This chapter does not, therefore, aspire to offer any "objective" solution to the question it began by posing. It is rather a kind of historical telescope which, by the isolation, magnification and foreshortening of certain aspects of the subject, may perhaps give them an artificial clarity and coherence.

Without trying to define the content of the Enlightenment, one may say that in its earlier, rationalist phase it challenged the claim of Christian theology to have explained the nature of man and his relationship to his natural environment, and in particular rejected the idea of religious persecution. It assumed that men enjoyed inalienable natural rights, such as unrestricted access to information, freedom of speech and freedom from arbitrary arrest; many of its spokesmen included economic liberalism as one of these natural rights. In a general sort of way, all this amounted to the belief that men would live with greater happiness and dignity if their social institutions were determined by what was considered reasonable or scientific rather than regulated by prescription—the assumption that attitudes, privileges and social arrangements acquired legitimacy, if not indeed divine sanction, by the mere fact of having existed for a long time. The Rousseauist revolution, which partly contradicted these attitudes and partly supplemented them, insisted that reason must accommodate itself to an inner moral sense, which in turn implied the duty of the individual to sacrifice his personal advantage to the moral welfare of the living community on which he depended. Although this community was the source of his own existence as a moral being, its legitimacy was, in the last resort, dependent on its satisfying the moral and material needs of the individuals who composed it.

We have seen that these ideas, in France, were most widely diffused among the nobility of Paris and Versailles, the agents of the royal bureaucracy and the professional classes. They made less impression on the business community and their impact on the anonymous mass of town artisans and peasants was indirect, if not insignificant. The Enlightenment, in both its rationalist and emotional aspects, was not primarily a political movement, except in the sense in which anticlericalism was a political program of a kind. The letters to Sophie Volland, in which Diderot describes in great detail the events of his everyday life and in particular the discussions *chez* d'Holbach, show very clearly that it was disinterested intellectual speculation rather than possible political action which really excited these people. This was equally true of their readers. Madame Roland found *Du contrat social* difficult and not very rewarding, whereas the *Nouvelle Héloïse* swept her off her feet. In England, the Whig leader, Fox, said of *Du contrat social* that he "believed it was one of the most extravagant of that author's works. So much so that he had only read the beginning." An obscure Arras lawyer, who still called himself *de* Robespierre, shared the general enthusiasm of the educated for the author of the *Nouvelle Héloïse.* A law case in the spring of 1789 allowed Robespierre to speculate on the Brave New World that seemed to be in the making.

> *You, generous nation, which alone among the peoples of the world, without a fatal revolution, without any bloody catastrophe, by your own magnanimity and the virtuous character of your king, have resumed the exercise of the sacred and imprescriptible rights that have been violated in every age. . . . Here is the basis of that social contract of which people talk so much, which is far from being an agreement produced by human volition; its fundamental conditions, written in heaven, were determined for all time by that supreme legislator who is the only source of all order, of all happiness and of all justice.*

Just as the Enlightenment was not primarily political, the origins of the French Revolution were not primarily ideological. . . . The crisis opened in 1787 when Calonne, making a virtue of financial necessity, tried to commit the French monarchy to the policies of reforming bureaucratic absolutism that Joseph II was struggling to implement in the Hapsburg Empire. The notables and the *Parlements* hoped to exploit the financial weakness of the crown in order to restore organs of collective aristocratic power—notably the provincial Estates—that had been destroyed or emasculated by Bourbon absolutism. Like the English parliamentarians of the previous century, they insisted that their objective was a return to an ancient constitution. During the pamphlet war that reached its climax in 1788 the majority seem to have based their claim on this appeal to prescription. Modern writers were pressed into service and a contemporary complained that "They put on show and repeat everything that Montesquieu and Rousseau have so well deduced against despotism." Montesquieu, himself a former member of the Bordeaux *parlement,* seemed to provide a theoretical justification for what might otherwise have seemed mere antiquarianism. But the conflict would probably have taken much the same course if *De l'esprit des lois* had never been written, and it does not seem to have spread far beyond the legal and aristocratic circles immediately concerned. Faced with an unsatisfactory choice between reforming absolutism and reactionary constitutionalism, the majority of the educated commoners remained aloof.

What transformed the debate and for the first time gave it a truly national resonance was the campaign for the election of deputies to the Estates General, in the winter of 1788–1789. This campaign was dominated by an assertion of the natural equality of man that was accompanied by a bitter outburst of hatred, directed against the nobility as a social order. The abbé Sieyès, in the most famous pamphlet of the time, so far forgot his Christian charity as to describe the nobility as "some horrible disease eating the living flesh on the body of some unfortunate man." The intensity of this passionate assertion of human equality, similar in some respects to the depth of feeling about racial equality at the present day, was the key to the first phase of the Revolution proper. It made an immediate impact on most of Europe, not merely in those countries where the nobility still formed a privileged caste, but also in England. It was this which led Wordsworth to write, long after his principles had changed:

Bliss was it in that dawn to be alive.

He expressed himself more prosaically, but to the same effect, in 1794. "Hereditary distinctions and privileged orders of every species, I think, must necessarily counteract the progress of human improvement." This new faith in human equality did not arise directly from the Enlightenment. However implicit in the argument of *Du contrat social* it may appear to the modern reader, Rousseau's own life and the idealized society portrayed in the *Nouvelle Héloïse* indicate a revolt against Parisian salon society rather than a specific protest against what the perceptive royalist journalist, Rivarol, defined in 1789 as *le préjugé de la noblesse*—which Rivarol identified as the essential cause of the Revolution. In a sense the new revolt was anti-Rousseauist, since its partisans aimed not to overthrow an artificial society but to open it to those who were gentlemen in the British sense without being *gentilhommes* in the French one.

Social equality in this limited sense of the equality of gentlemen and nobles raised very difficult problems in both practice and theory. The objective was a society roughly similar to that in Britain but whereas, in Britain, such social attitudes could be defended in the name of tradition, in France they could only be created by the rejection of tradition in the name of abstract principle. The principle involved, being of universal application, was bound to excite the whole of western Europe, whereas the British society that embodied it, however imperfectly, had appeared to be an insular anomaly of little relevance to the Continent. Since, in France, the conception of the natural inequality of man was the theoretical basis of a whole complex system of law, taxation and local government, its overthrow implied a complete reorganization of the country's institutions. The appeal to principle rather than to precedent also opened up a further problem: it was difficult to justify the equality of gentlemen and nobles without conceding that artisans and peasants were equal to gentlemen, however remote such "democratical principles" might seem from the social realities of 1789. Behind the principle that commended itself to the educated commoners of the Third Estate— and to an important minority of the nobles themselves—lay the shadow of political democracy which, it was generally assumed, would lead to an assault by the enfranchised poor against the unequal distribution of property.

On June 23, 1789 Louis XVI, to break the deadlock between the privileged orders and the Third Estate, promulgated a royal program of reform to which he was to adhere for the rest of his life. On every issue which could be considered directly related to the Enlightenment—parliamentary control of taxation, the abolition of *lettres de cachet,* the freedom of the press, internal free trade and the reform of the law—the king offered substantial concessions. Had French society resembled that of England, he gave enough ground for a settlement like that of 1688 to have been possible. On the issue of social equality, however, he returned a blunt negative. The first clause of his Charter declared, "The king wills that the ancient distinction between the three Orders of the state shall be maintained in its entirety as essentially bound up with the constitution of his kingdom." It was this which produced the crisis of July, the revolt of Paris and most of the towns of France, and it had very little indeed to do with the Enlightenment.

If the first phase of the Revolution, from 1789 to 1791, was not directly caused by the Enlightenment, it nevertheless transferred political power in France to the men who had been most influenced by the Enlightenment. As the moderate royalist leader of 1789, Mounier, wrote long afterwards, "It was not the influence of those principles which created the Revolution, it was on the contrary the Revolution which created their influence." The real rulers of France at the time of the Constituent Assembly came from those sections of society most influenced by the writing of the *philosophes:* members of the court nobility such as Lafayette, Noailles and La Rochefoucauld, intellectuals like the astronomer, Bailly, now mayor of Paris, Duport from the Paris *parlement,* Barnave, a lawyer from Grenoble. The Assembly reorganized the entire political shape of the country on principles of secularism, rationality, uniformity and election to office—even to such offices as those of bishop, parish priest and judge. With the abolition of *parlements* and manorial courts went an attempt to reform French law along the lines advocated by Beccaria. Duport and his political opponent, Robespierre, fought side by side in an unsuccessful attempt to obtain the abolition of the death penalty, but even though capital punishment was retained, the instrument invented by one of the deputies, Dr. Guillotin, was very different from the former barbarity of breaking on the wheel. As was to be expected with such men in control, the social consequences of the Revolution were somewhat limited. Economic privileges that depended exclusively on birth were abolished, together with such relics of personal servitude as had existed in 1789, but traditional payments connected with the occupancy of land were put in the sacrosanct class of property. The sale of the enormous estates of the Church on the whole benefited the well-to-do rather than the poorer peasants. Where the laity were concerned there was no expropriation of land and the abolition of the purely personal dues owed to manorial lords was of very limited scope. The Assembly defeated the advocates of both political and economic democracy. It curtailed the very broad franchise on which the Third Estate had been elected in 1789 and when a member asked why the new naval penal code provided corporal punishment for seamen but not their officers, he was told that the loss of honor which an officer incurred by the mere fact of punishment made any comparison of penalties irrelevant.

The combined effect of the Assembly's moderation in practice and the Rousseauist enthusiasm of its moral principles—such as open diplomacy and the renunciation of aggressive war—excited the admiration of most of the people in Europe who did not feel personally threatened in their privileges. This was particularly marked in Germany, where even men who had reacted against French classicism and corruption acknowledged with regret that the regenerated France had won the moral leadership of Europe. The aged Klopstock, in a poem on the Estates General, begged his pardon of the French people if "formerly turned towards the Germans, I called on them to shun what I now invite them to imitate." Herder, who had also reacted against French cultural imperialism in the past, preached in favor of the Revolution at Weimar even when his own prince had joined the Prussian army that was intended to suppress it. In Britain, the initial enthusiasm of Blake, Wordsworth, Coleridge, Southey and Burns expressed a new feeling of sympathy which in many cases overcame the tradition of political enmity.

This situation was radically, if not immediately, transformed by the outbreak of war between France and Austria and Prussia in 1792, extended to Britain, Holland and Spain in the following year. R. R. Palmer has shown, in the second volume of his penetrating *Age of the Democratic Revolution,* that although the war did not begin as an ideological crusade it gradually became one. Beleaguered France, attacked on all sides and invaded across every land frontier, was the scene of a second revolution which overthrew the king in 1792, executed him in the following year and subordinated every principle to national survival. Driven to depend on the support of those who were not gentlemen, the Republic introduced a democratic franchise, abolished the remaining manorial rights without compensation, imposed price controls in the interest of the poorer urban consumer and unleashed the Terror against its presumed enemies. Responding to the desperate enthusiasm of 1793–1794, one or two members of the Committee of Public Safety, notably Robespierre and Saint-Just, devotees of Rousseau, seemed to see France as the embattled Sparta/Geneva of Rousseau's dreams. By terror and extermination they hoped to create the kind of ideal moral community that had increasingly haunted the thinkers of the later Enlightenment. The actual struggling republic became the Ideal City, engaged in an inevitable war to the death against an old order in which moral corruption and political despotism were two faces of the same coin. "Monarchy", said Saint-Just, "is not a king, it is crime; the republic is not a senate, it is virtuo." Robespierre, in his speech of May 7, 1794 on "The relations between religious and moral ideas and republican principles" at last avenged Rousseau against the sophisticated *philosophes* who were alleged to have persecuted him. Contrasting the technical progress of the previous two thousand years with its moral stagnation, and castigating the Encyclopedists in passing, Robespierre aspired to regenerate France by dedicating the republic to a Supreme Being whose principles were those of the *vicaire savoyard* and whose worship was to fill the void described in the last chapter of *Du contrat social. Vertu* was to be the criterion of every aspect of public life. *Il faut moraliser le commerce.* Saint-Just, taking up Rousseau's conception of society as a means for reinforcing the morality of its members, wrote that it was for the legislator to shape men into what he wanted them to be. The final objective, for both of them, was a moral utopia in which the state as a repressive institution would have withered away, leaving a community of St. Preux and Wolmars to live in peace with itself and with its neighbors. Others, both in France and elsewhere, were more impressed by the fact that between April and June 1794 the revolutionary tribunal in Paris sent over 1,100 people to the guillotine.

Just as the war drove France to one extreme it pushed the allied nations, reluctantly or not, in the opposite direction. Pitt, although he had been unwilling to go to war, used methods against the Revolution, such as the printing of forged French currency, which he would probably have considered dishonorable if employed against a legitimate government. Francis II, who ruled over the Habsburg Empire from 1792, found it impossible to continue the struggle against his own aristocracy while waging an unpopular war against revolutionary France. Catherine II, whose enlightenment had always been something of an export commodity, pursued an increasingly repressive policy at home and she and Frederick William II overthrew the new Polish constitution in the name of the "Most Holy and Invisible Trinity" and of counterrevolutionary principle. Many of the European intellectuals—Kant being a striking exception—were repelled by the violence of the Revolution and its increasingly belligerent nationalism. Europe was less impressed by the offer of help to peoples striving to recover their liberty, towards the end of 1792, than by the renunciation of aggressive war two years earlier. Nevertheless, an important minority of discontented townsmen in Holland, Italy, and the Rhineland saw in French military success the means to their own social and political emancipation. When the Terror gave way to relatively moderate government in France in 1794, the Revolution appeared to the frightened governments of Europe to become more rather than less of a menace to their own authority.

Men of moderate opinions outside France saw the danger that military and political opposition to the French Republic might be accompanied by a blind repudiation of the Enlightenment as a whole, and fought against it as well as they could. One of them, Mallet du Pan, wrote in 1796, "There has been formed in Europe a league of fools and fanatics who, if they could, would forbid man the faculty to think or see. The sight of a book makes them shudder; because the Enlightenment has been abused they would exterminate all those they suppose enlightened. . . . Persuaded that without men of intelligence there would have been no revolution, they hope to reverse it with imbeciles." The moderates were to be disappointed, for the long war hardened attitudes all the time. French constitutional monarchists could make no peace with a Pretender who in 1797 declared his intention to bring the French "to the holy religion of their fathers and the paternal government that was so long the glory and happiness of France." As early as 1793, the abbé Maury, who had been a member of the Constituent Assembly, advised the Pope that when the counterrevolution should have triumphed it would no longer be necessary to tolerate French Protestants. Religious toleration had been introduced by Louis XVI before the Revolution—but the paladins of reaction prided themselves on being *plus royaliste que le roi.* Even in England, where the threat from France was least immediate, the poets—with the exception of Blake—soon migrated to the Establishment and the Government began dismantling those safeguards of individual liberty that had appealed so much to Voltaire and Montesquieu, with the Treasonable Practices Act, the Seditious Meetings Act and the suspension of *Habeas Corpus.*

Palmer has shown how the military conflict took the form of a struggle between the Enlightenment and an increasingly reactionary defense of a supposedly traditional order. As a direct consequence of the success of French arms, urban revolutionaries created sister republics in Holland, Switzerland, northern Italy, the Papal States and Naples. In so far as time permitted, these were reorganized on French lines, clerical and seigneurial privilege and local particularism giving way to unitary republican government, secular, egalitarian and reasonable. It was symbolic of the ideological clash that when the Second Coalition launched its attack on France in 1799 the decisive military contribution was made by Russia and the cause of throne and altar also benefited from the support of a Turkish contingent. The French won, but in the process Bonaparte seized power in Paris and his rule was to transform the nature of the confrontation.

As Revolutionary France became Imperial France in 1804 its impact on Europe became less ideological and more military. Napoleon himself, like his namesake in George Orwell's parable about another revolution, became increasingly indistinguishable from the kings and emperors whom he was fighting. He was, of course, by birth a noble, even if only a Corsican one. Once established in power he encouraged the French exiles to return, and not merely the more moderate, but men like Chateaubriand who considered themselves the sworn enemies of the Revolution. Napoleon's own rule became increasingly autocratic and monarchical. After his Habsburg marriage the servility and ceremonial of the Imperial Court rivalled any in Europe. Even after his overthrow the Powers treated the defeated Emperor as something more than a successful revolutionary. Within France Napoleon on the whole maintained the civil equality won during the Revolution, at least in the restricted sense in which birth conferred no formal privileges. Such of the legacy of the Enlightenment as related merely to national efficiency, for example internal free trade and advanced technical education, became a permanent part of French society. But much that the Enlightenment regarded as essential disappeared, notably freedom of the press and freedom from

arbitrary arrest. In many respects Napoleonic France was closer than
the France of Louis XV to Montesquieu's conception of despotism.
The almost continual warfare of the Napoleonic period at first led
to an extension of the Revolution, when most of Germany was reorganized after the collapse of Prussia in 1806. But French rule
became increasingly associated with conscription, economic dis-
crimination, censorship and police repression. More and more it came
to reflect efficient bureaucratic absolutism rather than the Enlightenment of Chastellux and Condorcet. For a short period it seemed as if
France's enemies might turn against her the ideological weapons
that had made her so formidable. Stadion, from Vienna, called for a
national revolt of Germany; the young Czar, Alexander I, fell fleet-
ingly under the influence of his reforming minister Speransky; Stein,
taking French experiments as his model, set about the reform of
Prussia. But where the Habsburg Empire and Russia were concerned,
this was a mere passing phase and the great crisis of 1812–1813
saw both intent on the restoration of the old order. The case of
Prussia is more complicated. Not merely did the government continue
rebuilding on more modern lines the state that had collapsed after
the battle of Jena in 1806; the war of liberties of 1813 made Prussia
for a time the focus of German hopes for some kind of a new order.
The Enlightenment, as we have seen, was not primarily a political
movement. Voltaire in particular, more concerned with what was done
than with who did it, would have had no objection to reform being
imposed from above by the descendant of his sometime friend,
Frederick II. But, as I hope to show at the end of this chapter, the
reshaping of Prussia corresponded to a new conception of the relationship between the individual and the state, whose theorists were
at pains to stress their dissociation from what they considered to be
the anarchic individualism of the Enlightenment.

It is impossible to regard the conflict that enveloped the whole of
Europe in 1814 as corresponding in any meaningful sense to a
struggle for the survival or extension of the principles of the Enlightenment. Napoleon was an autocrat without a pedigree, opposed by
governments intent on restoring the *ancien régime* as far as this was
still practicable. The latter considered themselves to be fighting
against the Enlightenment which they had come to identify with the
Revolution and the upstart Emperor. Napoleon was its defender only

to the extent that its more practical aspects proved useful to efficient absolutism. With his defeat and the restoration of the Bourbons in Paris in 1814 the last sparks of the Enlightenment as a political force sputtered out.

Suggestions for Additional Reading

The influence of the Enlightenment on the French Revolution has intrigued political analysts and historians from the late eighteenth century to our own time, and may be studied in a large variety of works. Many are available in English, but a majority are to be had only in the original French. The following bibliographies contain extensive listings of relevant studies: L. Villat, *La Révolution et l'Empire ("Clio"),* Vol. I (Paris, 1940); J. Godechot, *Les Révolutions, 1770–1799 ("Nouvelle Clio")* (Paris, 1963); L. Gershoy, *From Despotism to Revolution* (New York, 1957), bibliographical essay; C. Brinton, *A Decade of Revolution* (New York, 1958), bibliographical essay; P. Farmer, *France Reviews its Revolutionary Origins* (New York, 1963); A. Cobban, *Historians and the Causes of the French Revolution* (London, 1962).

The following general works on the intellectual history of the eighteenth century incidentally examine the influence of ideas: M. Leroy, *Histoire des idées sociales en France, de Montesquieu à Robespierre* (Paris, 1946); B. Groethuysen, *Philosophie de la Révolution française* (Paris, 1956); P. Hazard, *European Thought in the Eighteenth Century* (New Haven, 1954); K. Martin, *French Liberal Thought in the Eighteenth Century* (London, 1962); L. G. Crocker, *An Age of Crisis: Man and World in Eighteenth Century France* (Baltimore, 1959), and *Nature and Culture: Ethical Thought in the French Enlightenment* (Baltimore, 1963); J. Godechot, *La Pensée révolutionnaire, 1780–1799* (Paris, 1964). Carl L. Becker, *The Heavenly City of the Eighteenth Century Philosophers* (New Haven, 1932) has been extensively criticized but is still provocative and food for thought. On this work, see R. O. Rockwood, ed., *Carl Becker's Heavenly City Revisited* (Ithaca, 1958). The broader influence of the Enlightenment during the Revolution and later is discussed in A. Cobban, *In Search of Humanity: The Role of the Enlightenment in Modern History* (London, 1960). The motivation of the revolutionaries is debated in P. Gay, "Rhetoric and Politics in the French Revolution," *American Historical Review* 66 (1961):664–76, and C. Brinton, "Comment on Gay," *ibid.,* 677–81. The counter-revolutionary movement of the late eighteenth century is examined in P. H. Beik, "The French Revolution Seen from the Right," *Transactions of the American*

Philosophical Society 46, Part I (1956), and J. Godechot, *La Contre-Révolution, 1789–1804* (Paris, 1961).

Turning to writers who observed the Revolution in action and/or participated in it, Condorcet best represents the philosopher-revolutionary. His *Sketch for a Historical Picture of the Progress of the Human Mind* (New York, 1955) sets forth his basic ideology. On Condorcet, see L. Cahen, *Condorcet et la Révolution française* (Paris, 1904), and J. S. Shapiro, *Condorcet and the Rise of Liberalism* (New York, 1963). Among the many works on Edmund Burke, the following are valuable: E. Barker, "Burke and the French Revolution," in *Essays on Government* (Oxford, 1945); C. Parkin, *The Moral Basis of Burke's Political Thought* (Cambridge, 1956); A. Cobban, *Edmund Burke and the Revolt against the Eighteenth Century* (New York, 1060). The works on Thomas Paine are much less satisfactory: M. D. Conway, *Life of Thomas Paine,* 2 vols. (New York, 1892); A. O. Aldridge, *Man of Reason: The Life of Thomas Paine* (London, 1960); and R. R. Fennessy, *Burke, Paine, and the Rights of Man* (The Hague, 1963).

Several writers who observed the Revolution from abroad, usually from London, produced a variety of criticisms of the upheaval. One of the earliest was Chateaubriand's *Essai sur les révolutions* (London, 1797; English translation, 1815). Chateaubriand regarded the Enlightenment as a major cause of the Revolution, and found both good and bad elements in the movement as it developed. Jacques Mallet du Pan, also writing from London, was much more critical and viewed the *philosophes'* ideas as utterly pernicious and destructive in both church and state. See B. Mallet, *Mallet du Pan and the French Revolution* (London, 1902); A. P. d'Entrèves, "Mallet du Pan: A Swiss Critic of Democracy," *Cambridge Journal* 1 (1947): 99–108. The abbé Augustin de Barruel's *Mémoires pour servir à l'histoire du Jacobinisme,* 5 vols. (Hamburg, 1798–1799) gave important impetus to the idea that the Revolution stemmed from a monstrous conspiracy of *philosophes,* Freemasons, and Illuminati. A rebuttal appeared in Jean-Joseph Mounier, *On the Influence Attributed to Philosophers, Free-Masons, and to the Illuminati, on the Revolution of France* (London, 1801). See J. Egret, *La Révolution des notables: Mounier et les monarchiens* (Paris, 1950); and G. Weill, "Les Causes de la Révolution française d'après un témoin," *Revue de Synthèse* 59 (1939): 129–36.

The most important conservative French writers during this period were Joseph de Maistre and Louis de Bonald. For de Maistre's ideas on politics, see F. Bayle, *Les Idées politiques de Joseph de Maistre* (Paris, 1945); J. C. Murray, "The Political Thought of Joseph de Maistre," *Review of Politics* 11 (1949): 63–86; and Richard A. Lebrun, *Throne and Altar: The Political and Religious Thought of Joseph de Maistre* (Ottawa, 1965). Bonald held to a position similar to that of de Maistre but was a more systematic writer. For our purposes, one of his most significant works is his *Observations sur un ouvrage posthume de Condorcet intitulé Esquisse d'un tableau historique des progrès de l'esprit humain,* in Bonald, *Œuvres,* Vol. XIV (Paris, 1843), pp. 454–88.

Between 1815 and 1870, the role of ideas in causing the Revolution was given great emphasis by a number of liberal French writers. One of the most important was Mme de Staël, whose *Considerations on the Principal Events of the French Revolution* (New York, 1818) had considerable influence. See J. C. Herold, *Mistress to an Age: A Life of Madame de Staël* (New York, 1958). The historian François A. Mignet stated in his *History of the French Revolution,* 2 vols. (London, 1826) that the Enlightenment massively influenced events beginning in 1789. The socialist Louis Blanc likewise found the impact of ideas crucial in his *Histoire de la Révolution française,* 12 vols. (Paris, 1847–1862). And Edgar Quinet, writing from his exile in Switzerland during the Second Empire, argued in his work, *La Révolution, précédé de la critique de la Révolution,* 3 vols. (Paris, 1876), that the Enlightenment was the most potent factor leading to both the achievements and the excesses of the Revolution.

In studying the ideas of Alexis de Tocqueville, the indispensable instrument is the critical edition of his *Œuvres complètes,* edited by J. P. Mayer, 9 vols. (Paris, 1952–   ). The evolution of de Tocqueville's position concerning ideas as a cause of the Revolution is traced in M. Reinhard, "Tocqueville, historien de la Révolution," *Annales historiques de la Révolution française* 32 (1960): 257–65. See also J. Lively, *The Social and Political Thought of Alexis de Tocqueville* (Oxford, 1962); and R. Herr, *Tocqueville and the Old Regime* (Princeton, 1962).

Between 1871 and 1914, both the liberal and conservative views of the Enlightenment and its influence were deepened and strengthened. Shortly after the Franco-Prussian War, Hippolyte Taine began research for his volumes that would set forth the most thoroughgoing statement of the conservative position. See V. Giraud, *Essai sur Taine, son œuvre et son influence* (Paris, 1902); G. Monod, *Renan, Taine, Michelet* (Paris, n. d.); and A. Aulard, *Taine: historien de la Révolution française* (Paris, 1907).

The extent to which French historians and men of letters during the Third Republic differed concerning the relationship of the Enlightenment to the Revolution is indicated by the following debate. Charles Aubertin, in *L'Esprit publique au XVIIIe siècle* (Paris, 1873), and Felix Rocquain, in *L'Esprit révolutionnaire avant la Révolution, 1715–1789* (Paris, 1878; English translation, London, 1891), argued that the Revolution stemmed from practical problems and circumstances rather than ideas. They were answered by Ferdinand Brunetière, the literary critic, whose article, "Les Philosophes et la Révolution," *Revue des deux mondes* 29 (1878) reiterated the significance of ideas in shaping the Revolution. Somewhat later, Edme Champion ascribed little weight to ideas in his *Esprit de la Révolution française* (Paris, 1887) and *La France d'après les cahiers de 1789* (Paris, 1897). This was followed by Emile Faguet's *Questions politiques* (Paris, 1902) which denied that the Enlightenment had any influence whatsoever. Marius Roustan answered with his *Les Philosophes et la société française au XVIIIe siècle* (Lyon, 1906; English translation, London, 1926) which again ascribed major influence to the *philosophes*. Brunetière, in *Etudes sur le XVIIIe siècle* (Paris, 1906), analyzed Roustan's work, approved of it, and restated his earlier position.

Meanwhile, Lord Acton, one of the greatest liberal historians of the period, was arguing the decisive importance of ideas in history. In his "Inaugural Lecture on the Study of History," (*Lectures on Modern History,* chapter 1), he went so far as to state that ideas *determine* events, and applied this view to our problem in two lectures, "The Heralds of the Revolution" (*Lectures on the French Revolution,* chapter 1), and "The Background of the French Revolution" (*Essays on Freedom and Power,* chapter 8). On Acton, see L. Kochan, *Acton on History* (London, 1954); and G. Himmelfarb, *Lord Acton: A Study in Conscience and Politics* (Chicago, 1952).

Alphonse Aulard and his pupil Albert Mathiez differed considerably regarding the role of ideas in the eighteenth century. Aulard held that the Enlightenment was a major source of the principles of the Revolution. See G. Belloni, *Aulard, historien de la Révolution française* (Paris, 1949). Mathiez tended to discount ideas as motive forces but discussed their role in *Les Origines des cultes révolutionnaires (1789–1792)* (Paris, 1904), and "Les Philosophes et la séparation de l'église de l'état en France à la fin du XVIIIᵉ siècle," *Revue historique* 103 (1910): 63–79.

The anti-liberal view of the Enlightenment has found few supporters in the twentieth century. Louis Madelin's book, *The French Revolution* (New York, 1928), states that the *philosophes* exercised very extensive influence which was "purely destructive." Augustin Cochin reiterated this view in extreme form in *La Révolution et la libre-pensée: la socialisation de la pensée, 1750–1789; la socialisation de la personne, 1789–1792; la socialisation des biens, 1793–1794* (Paris, c. 1910), and *Les Sociétés de pensée et la démocratie* (Paris, 1921). Louis Gottschalk discussed the conspiracy thesis in "The French Revolution: Conspiracy or Circumstance?" in *Persecution and Liberty: Essays in Honor of George Lincoln Burr* (New York, 1931), pp. 445–72.

Georges Lefebvre, the most outstanding French historian of the revolutionary era in this century, examined the influence of the Enlightenment on the French Revolution in "La Révolution française et le rationalisme," *Annales historiques de la Révolution française* 18 (1946): 4–34, and "L'Encyclopédie et la Révolution française," *Annales de l'Université de Paris* 22² (1952): 81–90.

The year 1939, the one hundred-fiftieth anniversary of the outbreak of the French Revolution, witnessed the appearance of many studies which stressed the debt of the Revolution to the *philosophes.* Among these are Henri Berr, "Le Rôle des idées dans la Révolution," *Revue de Synthèse* 59 (1939): 191–98; J. Ray, "La Révolution française et la pensée juridique: l'idée du règne de la loi," *Revue philosophique* 128 (1939): 364–93; Philippe Sagnac, "Les Grands Courants d'idées et de sentiments en France vers 1789," *Revue d'histoire politique et constitutionnelle* 2 (1938): 317–41; "La Révolution française et la morale," *ibid.* 3 (1939): 169–85; "La Pensée sociale et l'œuvre de la Révolution française (1789–1792)," *ibid.* 3 (1939): 402–28; and Edouard Herriot, *The Wellsprings of Liberty* (New York, 1939).

Continuing interest in our problem since World War II is evidenced by the following articles: W. Gurian, "L'influence de l'ancien régime sur la politique religieuse de la Révolution," *Revue international d'histoire politique et constitutionnelle* 6 (1956): 259–77; P. H. Meyer,

"The French Revolution and the Legacy of the Philosophes," *The French Review* 30 (1956–57): 429–34; L. A. Loubère, "The Intellectual Origins of French Jacobin Socialism," *International Review of Social History* 4 (1959): 415–31; A. M. Wilson, "Why did the Political Theory of the Encyclopedists not Prevail? A Suggestion," *French Historical Studies* 1 (1960): 283–94; C. A. Gliozzo, "The Philosophes and Religion: Intellectual Origins of the Dechristianization Movement in the French Revolution," *Church History* 40 (1971): 273–83; C. G. Stricklen, Jr., "The *Philosophe's* Political Mission: The Creation of an Idea, 1750–1789," *Studies on Voltaire and the Eighteenth Century* 86 (1971): 137–228.

The statistical approach to the spread of ideas and their influence has rapidly gained favor in recent years. The pioneer work, still fundamental, was done by Daniel Mornet. He summarized his findings in "Les Origines intellectuelles de la Révolution française," *Annales de l'Université de Paris* 8 (1933): 307–19. See R. Herr, "*Histoire littéraire:* Daniel Mornet and the French Enlightenment," *Journal of Modern History* 24 (1952): 152–66. More recently, many French scholars have extensively developed the statistical method. F. Furet, G. Bollème, et al., *Livre et société dans la France du XVIIIᵉ siècle,* 2 vols., (Paris, 1965, 1970). The American scholar Robert Darnton has published two valuable articles on the social history of ideas: "The High Enlightenment and the Low-Life of Literature in Pre-Revolutionary France," *Past and Present,* no. 51 (May, 1971), pp. 81–115; and "Reading, Writing, and Publishing in Eighteenth-Century France: A Case Study in the Sociology of Literature," F. Gilbert and S. R. Graubard, eds., *Historical Studies Today* (New York, 1972), pp. 238–80.

Voltaire's influence during the Revolution is studied in R. Waldinger, *Voltaire and Reform in the Light of the French Revolution* (Geneva, 1959); R. O. Rockwood, "The Legend of Voltaire and the Cult of the Revolution, 1791," in R. Herr and H. T. Parker, eds., *Ideas in History: Essays Presented to Louis Gottschalk by his Former Students* (Durham, North Carolina, 1965).

The problem of Rousseau's influence on the Revolution is studied in the following: E. Champion, *J. J. Rousseau et la Révolution française* (Paris, 1909); A. Cobban, *Rousseau and the Modern State* (London, 1934); D. Williams, "The Influence of Rousseau on Political Opinion, 1760–1795," *English Historical Review* 48 (1933): 414–30; G. H. McNeil, "The Cult of Rousseau and the French Revolution,"

Journal of the History of Ideas 6 (1945): 197–212; and "The Anti-Revolutionary Rousseau," *American Historical Review* 58 (1953): 808–23; D. Higgins, "The Terrorists' Favorite Authors: Some Statistics from Revolutionary Literature," *Modern Language Review* 54 (1959): 401–404; A. Soboul, "Classes populaires et Rousseauisme sous la Révolution," *Annales historiques de la Révolution française* 34 (1962): 421–38; and "Jean-Jacques Rousseau et le jacobinisme," *Studi storici* 4 (1963): 3–22; G. May, *De Jean-Jacques Rousseau à Madame Roland* (Geneva, 1964); G. H. McNeil, "Robespierre, Rousseau and Representation," in *Ideas in History* (cited above); L. Sozzi, "Interprétations de Rousseau pendant la Révolution," in *Studies on Voltaire and the Eighteenth Century* 64 (1968): 187–223.

The following volumes of Rousseau studies contain valuable articles: *Jean-Jacques Rousseau (1712–1778): Pour le 250ᵉ anniversaire de sa naissance* (Gap, 1963); and *Etudes sur le Contrat Social,* in *Publications de l'Université de Dijon* 30 (Paris, 1964).

The view that Rousseau was a major progenitor of modern "totalitarian democracy" is presented in exaggerated form in J. L. Talmon, *The Origins of Totalitarian Democracy* (Boston, 1952).

9128